AF541788

Disaster Mitigation and Management

Disaster Mitigation and Management

Anshuman Sharma

RANDOM PUBLICATIONS
NEW DELHI (INDIA)

Disaster Mitigation and Management

ISBN 978-93-5111-491-8

Published in 2015 in India by

Reprint 2019

RANDOM PUBLICATIONS

4376-A/4B, Gali Murari Lal, Ansari Road
New Delhi-110 002
Phone : +9111-43580356, 011-23289044, 011-43142548
e-mail: sales@randompublications.com,
info@randompublications.com, randomexports@gmail.com

Type Setting by : Friends Media, Delhi-110089
Printed at : Mehra Printers, Delhi-110 092

Preface

Disaster can be defined as any occurrence, that causes damage, ecological disruption, loss of human life, deterioration of health and health services, on a scale sufficient to warrant an extraordinary response from outside the affected community or area. The damage caused by disasters is immeasurable and varies with the geographical location, climate and the type of the earth surface/degree of vulnerability. This influences the mental, socioeconomic, political and cultural state of the affected area.

Disaster management is the discipline of dealing with and avoiding risks. It is a discipline that involves preparing for disaster before it occurs, disaster response, as well as supporting, and rebuilding society after natural or human-made disasters have occurred. In general, any disaster management is the continuous process by which all individuals, groups, and communities manage hazards in an effort to avoid or ameliorate the impact of disasters resulting from the hazard.

Mitigation efforts attempt to prevent hazards from developing into disasters altogether, or to reduce the effects of disasters when they occur. The mitigation phase differs from the other phases because it focuses on long-term measures for reducing or eliminating risk. The implementation of mitigation strategies can be considered as part of the recovery process if applied after a disaster occurs.

The present book takes a multidimensional approach to the discussion of disaster mitigation and management, which involves preparing, supporting and rebuilding society when disasters occur. It provides full-fledged discussion of the practices, processes, techniques, equipment and managerial strategies involved, both in pre-as well as post-disaster conditions. It will be a useful reference for students, practitioners and anyone interested in international humanitarian response and recovery.

Author

Contents

1

Concepts of Disaster Mitigation

The term 'disaster', meaning 'bad star' in Latin, is defined as an impact of a natural or man-made hazard that causes human suffering or creates human needs that the victims cannot alleviate without assistance.The word's root is from astrology and implies that when the stars are in a bad position, a bad event is about to happen. In a recent document published by the United Nations Development Programme (UNDP) in the Americas, a disaster is defined as 'a social crisis situation occurring when a physical phenomenon of natural, socio-natural or anthropogenic origin negatively impacts vulnerable populations ... causing intense, serious and widespread disruption of the normal functioning of the affected social unit.' According to another widespread definition, disasters occur when hazards strike in vulnerable areas.

Types of Disasters

Generally, disasters are of two types—Natural and Man-made. Based on the devastation, these are further classified into major/minor natural disaster and major/minor manmade disasters.

Natural hazards are naturally occurring physical phenomena caused either by rapid or slow onset events which can be geophysical (earthquakes, landslides, tsunamis and volcanic activity), hydrological (avalanches and floods), climatological (extreme temperatures, drought and wildfires), meteorological (cyclones and storms/wave surges) or biological (disease epidemics and insect/animal plagues).

Technological or man-made hazards (complex emergencies/conflicts, famine, displaced populations, industrial accidents and transport accidents) are events that are caused by humans and occur in or close to human settlements. This can include environmental degradation, pollution and accidents.Technological or man-made hazards (complex emergencies/ conflicts, famine, displaced populations, industrial accidents and transport accidents)

There are a range of challenges, such as climate change, unplanned-urbanization, under-development/poverty as well as the threat of pandemics, that will shape humanitarian assistance in the future. These aggravating factors will result in increased frequency, complexity and severity of disasters.

Though, all kinds of disaster require more or less similar skill-sets and rescue-efforts at least a few days after the event, it is important to understand various kinds of disasters. Depending upon the actual nature of disaster, the immediate reaction needs to be different.

Also, the first few moments of disasters are distinctly different for each kind of disasters. Thus, understanding of each kind of disaster might also help in identifying the onset of a disastrous event, so that a trained person can undertake some key actions, during the initial few moments. This could have a major impact on the final outcome in terms of amount of final loss.

Some of the disasters are listed below:

Major natural disasters

- Flood
- Cyclone
- Drought
- Earthquake

Minor natural disasters

- Cold wave
- Thunderstorms
- Heat waves
- Mud slides
- Storm

Major manmade disasters

- Setting of fires
- Epidemic
- Deforestation
- Pollution due to agriculture
- Chemical pollution
- Wars

Minor manmade disasters

- Road / train accidents, riots
- Food poisoning
- Industrial disaster/ crisis
- Environmental pollution

Disaster Impacts

A disaster occurs when an extreme event exceeds a community's ability to cope with that event. Understanding the process by which natural disasters produce community impacts is important for four reasons. First, information from this process is needed to identify the preimpact conditions that make communities vulnerable to disaster impacts. Second, information about the disaster impact process can be used to identify specific segments of each community that will be affected disproportionately. Third, information about the disaster impact process can be used to identify the event-specific conditions that determine the level of disaster impact. Fourth, an understanding of disaster impact process allows planners to identify suitable emergency management interventions. The process by which disasters produce community impacts can be explained in terms of models proposed by Cutter and Lindell and Prater.

Figure 1 indicates the effects of a disaster are determined by three preimpact conditions—hazard exposure, physical vulnerability, and social vulnerability. There also are three event-specific conditions, hazard event characteristics, improvised disaster responses, and improvised disaster recovery. Two of the event-specific conditions, hazard event characteristics and improvised disaster responses, combine with the preimpact conditions to produce a disaster's physical impacts.

The physical impacts, in turn, combine with improvised disaster recovery to produce the disaster's social impacts. Communities can engage in three types of emergency management interventions to ameliorate disaster impacts. Physical impacts can be reduced by hazard mitigation practices and emergency preparedness practices, whereas social impacts can be reduced by recovery preparedness practices.

Hazard Exposure

Hazard exposure arises from people's occupancy of geographical areas where they could be affected by specific types of events that threaten their lives or property. For natural hazards, this exposure is caused by living in geographical areas as specific as floodplains that sometimes extend only a few feet beyond the floodway or as broad as the Great Plains of the Midwest where tornadoes can strike anywhere over an area of hundreds of thousands of square miles. For technological hazards, exposure can arise if people move

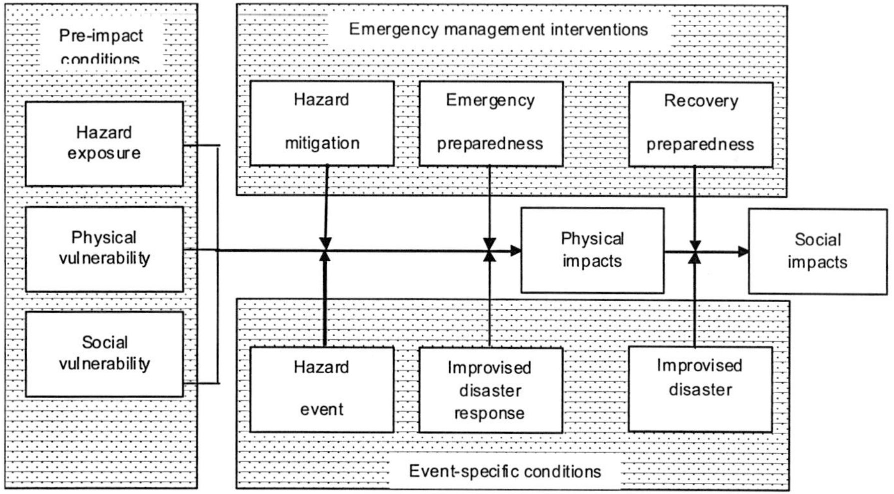

Figure 1. Disaster Impact Model

into areas where they could be exposed to explosions or hazardous materials releases.

In principle, hazard exposure can be measured by the probability of occurrence of a given event magnitude, but these exceedance probabilities can be difficult to obtain for hazards about which the historical data are insufficient to reliably estimate the probability of very unusual events. For example, many areas of the US have meteorological and hydrological data that are limited to the past 100 years, so the estimation of extreme floods requires extrapolation from a limited data series. Moreover, urbanization of the watersheds causes the boundaries of the 100-year floodplains to change in ways that may be difficult for local emergency managers to anticipate. Even more difficult to estimate are the probabilities of events, such as chemical and nuclear reactor accidents, for which data are limited because each facility is essentially unique. In such cases, techniques of probabilistic safety analysis are used to model these systems, attach probabilities to the failure of system components, and synthesize probabilities of overall system failure by mathematically combining the probabilities of individual component failure.

The greatest difficulties are encountered in attempting to estimate the probabilities of social hazards such as terrorist attacks because the occurrence of these events is defined by social system dynamics that cannot presently be modeled in the same way as physical systems. That is, the elements of social systems are difficult to define and measure. Moreover, the interactions of the system elements have multiple determinants and involve complex lag and feedback effects that are not well understood, let alone precisely measured. Indeed, there are significant social and political constraints that limit the collection of data on individuals and groups.

Physical Vulnerability

Human Vulnerability

Humans are vulnerable to environmental extremes of temperature, pressure, and chemical exposures that can cause death, injury, and illness. For any hazard agent—water, wind, ionizing radiation, toxic chemicals, infectious agents—there often is variability in the physiological response of the affected population. That is, given the same level of exposure, some people will die, others will be severely injured, still others slightly injured, and the rest will survive unscathed. Typically, the most susceptible to any environmental stressor will be the very young, the very old, and those with weakened immune systems.

Agricultural Vulnerability

Like humans, agricultural plants and animals are also vulnerable to environmental extremes of temperature, pressure, chemicals, radiation, and infectious agents. Like humans, there are differences among individuals within each plant and animal population. However, agricultural vulnerability is more complex than human vulnerability because there is a greater number of species to be assessed, each of which has its own characteristic response to each environmental stressor.

Structural Vulnerability

Structural vulnerability arises when buildings are constructed using designs and materials that are incapable of resisting extreme stresses (e.g., high wind, hydraulic pressures of water, seismic shaking) or that allow hazardous materials to infiltrate into the building. The construction of most buildings is governed by building codes intended to protect the life safety of building occupants from structural collapse—primarily from the dead load of the building material themselves and the live load of the occupants and furnishings— but do not necessarily provide protection from extreme wind, seismic, or hydraulic loads. Nor do they provide an impermeable barrier to the infiltration of toxic air pollutants.

Social Vulnerability

The social vulnerability perspective represents an important extension of previous theories of hazard vulnerability. As a concept, social vulnerability has been defined in terms of people's "capacity to anticipate, cope with, resist and recover from the impacts of a natural hazard". Whereas people's physical vulnerability refers to their susceptibility to biological changes (i.e., impacts on anatomical structures and physiological functioning), their social vulnerability refers to their susceptibility to behavioral changes. As will be discussed in greater detail below, these consist of psychological, demographic, economic, and political impacts.

The central point of the social vulnerability perspective is that, just as people's occupancy of hazard prone areas and the physical vulnerability of the structures in which they live and work are not randomly distributed, neither is social vulnerability randomly distributed—either geographically or demographically. Thus, just as variations in structural vulnerability can increase or decrease the effect of hazard exposure on physical impacts (property damage and casualties), so too can variations in social vulnerability. Social vulnerability varies across communities and also across households within communities. It is the variability in vulnerability that is likely to be of greatest concern to local emergency managers because it requires that they identify the areas within their communities having population segments with the highest levels of social vulnerability.

Importance of Disaster Management

In development circles today, disaster management is often treated holistically rather than as a single issue. It is an essential component of any development framework. Proper disaster management has been recognized as a key requirement towards achieving the Millennium Development Goals (MDGs) by the specified target of 2015.

Recent events have shown that there is no country that does not stand the threat of a disaster, though they may be threatened at different levels.Therefore, disaster preparedness is no longer a choice; it is mandatory irrespective of where one lives. Risk types vary and increase depending on a country's geographic location. For instance, countries like China, Indonesia, Iran and Pakistan are prone to earthquakes. Small island states in the Pacific region and countries like the Maldives are prone to various types of threats from the sea. Bangladesh and parts of China and India experience floods each year. Some countries have also encountered man-made hazards recently (e.g. river pollution in China). Environmental pollution taking place today could be the origin of many man-made disasters in the coming years. In addition, with the increased mobility of people, there is always the danger of a serious outbreak of a fatal disease (e.g. avian flu, mad cow disease and SARS). This too may lead to disastrous situations.

Disaster Management Cycle

There are no standardized rules defining the different phases of the disaster management cycle. Different agencies use different cycles depending upon their objectives. However, while approaches vary, it is agreed that disaster management activities should be carried out in a cycle. Figure 2 illustrates the phases of the disaster management cycle, which are described as follows:

1. *Mitigation*: any activity that reduces either the chance of a hazard taking place or a hazard turning into disaster.
2. *Risk reduction:* anticipatory measures and actions that seek to avoid future risks as a result of a disaster.
3. *Prevention*: avoiding a disaster even at the eleventh hour.
4. *Preparedness*: plans or preparations made to save lives or property, and help the response and rescue service operations. This phase covers implementation/operation, early warning systems and capacity building so the population will react appropriately when an early warning is issued.
5. *Response:* includes actions taken to save lives and prevent property damage, and to preserve the environment during emergencies or disasters. The response phase is the implementation of action plans.
6. *Recovery*: includes actions that assist a community to return to a sense of normalcy after a disaster.

These six phases usually overlap. ICT is used in all the phases, but the usage is more apparent in some phases than in others.

Disaster Management is the discipline that involves preparing, warning, supporting and rebuilding societies when natural or man-made disasters occur. It is the continuous process by which all individuals, groups and communities manage hazards in an effort to avoid or minimize the impact of disasters resulting from hazards. Effective disaster management relies on thorough integration of emergency plans at all levels of government and non-government involvement. Activities at each level (individual, group, community) affect the other levels.

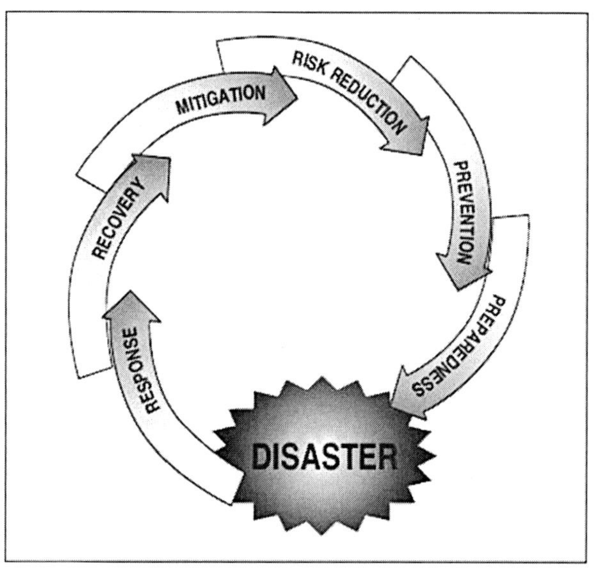

Figure 2. The Disaster Management Cycle

Events over the last two years have shown that there is no country that does not stand the threat of a disaster. Countries like China, Indonesia, Iran and Pakistan are prone to earthquakes. Small Islands States in the Pacific region and countries like Maldives are prone to various types of threats from the sea. Bangladesh and parts of China and India experience floods each year. Therefore, disaster preparedness is no longer a choice; it is mandatory irrespective of where one lives.

It is somewhat surprising that no Millennium Development Goal (MDG) directly addresses the issues related to disaster management. Perhaps it is because it is so obvious that building a safer world is a prerequisite for the achievement of all the eight MDGs. Poverty eradication, freedom from hunger, primary education, freedom from disasters, and building a sustainable world etc. are all key aspects of the disaster management process. It has been shown that any nation should have effective disaster reduction and recovery processes in place to achieve the MDGs by the expected deadline of year 2015.

What is Disaster Mitigation ?

Mitigation means taking actions to reduce the effects of a hazard before it occurs. The term mitigation applies to a wide range of activities and protection measures that might be instigated, from the physical, like constructing stronger buildings, to the procedural, like standard techniques for incorporating hazard assessment in land-use planning.

The 1990s will be a decade of major effort to encourage the implementation of disaster mitigation techniques in development projects around the world. The United Nations has adopted the decade of the 1990s as the International Decade for Natural Disaster Reduction. The aim is to achieve a significant reduction in the loss of life and material damage caused by disasters by the end of the decade.

A useful analogy with the recently developing science of disaster mitigation is the implementation of public health measures that began in the mid 19th century. Before that time tuberculosis, typhoid, cholera, dysentery, smallpox and many other diseases were major causes of death and tended to assume epidemic proportions as the industrial development of cities fuelled increasing concentrations of population. These diseases had a major effect on life expectancy at the time and yet were regarded as just part of the everyday risks of living. The apparent randomness with which the diseases struck and the unpredictability of epidemics meant that superstition, mythology and a certain amount of fatalism was the only public response to the hazards: the high risk of disease was generally accepted because there was little alternative. As the understanding of what caused diseases increased, chiefly through the efforts of scientists and epidemiologists in the 19th century, so the incidence of epidemics and illnesses generally became demystified.It became evident that disease was preventable and gradually the concept of public protection against disease became accepted.

Sanitation, purification of the water supply, garbage disposal and public hygiene were key issues for public health. The measures necessary to reduce the risk of disease were expensive-massive investment in infrastructure was needed to build sewers and clean water supply networks-and required major changes in public practices and attitudes. Social historians refer to this as the "Sanitary Revolution". Garbage collection and disposal had to be organized. It became socially unacceptable to throw garbage or to dispose of sewage in the streets. Personal hygiene, washing and individual sanitation practices became important. Initially encouraged by public awareness campaigns, they gradually became part of the social norms and were taught by parents to their children. Attitudes changed from the previous fatalism about disease to a public health "safety culture", where everyone participated in reducing the risk of communal disease.

Public health advances went hand-in-hand with public medicine, medical care, vaccination, preventive health care and a health industry that in most developed countries today consumes a very significant proportion of national economic production. Today public epidemics are unacceptable. High levels of risk from disease are not tolerated and outbreaks of disease are followed by outbursts of public opinion demanding medical and government response to protect them. Everyone now considers it normal to participate in their own protection against health hazards and accepts the high levels of cost involved in society's battle against disease. The level of risk from public health hazards that is judged acceptable by modern society is far lower than it was three or four generations ago.

Disasters today are seen in much the same way as disease was in the early 19th century: unpredictable, unlucky and part of the everyday risk of living. Concentrations of people and rising population levels across the globe are increasing the risk of disasters and multiplying the consequences of natural hazards when they occur. However, the "epidemiology" of disasters-the systematic science of what happens in a disaster-shows that disasters are largely preventable. There are many ways to reduce the impact of a disaster and to mitigate the effects of a possible hazard or accident.

Just like the fight against disease, the fight against disasters has to be fought by everyone together and involves public and private sector investment, changes in social attitudes and improvements in the practices of individuals. Just as the Sanitary Revolution occurred with the development of a "safety culture" for public health, so disaster mitigation has to develop through the evolution of an equivalent "safety culture" for public safety. !Governments can use public investment to make stronger infrastructure and a physical environment where a disaster is less likely to occur, but individuals also have to act to protect themselves. Just as public health depends on personal hygiene, so public protection depends on personal safety. The type of cooking stove an individual uses, and an awareness that a sudden earthquake could tip it over is more important in reducing the risk of conflagration than the community maintaining a large fire brigade.

The science of disasters is in a similar state of development to that of epidemiology in the latter half of the 19th century: the causes, mechanisms and processes of disasters are becoming understood rapidly. As a result of this understanding, the more developed countries have begun to implement individual measures to reduce the risk of future disasters. A catalogue of techniques are known for disaster mitigation, and their relevance to the countries that need them most is now clear.

Disasters are very largely a developmental issue. The great majority of casualties and disaster effects are suffered in developing countries. Development achievements can be wiped out by a major disaster and economic growth reversed. The promotion of disaster mitigation in the projects and planning activities of development protects development achievement and assists populations in protecting themselves against needless injury.

UNDERSTANDING HAZARDS

The most critical part of implementing mitigation is the full understanding of the nature of the threat. In each country and in each region, the types of hazards faced are different. Some countries are prone to floods, others have histories of tropical storm damage, and others are known to be in earthquake regions. Most countries are prone to some combination of the various hazards and all face the possibility of technological disasters as industrial development progresses. The effects these hazards are likely to have and the damage they are likely to cause depends on what is present in the region: the people, their houses, sources of livelihood and infrastructure. Each country is different. For any particular location or country it is critical to know the types of hazards likely to be encountered.

The understanding of natural hazards and the processes that cause them is the province of seismologists, volcanologists, climatologists, hydrologists and other scientists. The effects of natural hazards on structures and the man-made environment is the subject of studies by engineers and risk specialists. Death and injury caused by disasters and the consequences of damage in terms of the disruption to society and its impact on the economy is a research area for medical practitioners, economists and social scientists. The science is still relatively young-most of the recordings of damaging earthquakes by strong motion instruments were obtained in the past twenty years, for example, and only since satellite photography has it been possible to routinely track tropical storms. The understanding of the consequences of failure of social organizations and regional economies is even more recent. However there are now many books and case studies that document the incidence of disasters and a growing body of knowledge about hazards and their effects.

Understanding hazards involves comprehension of:

— how hazards arise
— probability of occurrence and magnitude
— physical mechanisms of destruction
— the elements and activities that are most vulnerable to their effects
— consequences of damage.

These demonstrate that hazards have different effects on different parts of the community, sectors of the economy and types of infrastructure: floods tend to destroy agricultural produce but cause less damage to the structure of buildings; earthquakes tend to destroy structures but have little impact on crops growing in fields. The vulnerability of people, buildings, roads, bridges, pipelines, communications systems and other elements is different for each hazard.

Saving Life and Reducing Disruption

The worst effects of any disaster are the deaths and injuries caused. The scale of disasters and the number of people they kill are the primary justifications for mitigation. Understanding the way that people are killed and injured in disasters is a prerequisite for reducing casualties. Among the sudden onset disasters, floods and earthquakes cause the most casualties worldwide, with storms and high winds being less deadly but far more widespread.

In earthquakes over 75% of fatalities are caused by building collapse. In floods deaths occur by drowning, mainly outdoors and in fast flowing currents or in turbulent water. Saving lives in earthquakes means focusing on prevention of building collapse. Reducing fatalities from floods means limiting the exposure of people to rapid inundation-either by keeping people out of the track of potential water flows or by preventing the flows from occurring.

The consequences of physical damage are often more important than the damage itself. A damaged factory can no longer continue to manufacture jobs. The jobless have no income to spend in their local shops and the whole local economy suffers. Damage to infrastructure and to the means of production depresses the economy.

Mitigation also entails the protection of the economy from disasters. Economic activity in the more industrialized societies is complex and interdependent, with service industries dependent on manufacturing, which in turn relies on supplies of raw materials, labour, power and communications. This complex interdependency is extremely vulnerable to disruption by hazards affecting any one link in the chain. Newly industrializing societies are most vulnerable of all.

Agricultural sectors of the economy are most vulnerable to drought but also to floods and high winds, disease and pest attack and pollution. Industry is more vulnerable to earthquake damage and the disruption of transportation and utilities networks. Commerce and finance are most vulnerable to disruption of production, population migration and to breakdowns in communications systems. Mitigation measures that focus on protecting the most vulnerable elements and activities–the weakest links– in the different sectors of the economy will help protect the achievements of economic development.

Targeting Mitigation

If there were no human settlements or economic activities affected, an earthquake would be a harmless act of nature. The combination of settlements (elements) and earthquake (hazard) makes the disaster possible. Some elements are more vulnerable to earthquake effects than others. Identifying which these are–he elements most at risk–indicates priorities for mitigation.

Disasters are often the result of combinations of factors occurring together: a fire source, a dense residential area and combustible houses for example, or a seismic fault rupturing close to a city formed of high occupancy weak buildings. The contributory factors of past disasters can be identified to highlight similar conditions elsewhere. This is the process of risk analysis.

Identifying situations where combinations of risk factors coincide indicates the elements most at risk. The elements most at risk are the buildings, community services, infrastructure and activities that will suffer most from the effects of the hazard or will be least able to recover after the event. At a regional level, the concentrations of population and infrastructure in large cities make it likely that the losses inflicted by even low levels of hazard will exceed the total losses inflicted by severe levels of hazard on all the villages in the region. Mitigation measures in the city may have the most effect in reducing future losses. The portions of the housing stock in the city most likely to be damaged can be identified and mitigation measures applied to that sector will have the effect on reducing risk. The number of elements likely to be affected by a hazard, together with their vulnerability to the hazard will identify where mitigation is most effective.

Houses built form cane and thatch that can be blown apart in a tropical storm are more vulnerable to wind loads than a brick building. A brick building is more likely to disintegrate with the violent ground shaking of an earthquake than a strong reinforced concrete frame structure and is more vulnerable to earthquake hazard. Vulnerability is the degree of expected damage form a particular hazard. Targeting mitigation efforts relies heavily on correctly assessing vulnerability.

This concept of vulnerability assessment can also be extended to social groups or economic sectors: People who rent their houses rely on a landlord to repair the damage and are more likely to be made homeless in the event of a disaster. Correctly identifying the groups of tenants and establishing rights of tenure and landlords' obligations to repair may reduce the number of people made homeless in a disaster. Similarly, food growers sending their produce to market through a single mountain pass will be unable to sell their produce if the pass is blocked. Developing an alternative route to market will reduce the vulnerability of the agricultural sector to damage by disaster.

Mitigation Actions

The techniques or measures that an authority might consider in assembling an appropriate package for disaster mitigation can be classified as:

— Engineering and construction

— Physical planning

— Economic

— Management and institutional

— Societal

Engineering and Construction Measures

Engineering measures are of two types. Those that result in stronger individual structures that are more resistant to hazards, and those that create structures whose function is primarily disaster protection-flood control structures, dikes, levees, infiltration dams, etc.

Actions of the first type are mainly actions on individual buildings and structures and are sometimes referred to as "hardening" facilities against hazard forces. Improving the design and construction of buildings, agricultural structures, infrastructure and other facilities can be achieved in a number of ways. Design standards, building codes and performance specifications are important for facilities designed by engineers. Engineering design against the various hazards may include design for vibration, lateral loads, load surcharges, wind loads, impact, combustibility, flood resistance and other safety factors. Building codes are the critical front line defense for achieving stronger engineered structures, including large private buildings, public sector buildings, infrastructure, transportation networks and industrial facilities.

Disaster-resistance based building codes are unlikely to result in stronger buildings unless the engineers who have to implement the code accept its importance and endorse its use, understand the code and the design criteria required of them and unless the code is fully enforced by authorities through checking and penalizing designs that do not comply. A code has to fit into an environment prepared to receive it. Part of the measures necessary to achieve the "engineering" mitigation measures may include increased levels of training for engineers and designers, explanatory manuals to interpret the code requirements and the establishment of an effective administration to check code compliance in practice: the recruitment of ten new municipal engineers to enforce an existing code may have more effect in increasing construction quality in a city than proposing higher standards in building codes.

A large number of the buildings likely to be affected in a disaster, and those most vulnerable to hazards are not designed by engineers and will be unaffected by safety standards established in the building codes. These are houses, workshops, storerooms and agricultural buildings built by the owners themselves or by craftsmen or building contractors to their own designs. In many countries these non-engineered buildings make up a large percentage of the total building stock. The "engineering" measures that are needed to improve the disaster-resistance of non-engineered structures involve the education of builders in practical construction techniques. The resistance of houses to cyclone winds is ultimately dependent on how well the roofing sheets are nailed down, and the quality of the joints in the building frame and its attachment to the ground. Training techniques to teach builders the practicalities of disaster resistant construction are now well understood and form part of the menu of mitigation actions available to the disaster manager.

Persuading owners and communities to build safer, more disaster-resistant structures and to pay the additional costs involved is required to make builder training effective. The building contractor may play a role in persuading the client to build to higher specifications, but unless this is carried out within a general public awareness of the disaster risk and acceptance of the need for protection, the contractor is unlikely to find many customers. Grant systems, preferential loans and supply of building materials have also been used as incentives to help improve the hazard-resistance of non-engineered buildings. Legalizing land ownership and giving tenants protective rights also encourages people to upgrade building stock with security of tenure and a stake in their own future.

Apart form new buildings, the existing building stock also may need to be "hardened" against future hazard impacts. The vulnerability of existing buildings can be reduced to some degree by regular maintenance and the cost of adding strength to an existing building tends to be more expensive than making new building design stronger, so strengthening is unlikely to be an economic option for the large majority of the building stock; for average buildings, with relatively short life expectancies (10 to 50 years), it may be better to take a long-term view of building stock upgrading, waiting until buildings come naturally to the end of their useful lives, demolishing them and buildings new structures in their place that conform to building code safety requirements.

For special structures, critical facilities or historic buildings with long expected life spans, retrofit strengthening techniques are now well established and a considerable amount of expertise has been developed in this field, though these are generally too costly to be useful in development projects.

The engineering of large-scale flood control and water-supply measures is complex, lengthy and capital-intensive; and their construction frequently has adverse consequences for those they are intended to protect, for example some people may be forced off their land, land-use patterns may be changed and other adverse effects felt.

Experience has shown that small-scale flood control measures which can be managed by community-based organizations can be effective in risk mitigation while simultaneously achieving other development goals. They tend to make use of local materials, labour and management resources to build on traditional mitigation knowledge rather than replacing it, and to enhance the community's own self-reliance rather than undermining it. Such measures can play an important role in disaster-mitigation within integrated agricultural or rural development projects.

Physical Planning Measures

Many hazards are localized with their likely effects confined to specific known areas: Floods affect flood plains, landslides affect steep soft slopes, etc. The effects can be greatly reduced if it is possible to avoid the hazardous areas being used for settlements or as sites for important structures. Most urban masterplans involving land use zoning probably already attempt to separate hazardous industrial activities from major population centers.

Urban planning needs to integrate awareness of natural hazards and disaster risk mitigation into the normal processes of planning the development of a city.

Location of public sector facilities is easier to control than private sector location or land use. The careful location of public sector facilities can itself play an important role in reducing the vulnerability of a settlement–schools, hospitals, emergency facilities and major infrastructural elements like water pumping stations, electrical power transformers and telephone exchanges represent a significant proportion of the functioning of a town.

An important principle is deconcentration of elements at risk: services provided by one central facility are always more at risk than those provided by several smaller facilities. The collapse of the central telephone exchange in the Mexico City earthquake of 1985 cut communications in the city completely. In the reconstruction, the central exchange was replaced by a number of mini exchanges in different locations around the city to make the telephone system less vulnerable. The same principle applies equally to hospitals and schools, for example as it does to power stations and water treatment plants.

The principle of deconcentration also applies to population densities in a city: a denser concentration of people will always have more disaster potential than if they are more dispersed. Where building densities can be controlled the urban masterplan should reflect the spatial distribution of hazard severity levels in its zoning for permitted densities of development. Indirect control of densities is sometimes possible through simpler methods such as using wide roads, height limitations and road layouts that limit the size of plots available for development. Creation of park lands reduces urban densities, and also provides space in the city, greenery, allows drainage to decrease flood risk, provides refuge areas for the population in the event of urban fires and may provide space for emergency facilities in the event of a disaster.

At a regional level, the concentration of population growth and industrial development in a centralized city is generally less desirable than a decentralized pattern of secondary towns, satellite centers and development spread over a broader region.

The design of service networks-roads, pipelines, and cables also needs careful planning to reduce risk of failure. Long lengths of supply line are at risk if they are cut at any point. Networks that interconnect and allow more than one route to any point are less vulnerable to local failures provided that individual sections can be isolated when necessary. Vehicle access to a specific point is less likely to be cut by a road blockage in a circular road system than in a radial one.

Urban planners may also be able to reduce risks by changing the use of a vulnerable building being used for an important function-a school in a weak building could be moved to a stronger building and the weak building used for a less important function, like storage.

The location of public sector facilities is easier to control than those in the private sector. In many rapidly developing cities, the control of private sector land use through urban masterplanning and development permissions is almost impossible. It is often private sector land use, the informal sectors and shanty towns that pose the highest risks of disaster. Flood plains and steep slopes are often the marginal lands that are available to the lower-income communities and the most vulnerable social groups.

The economic pressures that drive these groups, first to the city for jobs and opportunity, and second to the marginal lands to live, need to be fully understood as the context for reducing their risk. Prohibition or measures to clear settlers from hazardous areas are unlikely to be successful for long if the background pressures are not addressed. Some indirect measures may be effective, such as making safer land available, or making alternative locations more attractive. This may be through better provision of income sources, access to public transport and better service provision. Deterring further development in unoccupied areas by declaring areas clearly as hazard zones, denying services, reducing accessibility and limiting availability of building materials may also be effective. Ultimately, however, it is only when the local community recognizes the true extent of the hazard and accepts that the risk outweighs the benefit to them of being in that location that they will locate elsewhere or protect themselves in other ways.

Economic Measures

Equitable economic development is the key to disaster mitigation. A strong economy in which the benefits are shared throughout the society is the best protection against a future disaster. A strong economy means more money to spend on stronger buildings and larger financial reserves to cope with future losses. The interdependency between Disasters and Development is the subject of another module in this training course.

Mitigation measures that help the community reduce future economic losses, help members withstand losses and improve their ability to recover after loss and measures that make it possible for communities to afford higher levels of safety are important elements of an overall mitigation program. Inevitably it is those who have least that, proportionally, lose most in a disaster. The weakest members of the economy have few economic reserves. If they lose their house or their animals they have no means of recovering them. They are unlikely to have insurance or access to credit and can quickly become destitute. Large scale drought or flood disasters in rural areas can result in an acceleration of urbanization in the region and possibly increased risks as families with their livelihoods destroyed migrate to the towns in search of better opportunities. The destruction of industries and loss of jobs and incomes may well make recovery of the region a long and slow process or make it more vulnerable to a future disaster. Reconstruction plans often extend generous loans to victims to aid their recovery but a family without an income has little prospect of making repayments and is therefore unable to benefit.

Economic development is likely to be the main objective of any regional planner or national government agency, regardless of disaster mitigation objectives. The processes of economic development are complex and beyond the direct focus of this training course, however, disaster mitigation should be seen as a part of the process of economic development.

Some aspects of economic planning are directly relevant to reducing disaster risk. Diversification of economic activity is as important an economic principle as deconcentration is in physical planning. A single industry (or single-crop) economy is always more vulnerable than an economy made up of many different activities. The linkages between different sectors of an economy-the transportation of goods, the flow of information, the labour market-may be more vulnerable to disruption from a disaster than the physical infrastructure that is the means of production. Tourism as an economic sector is extremely vulnerable to disaster, or even the rumour of a potential disaster. The reliance of industry and the economy on infrastructure-the roads, transportation networks, power, telephone services etc., means that a high priority should be placed on protecting these facilities: the consequential losses of failure are costly to the whole community.

Economic incentives and penalties are an important part of the powers of any authority. Grants, loans, taxes, tax concessions and fines can be used to influence the decisions people make to reduce disaster-related risks. Industrial location is commonly influenced by government incentives which can be used to attract industry to safer locations or to act as a focus for and loans can be offered to assist owners to upgrade their property and make buildings more disaster resistant.

In industrialized countries, insurance is one of the major economic protection devices. If the risk of economic loss is spread widely over a large number of premium payers, the loss is safely dissipated. Commercial insurance is expensive and its viability is determined by accurate calculation of risk. With only a small number of premium payers, premiums remain high and are prohibitive to potential policy holders. The more widespread policy holding becomes, the lower the premiums are and the more widespread insurance use is likely to be. Encouragement of people to protect themselves through insurance ensures that a level of protection is built up. Compulsory insurance schemes have not been successful and national governments rarely have the financial resources to dedicate to disaster insurance guarantees, although many countries build up a disaster reconstruction fund through general taxation. Disaster insurance is high-risk finance and only multinational insurance companies can gather the resources to cover the losses of any sizeable disaster. It is unlikely to be available to protect poorer or rural communities and their disaster-protection investments unless backed by a large development agency.

Management and Institutional Measures

Disaster mitigation also requires certain organizational and procedural measures. The time span over which a significant reduction can be achieved in the potential for disaster is long. Changes in physical planning, upgranding structures and changes in the characteristics of building stock are processes that take decades.

Education, training and professional competence, and political will, are necessary aspects of institutionalizing disaster mitigation. The professional training of engineers, planners, economists, social scientist and other managers to include hazards and risk reduction within their normal area of competence is gradually becoming common. Increasing the exposure of these groups to international expertise and transfer of technology in disaster mitigation is an important part of building capability in the affected country.

Information is a critical element in planning for disaster mitigation, but there are many hazard-prone countries where the basic meteorological and geological observatories to monitor hazards have not been established or do not have the resources to carry out their job. Research, technical expertise and policy-making organizations are important resources for developing mitigation strategies both nationally and locally.

Administrative and organizational powers for disaster mitigation include the checking procedures and planning powers to realize mitigation plans, consultation procedures and representation of the community in mitigation decisions and management of the implementation of mitigation activities.

Additional staff resources and organizational structure may be needed to implement mitigation plans. Some countries have established Ministries of Civil Protection or sub-departments whose responsibilities are disaster management and the development of protection measures. It may not be necessary to establish an autonomous unit for disaster mitigation, and it is often argued that disaster mitigation is better integrated within existing activities than carried out as a separate exercise. An administration that carries policy through to implementation is essential.

At the local level, community-based mitigation requires the strengthening of the capability of the local institutions to carry out local protection measures-such training and support can often be carried out most effectively by national or international NGOs.

Societal Measures

The mitigation of disasters will only come about when there is a consensus that it is desirable, feasible and affordable. In many places, the individual hazards that threaten are not recognized, the steps that people can take to protect themselves are not known and the demand of the community to have themselves protected is not forthcoming. Mitigation planning should aim to develop a disaster "safety culture" in which the people are fully aware of the hazards they face, protect themselves as fully as they can and fully support efforts made on their behalf to protect them.

Public awareness can be raised in a number of ways, from short-term, high-profile campaigns using broadcasts, literature and posters, to more long-term, low-profile campaigns that are carried out through general education. Education should attempt to familiarize and de-sensationalize. Everyone who lives in a hazard-prone area should understand hazards as a fact of life. Information about hazards should be part of the standard curriculum of children at school and be part of everyday information sources, with occasional mentions of them in stories, TV soap operas, newspapers and other common media. The objective is to develop and everyday acknowledgment of hazard safety where people take conscious, automatic precautions through being aware of, but not terrified of, the possibility of hazard occurrence. Their understanding should include being aware of what to do in the event, and a sense that their choice of house, the placement of that bookcase or stove and the quality of construction of the garden wall around their children's area all affect their own safety. Awareness of risk locally is aided by reminders of past events: a bollard erected with marking to show the high water mark of past floods; the ruins of a building preserved as a monument to a past earthquake.

It is also important to de-sensationalize hazards. Most occurrences of hazards are not disastrous. Reporting only catastrophic hazards causes fear and fatalism: "If an earthquake lays waste a town, what difference does it make where I put my bookcase?". The treatment of fictional hazards in the media should be aimed at showing how a household copes or doesn't cope with a disruptive occurrence of the hazard, not the annihilation of the soap opera family through cataclysm.

Involvement of the community in mitigation planning processes may involve public meetings and consultations, public inquiries and full discussion of decisions in the normal political forum.

Further awareness is developed through drills, practice emergencies and anniversary remembrances. In hospitals, schools and large buildings it is often common to have evacuation practices to rehearse what the occupants should do in the event of fire, earthquake or other hazard. In schools children may practice earthquake drills by getting under desks. This reinforces awareness and develops behavioural responses.

In some countries, the anniversary of a major disaster is remembered as Disaster Awareness Day-1 September in Japan, 20 September in Mexico, and the month of April in California, USA. On this day drills are performed, ceremonies and activities held to promote disaster mitigation. The United Nations General Assembly in its adoption of the International Decade for Natural Disaster Reduction designated the second Wednesday of October as an International Day for Natural Disaster Reduction which may be an opportunity for many other countries to carry out disaster awareness activities.

Mitigation Strategies

The aim of a mitigation strategy is to reduce losses in the event of a future occurrence of a hazard. The primary aim is to reduce the risk of death and injury to the population. Secondary aims include reducing damage and economic losses inflicted on public sector infrastructure and reducing private sector losses in as far as they are likely to affect the community as whole. The objectives are likely to include encouragement for people to protect themselves as far as possible.

A set of actions that includes some engineering measures, some spatial planning, and a degree of economic, management and societal inputs will be needed to bring about effective mitigation. A mitigation program that concentrates solely on any one of these five aspects will be unbalanced and is unlikely to achieve its aims.

A mitigation strategy has to be designed for its proposed application. Disaster mitigation programs carried out in the Philippines are unlikely to be directly transferrable to Peru. There are few standard solutions. Some individual elements and techniques of mitigation will be transferrable-compulsory purchase techniques for widening roads in dense urban areas that have been used in Peru may be of interest to the planners in the Philippines-but the full range of measures needed to reduce disaster potential for an individual application is likely to be unique. In each country the range of hazards faced are likely to be different. The types of infrastructure, houses and other elements at risk will have their own characteristics. The types of actions that are possible including the legislative framework, the social attitude to the problem and the budget that is available will specify what constitutes an effective mitigation program.

Economics of Mitigation

Perhaps the greatest difference likely to be encountered between the various countries served by UNDP and DHA, and between the various societies threatened by disasters, is the budgetary constraints on spending for mitigation. The Japanese Government spends over $2 billion a year on disaster mitigation and preparedness. This is more than the total annual government revenue of half the world's nations.

In most of the developing nations threatened by disaster, capital for investment is at a premium. Investment in agricultural irrigation projects or in industrial manufacturing capability has a demonstrable effect in increasing economic output. Investing in disaster mitigation is likely to mean fewer resources left for irrigation projects, industry and hospitals. And yet not spending on disaster mitigation means that the investment in irrigation projects, industry and hospitals will be wasted if they are destroyed in a future occurrence of a hazard. The spending of a few percent extra on a new facility to build it a little stronger and protect it against a future threat is usually seen as prudent. Mitigation investment has to be seen in terms of the price of protecting existing and future infrastructure.

The level of investment that is justified to protect society, its economic activities and its built environment is a matter of political decision making, and the economics of risk. Choosing an appropriate level of safety for building codes, for example, is a matter of considerable debate in the engineering profession. The cost of providing safety is considerable and the stronger a building is, the more it costs. Structural resilience standards written into code requirements in United States, where GNP per capita is about $20,000 may not be directly applicable in countries with income levels of $1,000 GNP per capita, but the attitude to safety that the code espouses is applicable. Appropriate levels of investment in safety need to be defined for each country.

Decision making on appropriate levels of investment in disaster mitigation depends on how likely the hazard is to occur, and what would be the impact of the hazard if it does occur. The assessment of risk and use of vulnerability evaluation in decision-making is covered in the module on Vulnerability and Risk Assessment.

The costs and benefits of alternative investment strategies need to be carefully evaluated. In a number of evaluations of disaster mitigation projects, it has been demonstrated that well-targeted investment will repay itself several times in the event of a disaster in reduced levels of direct damage cost. It will also have the additional benefits of saving life and reducing consequential losses to the economy and the costs of emergency operation. The use of a systematic framework of risk assessment to establish which hazards are most likely to occur and the probable effects will help define the priorities of a mitigation program-whether to build flood protection barriers or to establish a public information campaign for cyclone-resistant housing, for example.

Practicalities of Mitigation

Successful mitigation entails a number of fundamental changes in the attitudes of the people at risk, in the processes of creating and modifying the physical environment and in the physical layout of a community. These changes take time.

The nature of political administrations requires that projects resulting in tangible or demonstrable outputs within the lifetime of the administration (two, three, four years) are preferred. Many visible elements of mitigation can be achieved within that time span; engineering projects for hazard mitigation, building strengthening, changing the use of vulnerable structures, widening streets, for example, but these alone are unlikely to result in a sustainable reduction in risk. A balance of both immediately visible outputs and long term, sustainable benefits is needed.

Financial incentive schemes to reduce disaster risk requires a considerable government budget for disaster mitigation. The scale of the problem faced in trying to combat a large-scale hazard like earthquakes or tropical storms is the geographical extent of the zone at risk and the number of elements at risk in the region. Programs for housing upgrading, hazard education or community action is likely to involve millions of households. The resources necessary to accomplish this may be considerable.

Opportunities for Mitigation

Occasionally mitigation projects are prompted by predictions and studies of the likely consequences of hazards but in many cases implementation of mitigation comes about mainly in the aftermath of disaster. Rebuilding what has been destroyed and a recognition that the damage was avoidable can generate protection against a future disaster. Public support for mitigation action is strong with the visible evidence and recent memory of the disaster, or the knowledge of a disaster elsewhere.

For most hazards, mitigation projects tend to focus on the reconstruction area, even if other areas are more at risk: An area damaged by an earthquake is likely to be targeted for immediate mitigation measures despite the fact that the next earthquake may be unlikely to strike the same place, but is more likely to occur elsewhere in the region. This may not be true for some hazard types especially floods which tend to reoccur in the same locations. The experiences of the disaster, the reconstruction and the mitigation measures it engenders should be exported with relevant adaptations to the places that need it most. The fact remains that reconstruction activities with large amounts of investment being put into the area and the opportunities for change represent significant opportunities to carry out mitigation. The techniques learned and the expertise developed will be applicable elsewhere in the country. It is important that the mitigation actions are promoted as far as possible beyond the reconstruction area to other areas at risk from similar hazards, and that mitigation encompasses all the hazards likely to be encountered. The experiences of the disaster, the reconstruction and the mitigation measures it engenders should be exported with relevant adaptations to the places that need it most.

Community-based Mitigation

It has been argued that governments and large development agencies tend to adopt a "top-down" approach to disaster mitigation planning whereby the intended beneficiaries are provided with solutions designed for them by planners rather than selected for themselves. Such "top-down" approaches tend to emphasize physical mitigation measures rather than social changes to build up the resources of the vulnerable groups. They rarely achieve their goals because they act on symptoms not causes, and fail to respond to the real needs and demands of the people. Ultimately they undermine the community's own ability to protect itself.

An alternative approach is to develop mitigation policies in consultation with local community groups using techniques and actions which they can organize themselves and manage with limited outside technical assistance. Such community-based mitigation programs are considered more likely to result in actions which are a response to people's real needs, and to contribute to the development of the community, its consciousness of the hazards it faces and its ability to protect itself in the future, even though technically the means may be less effective than larger-scale mitigation programs. They will also tend to maximize the use of local resources, including labour, materials and organization.

Applying such community-based policies depends on several factors- the existence of active concerned local community groups and agencies able to provide technical assistance and support at an appropriate level, for example, are crucial to success.

Nevertheless, opportunities for community-based mitigation actions should always be sought in developing a comprehensive mitigation strategy. They will certainly be cheaper and may be more successful than alternative larger-scale programs.

Mitigation and Community Empowerment

Successful mitigation practices must involve collaboration between the local community and larger-scale development agencies. The local community must be aware of the risk and concerned to take action to prevent it: in this they may need technical assistance, material assistance and help in building their own capabilities. These forms of assistance may not be available in which case they need to be provided by external agencies. One of the most effective ways in which such an agency can help promote community protection is by enabling communities to formulate their own project proposals and negotiate with government and the larger development agencies (or government agencies) for the necessary government actions and the material assistance they need. This is especially true for technologically based engineering projects, such as large embankments, spillways, and diversion works. For example construction of community defenses based solely on hand-labour and local materials alone may result in poor disaster defenses. But local labour supplemented by heavy machinery, and local materials bonded by factory-made materials (e.g. cement or wire mesh) provided from external sources can result in lasting defenses which the local community will be able to trust and maintain in the long term. Similarly a community-based mitigation program may need government action to provide land for safer resettlement of the most vulnerable, which can most effectively be determined by the community itself. The empowerment of the community created by achieving such goals and obtaining assistance from government agencies is likely to be a lasting development benefit.

Implementing Organisations

Building-up Skills and Institutions

Disasters are an international problem. The scale of a major disaster often exceeds the capabilities and resources of a national government. The international community is usually quick and generous in its response. Protection from disasters is similarly an international concern. Disasters are, with a few notable exceptions, infrequent and a country is unlikely to have regular experience or to have built up expertise in dealing with all of the wide range of hazards it is likely to experience. That expertise is available on an international level. Countries that have recently experienced a volcanic eruption may be best placed to assist another country anticipating volcanic activity, for example. International organizations are important vehicles for facilitating international exchanges of expertise and developing an international approach to disaster mitigation. Some of the important actors are DHA, UNDP, NGOs and regional organizations.

One of the most important long-term, sustainable aspects of disaster mitigation is the development of skills and technical capacitation in-country. Professional development and a pool of expertise in disaster mitigation techniques will allow longer term development of the issue. Helping to build national institutions and formal structures that will perpetuate the mitigation program is an important element of the UN's initiative in providing disaster management assistance. In a number of countries, the response to any individual disaster is to set up a special disaster committee to handle the emergency. At the end of the emergency of reconstruction, the committee or government department has the advantage of retaining these skills and experiences. This allows some emphasis to be switched from post-disaster assistance to pre-disaster preparedness. Institutions which gather and analyse information are fundamental to the development of the skills required in any nation to reduce its risk against future disaster. Examples of institutions that would make up a national technical capability could include:

— Meteorological observatory
— Seismological observatory
— Volcanology institution
— Hydraulics and hydrology laboratories
— Engineering council
— Industrial safety inspectorate
— Chamber of architects
— Institution of urban and regional planners
— Research institutions
— Associations of economists, geographers, social scientists
— National standards committee

The hazard observatories are the first requirements for a national capability in hazard defense. Often these institutions have few resources and are perceived as low priority or as esoteric research institutes. Equipment needs may be critical. Observatories need networks of sophisticated instrume-ntation maintained in the field, and are likely to need advanced computing facilities and software to analyse results. Training of technicians and staff members in developments in instrumentation and scientific methods may be important. The output of the various professional institutions is often highly technical and there is a need to persuade technical specialists to present their findings in simplified forms, comprehensible to laymen and to professionals in other disciplines-the interdisciplinary interfaces are important in developing an integrated mitigation program.

References

Carter, Nick. (1991). *Disaster Management: A Disaster Manager's Handbook.* Manila: Asian Development Bank.

Environment Waikato, (1999). Volcanic Risk Mitigation Plan, *Environment Waikato Policy Series* 1999/10.

Haddow, George D. and Jane A. Bullock, (2003). *Introduction to Emergency Management*, Amsterdam: Butterworth-Heinemann.

Maskrey, Andrew. (1989). *Disaster Mitigation: A Community Based Approach.* Development Guidelines No.3.Oxford: Oxfam Print Unit.

UNDRO. (1984). Disaster Prevention and Mitigation. Vol. 11, Preparedness Aspects. New York: United Nations.

2

Disaster Vulnerability Analysis

In recent years there has been a welcome growth in the literature on disasters that recognises the significance of people's vulnerability to hazards, rather than retaining a narrow focus on the hazards themselves. If we accept the equation that *Disaster = Hazard + Vulnerable people*, then we clearly need to know as much about vulnerability as we do about hazards. More than that, we need to know a great deal more about the interaction of hazards and people's vulnerability. Historically there has been a split in disasters work which sees these two - hazards and vulnerability - as separate arenas, each with their own specialists. Inherent in this is the danger that those who specialise in dealing with hazards tend not to deal with vulnerability (let alone the interaction). Many hazard specialists also tend to deal in one type of hazard, and to be rooted in a physical science where knowledge of (or even interest in) the social sciences is minimal.

At the same time, with the emergence of a wider awareness of vulnerability issues, there is also the danger that it is being used crudely or simplistically, and incorporated into disaster work in depoliticised and inadequate ways. This is particularly significant as the word itself implies people being potential victims, in need of assistance and incapacitated. For instance, the British Red Cross use the word to mean 'people in need and crisis', which is little different from the term 'victim' and has no sense of prediction. It is therefore crucial to recognise that vulnerability is balanced by peoples' capabilities and resilience, and that if they are perceived only or mainly as victims then the problem of what causes vulnerability may be evaded. Another problem is that vulnerability analysis risks being regarded as politically neutral and devoid of contention and conflict, its connotation being that it is simply about incorporating people into the equation in a more prominent manner. If this is the case, then vulnerability has now become one of those buzzwords akin to 'sustainability', used in so many contexts that it is in danger of becoming useless.

This makes an attempt to specify and operationalise what is meant by vulnerability particularly important. We need to disaggregate it, make it apparent that it is derived largely from a political, economic and social context and is not simply about people who are 'victims' in some aggregated and apolitical manner. The key issue is that people's own (very variable) characteristics - their capacities, resilience and vulnerabilities - are recognised as a significant part of the disaster equation. Moreover, vulnerability needs to be appraised in terms of the differential impacts of various types of hazard impacts, and operationalised so that the factors that constitute vulnerabilty can be measured and taken into account prior to a hazard striking.

Vulnerability analysis is developed from a range of socio-economic approaches to hazards and what we could call 'the disaster of everyday life'. Pelling's work on floods in Guyana sees vulnerability as 'an ongoing state rather than a status to be identified in relation to a specific hazardous event'. In other words, vulnerability analysis begins with the crucial acceptance that vulnerability is often part of the normal, becoming apparent and obvious to some only with the impact of a hazard. It overlaps with and is derived from other perspecitves including (among others) Amartya Sen's work on famine and entitlements, the UK Save the Children Fund's project on famine warning through the software system RiskMap and a great deal of other work on food systems and coping strategies. It is vital to recognise that vulnerability should be treated as a condition of people that derives from their political-economic position. It is therefore 'dangerous' to use it loosely or as a characteristic of exposure to hazards alone, since this allows for the key components of power and income distribution to be played down and prominence given to technical fixes.

Vulnerability Analysis

The assumption that 'natural' disasters are inherently and predominantly natural phenomena has tended to exclude the social sciences from consideration in much of the spending that is done in disaster preparedness. This is despite the fact that over the last twenty years a considerable literature on disasters has emerged from human geography, sociology, anthropology and (to a lesser extent) economics. For many years, social science has contributed to policy formation for disasters (especially in the Third World) through the activities of many Non-Government Organisations (NGOs). The initial development of vulnerability analysis is then rooted in social science, and in a sense has constituted a political economy of disasters to the analysis of devastating events that are normally associated with natural hazards. At its most simplistic, vulnerability analysis asserts that for there to be a disaster there has to be not only a natural hazard, but also a vulnerable population. Much of the conventional work on disasters has been dominated by 'hard science', and has been a product of the prominence that natural phenomena have acquired in the disaster causation process. But this 'physicalist' approach is also a result of the social construction of disasters as events that demonstrate the human condition as subordinate to Nature. Within such a framework, there is the inherent danger that people are perceived as victims rather than being part of socio-economic systems that allocate risk differently to various types of people. People therefore often become treated as 'clients' in the process of disaster mitigation and preparedness, and as passive onlookers in a process in which science and technology do things to them and for them, rather than with them.

Political Economy and Vulnerability Analysis

In the last five years or so, the term vulnerability analysis has become more widely used, and in some disaster disciplines the notion of vulnerability has become common. The notion is that the analysis of the vulnerability (of people and not only physical structures) would allow some measure of mitigation and preparation, if not socio-economic restructuring. So a key element of the term is that it should be prescriptive and predictive. The focus should be on its political economy determinants and their effects in differentiating people (into groups that are differentially exposed to risk), and not simply structures that happen to be in places where a particular hazard (or various hazards) is likely to strike.

Most usages of the idea of vulnerability accept that it is part of a continuum or ranking of people, and that being vulnerable is at the 'negative' end of such a scale. Granger has suggested that 'vulnerability of each element at risk within the community can be measured along a contunuum from total resilience at one end to total susceptability at the other.' The term in its political economy usage implies that while there can be a ranking of people from more to less vulnerable (with capabilities and resilience at the positive end), the continuum must be related to various political, social and economic components of vulnerability, and that there can be different types of vulnerability according to the different hazards that might affect a given place (for instance a particular family may be more vulnerable to wildfire than to earthquake in the same place.)

This means that vulnerability analysis is complex and dependent on large data sets, and on qualitative analysis that requires the involvement of the people concerned in the evaluation of their vulnerability. The focus is either on groups of people who prima facie are vulnerable in the sense that they are clearly low on all or most socio-economic indicators (a 'disaster waiting to happen'), or in places where conventional civil defence approaches are seen as inadequate, and community-led responses are possible. In the first type of situation, examples include the work of Intermediate Technology in Peru, and the Central America survey of the early 1990s. Much of the most innovative work is going on in Third World countries, where NGOs have become aware of the restrictions of the 'hard science' approach.

Vulnerability Modelling

The dominance of hard science in work on disasters has tended to mean that most mitigation proposals are dominated by a 'technical fix' approach. These tend to address only limited components of peoples' vulnerability, mainly in Societal Protection and in providing the technical capability (but often not the means for implementation) for Self-protection. In other words, and especially in Third World contexts, dealing with peoples' livelihood resilience (their strength pre-hazard and their recovery capacity post-hazard impact) is not regarded as susceptible to technical interventions and so is 'defined out' of the problem. Moreover, since the main components of what causes these forms of vulnerability is governed by politics and economics, vulnerability analysis is avoided as being 'not relevant to science' or 'too difficult to get involved in'. In effect, what happens then is that vulnerability is addressed only in aspects that are susceptible to technical interventions, but because the main causes are ignored these interventions themselves sometimes reinforce the conditions that generate vulnerability.In relation to riverine and rainfall floods, technical interventions have usually meant storm drains and channel modifications in urban environments, and river training and embanking elsewhere. Although the issues of land modification and changes to runoff from built-up areas have led to policies of land-use zoning to avoid e.g. flood plain risks, it seems clear that commercial pressures or inadequate implementation in some countries has reduced the efficacy of such engineering. And the issue of river training and embanking has become extremely controversial, especially after floods of the Mississippi, and the Rhine and its tributaries in Germany and the Netherlands in recent years.

But the issue is not really about whether Nature can be 'controlled' and subdued or not (in many cases it clearly can, for a price), but the type of control and set of choices that are presumed to be available within a given socio-economic system. In most capitalist and communist contexts, this has generally meant an overwhelming focus on practices that emerge from and reinforce that socio-economic system, rather than being able to think about how real people with actual vulnerabilities are interacting with hazards. As a result, huge capital investments are made in river training schemes with little consideration for the opportunity costs and how that capital might be spent in other ways to deal with the forces that generate peoples' vulnerability. The current environmentalist arguments about restoring rivers to flow more naturally and accept that people should 'live with floods' may well redress the errors of ineffective capital spending on hardware approaches. But they do not necessarily deal with the political economy of people and their vulnerabilities. The same must be said of vulnerability analysis: while it may be technically possible to do it, how are the causes of peoples' vulnerabilites - the political, economic and social roots of it - going to be addressed? It is largely because power structures want to avoid dealing with such issues that the 'tech-fix' approach is so dominant (it both avoids having to deal with socio-economic causes, and through capital spending and the enhanced role of the state it usually reinforces the political-economic status quo).

Modelling the vulnerability of people will require the collection and analysis of data in quantitative and qualitative terms, with a combination of surveys of households, institutional analysis (local governments, insurance companies, voluntary organisations, businesses and employers), livelihood and welfare analysis (of income sources and employment patterns), and surveys of physical structures and infrastructure (with the emphasis not only on property damage, but also the impact of floods on welfare and income earning opportunities). Attempts to design methodologies for this are being made, especially in Australian disaster management). Cross-cultural analysis of vulnerability and potential losses are also being worked out.

The vulnerability modelling will include not only the area at threat of inundation with given flood scenarios, but also surrounding areas that may suffer various forms of disruption for other categories of vulnerable people. For instance, loss of a significant employer through building damage will cause not only a loss to the business (and the insurer), but also widespread disruption of livelihoods and earning capacity for employees, whose vulnerability may be high. On the other hand, some communities may have more 'social capital' in the form of local organisations that enable people to recover more quickly than elsewhere. Although such organisations are not designed to deal with floods, they may permit greater social cohesion and higher morale.

Vulnerability can be considered on a scale from high to low levels for a number of components. These components recognise not only the negative ends of the scale (vulnerabilities), but also how they can constitute the positive capabilities of an individual or group to survive and recover from a given hazard impact of a given severity (see also Anderson and Woodrow, 1998 regarding the significance of capacities and vulnerabilities).

Vulnerability can be considered in terms of five components:

1. Initial well-being,
2. Self-protection,
3. Social protection,
4. Livelihood Resilience, and
5. Social Capital.

It should be noted that each one of these is crucially linked to the likely severity of impact of a given hazard, and yet primarily they are all determined by political, economic or social processes. Each of these contains the possibility of both vulnerabilities and capabilities, with these varying over time (as individuals and groups subsist and compete within given livelihood possibilities), and being affected in regard to different types of natural hazards. Of course, these components are also part and parcel of everyday life, and are not only related to the likely (or unlikely) impacts of different natural hazards. They are also of relevance to a person or group's ability to withstand (or be involved with) other forms of short-term shock or unforseen circumstances (such as civil conflicts and war, or Man-made hazards, or complex emergencies which combine either or both of these with natural hazards).

If we examine these in more detail, we can see that they each depend on a complex interaction between the actions (or inactions) of individuals, and of higher-level institutions. It is entirely possible for the capabilities of one person or group to be exercised at the expense of others, and for the higher-level activities to both negate or neutralise (as well as reinforce) the resilience of people. (This is important to recognise, as there is a danger in some of the literature on capacities and resilience to suggest that there are rather undifferentiated 'communities' which are inherently benign and positive in their composition, and their response to disasters.)

The five components of the level of vulnerability are then:

1. *Initial well-being, strength and resilience.* This evaluates the initial nutritional and health status (both physical and mental) of people in everyday life (or before the impact of a hazard). It is indicative of their capacity to cope with illness and some types of injury resulting from a hazard. It should include their potential for mental disturbance and recovery in the wake of a disaster, which might intensify existing stresses. A person's resilience may relate to having a faith or spiritual confidence, or a predisposition to self-reliance.
2. *Livelihood resilience.* A measure of the capacity of an individual and/or their household to cope with the aftermath of a given hazard impact, and to reinstate their earning or livelihood pattern. This might include their likely continued employment, level of savings, loss of welfare benefits, loss or injury of supportive family members, hazard damage to their normal livelihood activity (for example in floods this might include damage to agricultural land by sediment deposits, sea-water incursion, toxic or sewage contamination).
3. *Self-protection* concerns the ability or willingness of an individual and/or household (with a given level of knowledge of apparent risks) to provide themselves with adequate protection, or to be able to avoid living or working in hazardous places. It will be influenced by the level of knowledge of physical measures, and the capacity of people to implement them.

4. *Societal protection* refers to the ability or willingness of social and political structures at political or social levels above the individual or household, to provide protection (especially structural and technical preparations) from particular hazards. This might include local government, national government, relevant organisations (e.g. fire department, civil defence), or community-based initiatives.
5. *Social capital* involves the 'soft' security provided by group or community capacities to enhance (or reduce) a person's resilience. This may include the degree of cohesion or rivalry that might affect rescue and recovery. There are various forms of social capital that may enhance or hinder recovery. These include support networks (belonging to a church or other group), some of which may provide mutual aid in times of hardship. The character and quality of social capital may depend to a large extent on the type of state power and the capacity for civil society to develop

As can be seen, these five components place someone in the spectrum from highly vulnerabe to being secure and are a complex mix of an individual's characterstics, social factors and economic and political processes, and the type of hazard to which they might be exposed. They involve both 'hard', generally hazard-specific technical interventions like warning systems and physical structures like cyclone shelters and flood embankments, and 'soft' socio-economic factors (including income distribution, access to livelihood resources, discrimination in the receipt of assistance). Various processes and factors determine the extent to which a person or group is made vulnerable or secure in relation to each of these components of vulnerability.

These components must then be cross-related to a series of social factors and political characteristics that can be considered to affect them positively or negatively (determinants), so generating different levels of vulnerability for each of the components. The social factors include economic class (or income group as its surrogate), gender, ethnicity, and age. The political characteristics of different societies can be interpreted in four ways: firstly the type of state system (democratic, redistributive, pro-corporation, authoritarian, kleptocratic, religious, etc.); secondly the state's capacity to act (its 'reach', whether it has adequate revenue, its efficiency); thirdly the strength of civil society that the state enables or permits; and fourthly other factors which lead to cohesion or cleavages, such as whether a participatory society is fostered or forbidden, how much dependency there is on religious or political allegiances, and how these are organised in opposition or support for the state.

These social factors also affect the way that scientific and technical knowledge of hazards (and how to prepare for them) is used, how good it is and how that science and technology is 'distributed' between different groups of people. In other word, it is common to talk about income and asset distribution and the way these affect different groups of people. But we can also speak about 'scientific and technical distribution' as well, since it can operate within power relations that make knowledge unequally available to different types of people, leaving them more or less vulnerable.

There is no simple correlation between someone enjoying a low level of vulnerability and the normal 'advantaged' conditions of the rich, of men, or of dominant ethnic groups. There are occasions when being rich or male can generate more exposure to hazard risk, and vulnerability is not necessarily the same as poverty or marginalisation, though it appears that in most cases there is a reasonable parallel.

Mapping Hazard Exposures

States and local jurisdictions across the world vary in their exposure to the hazards. Consequently, an important objective for a local emergency manager is to identify the hazards that his or her community should set as priorities for its emergency management program. There are many useful sources of information about the regional incidence of these hazards, one of which is the set of maps contained in the US Federal Emergency Management Agency's (FEMA) Multi Hazard Identification and Risk Assessment. This source has an extensive set of maps describing exposure to natural hazards and also addresses some technological hazards.

The maps of natural hazard exposures contained in Multi Hazard Identification and Risk Assessment can be supplemented by visiting the Web sites of FEMA, the US Geological Survey, and the National Weather Service. These maps provide a good start toward assessing the potential impacts of disasters, but they have three limitations. First, many of these large scale maps are designed to compare the relative risk of broad geographical areas. This information enables local emergency managers to identify the hazards that could strike their jurisdictions, but it does not provide enough resolution to tell them which areas within their jurisdictions are most likely to be struck by a disaster.

Second, these maps vary from one hazard to another in terms of whether they define risk areas in terms of event magnitudes or in terms of recurrence intervals. For example, hurricane risk area maps identify areas that are expected to be affected by Category 1-5 hurricanes. However, these maps provide no information about the probability that each of these different hurricane intensities would occur.

By contrast, US Geological Survey earthquake hazard maps plot the peak ground acceleration (PGA) with a 2% probability of exceedance in 50 years. Thus, these maps provide useful information about the areas in which buildings are most likely to collapse and some indication likelihood of a disaster. However, trained engineers would be needed to use this quantitative information to assess the probabilities of building failure.

Third, these maps are insufficient for local HVAs because local emergency managers also need to assess the relative risk of different hazards for a given geographical area. That is, emergency managers need to know whether their jurisdictions are at risk for certain hazards, but they also need to know what is the likelihood of a flood in comparison to a tornado, an earthquake, or a toxic chemical release.

As a result of these limitations, local emergency managers must often settle for qualitative comparisons of the relative risk of different hazards. That is, they must typically categorize the probability of disaster impact as high, medium, or low . Such categorization provides only a "rough screen" for determining which hazards require the most attention, but this limitation is often more apparent than real because many hazards impose similar demands on the community, especially during the emergency response phase.

Specifically, the equipment and methods used for emergency assessment and hazard operations might differ among the meteorological, hydrological, geophysical, and hazardous materials hazards, but the equipment and methods used for population protection and incident management will be quite similar. Consequently, differences in hazard probability are often unimportant because preparedness for one provides preparedness for many, if not all, other hazards. Nonetheless, many mitigation measures are hazard-specific, so an understanding of the relative risk from different hazards can provide valuable guidance in determining which investments are most likely to reduce a community's vulnerability.

Incidents involving fires, explosions, or chemical releases can be initiated by internal (accident or sabotage) or external (geophysical, meteorological, or hydrological events, or terrorist attacks) causes. The types of hazards that can occur at a chemical facility, their initiating events, their consequences, and their likelihoods of occurrence can be assessed using hazard analysis. This process begins by identifying dangerous chemicals (i.e., those that are threats because of their flammability, reactivity, or toxicity), their locations, and the quantities stored at those locations.

Once the chemical inventory has been developed, this information can be used to assess the threats these chemicals pose to the facility, its workers, its neighbors, and the environment. In the case of Extremely Hazardous Substances (EHSs), Vulnerable Zones (VZs) can be computed using data on the chemical's toxicity, its quantity available for release, the type of spill (liquid or gaseous), the postulated release duration (e.g., 10 minutes), assumed meteorological conditions (wind speed and atmospheric stability), and terrain (urban or rural).

Emergency managers also should work with their Local Emergency Planning Committees (LEPCs) to identify the highway, rail, water, and air routes though which hazardous materials are transported. Once these routes have been identified, the number of tank trucks, railroad tankcars, and barges carrying each type of hazardous material can be counted in a commodity flow study. Once the chemicals being transported have been identified, analysts can use the same procedures that were used for fixed site facilities.

Emergency managers should recall that some disaster impacts can initiate others.Earthquakes can cause surface faulting, ground failure, landslides, fires, dam failures, and hazardous materials releases in addition to the expected structural failures caused by ground shaking. One method of identifying areas exposed to multiple hazards is to use a GIS to overlay the areas subject to these different hazards. This is accomplished by entering all of the data on primary and secondary hazard exposures and special facilities into a GIS that creates separate layers for fault lines; areas prone to the highest levels of ground shaking, subsidence, and landsliding; hazardous facility Vulnerable Zones; and locations of sensitive facilities. Next, these layers are intersected to produce composite maps displaying the areas subject to multiple hazards. Finally, the layers identifying the locations of residential, commercial, and industrial areas, and sensitive facilities are overlaid to produce the final maps.

Table 1. Primary and Secondary Hazards

Primary Hazard	*Secondary Hazards*
Severe storms	Floods, tornadoes, landslides
Extreme summer weather	Wildfires
Tornadoes	Toxic chemical or radiological materials releases
Hurricane wind	Toxic chemical or radiological materials releases
Wildfires	Landslides (on hillsides in later rains)
Floods	Toxic chemical or radiological materials releases
Storm surge	Toxic chemical or radiological materials releases
Tsunamis	Toxic chemical or radiological materials releases
Volcanic eruptions	Floods, wildfires, tsunamis
Earthquakes	Fires, floods (dam failures), tsunami, landslides, toxic chemical or radiological materials releases
Landslides	Tsunami

Assessing Physical Vulnerability

Information on hazard exposure needs to be supplemented with information on physical vulnerability of structures and people. This makes it necessary to identify the types of structures and populations that are located in the areas exposed to environmental hazards.

Structural Vulnerability to Wind, Seismic, and Water Forces

Structures can be vulnerable to environmental hazards because of inadequate designs, inadequate construction materials, or both. Older homes have been constructed under earlier building codes and most neighborhoods are relatively homogeneous with respect to age, so identifying older neighborhoods in hazard-prone areas will help set priorities of emergency management interventions. For example, many areas of the country have homes, built during the early part of the 20th Century using unreinforced masonry (brick walls constructed without steel reinforcing rods), that are especially vulnerable to earthquakes. Similarly, older homes are usually less weathertight, so they are much more prone to infiltration of hazardous materials.

There are three major issues in assessing structural vulnerability. First is the question of whether the structure has the strength or resilience to withstand environmental forces such as wind, seismicity, or water. In this case, the concern is about the impact on the structure itself and, consequently, the loss of function and the time and cost of rebuilding. The second issue concerns the ability of the structure to protect the contents. This issue is distinct from the first one because in earthquakes, for example, buildings that survive ground shaking without damage can transmit the motion to light fixtures, cabinets, and furniture—possibly damaging these items. The third issue concerns the ability of the structure to protect the occupants. This is especially important in connection with hazardous materials because they can infiltrate into a structure and kill the occupants without damaging the building.

Once the areas at risk from environmental hazards have been identified, emergency managers should identify the types of residential, commercial, and industrial land uses located within them. It is particularly important to determine if there are any facilities within each VZ that have highly vulnerable populations.

The assessment of structural vulnerability usually involves all three issues. For riverine flooding and hurricane storm surge, structures—especially concrete structures with well-anchored foundations—resist battering waves to protect the structure and provide the height to escape the rising water that could threaten contents and occupants.

In other cases, it is the strength of construction in resisting wind loads (tornadoes and hurricanes), blast forces (explosions and volcanic eruptions) and ground shaking (earthquakes) that protects the structure, contents, and occupants. For chemical, radiological, and volcanic ash threats, it is the tightness of construction in preventing the infiltration of outside (contaminated) air into the structure that is the important protective feature. Finally, in the case of exposure to a cloud of radioactive material, the construction material can provide shielding from penetrating radiation and from surface contamination.

In high wind (including tornadoes and hurricanes) and explosions (usually technological in origin, but also including some volcanic eruptions), a substantial increase in air pressure can cause structures to collapse. Such structural failures are caused by deficiencies in either design or materials, or both.

Fortified homes provide for installation of connections and braces to reinforce roofs and gable-end walls against wind attack. In addition to positive pressure on upwind walls, high wind creates negative pressure, or suction, as it is forced to flow up and over the roof. This suction is greatest in flat roofs, intermediate in gable-end roofs (which slope in two directions), and least in hipped roofs (which slope in four directions). Suction tends to lift the roof from the walls unless resisted by adequate connections to the walls—which in turn, must have adequate connections to the foundation. Adequate designs and materials also provide protection to building openings such as windows and doors, thus preventing the wind from pressurizing the interior and adding to the stress on roof and walls. The need for window and sliding glass door shutters is widely recognized because the shutters resist the direct pressure of the wind and the impact of flying debris. However, door reinforcement is also important—especially for double-wide (two-car) garage doors that are highly susceptible to failure because their great width allows the wind to deflect them inward and pull the rollers out of their tracks.

Similar observations apply to earthquakes; building damage typically results from the lateral pressures (ground shaking, surface faulting, and soil failure) exerted against a structure that was designed principally to resist the vertical loads resulting from the weight of the occupants, furniture, upper stories, and roof. Rigid structures such as unreinforced masonry are extremely vulnerable, whereas wood frame dwellings are much safer. In the latter case, there might be rigid portions of a structure, such as brick chimneys, that separate from the rest of the structure and collapse into the living area. In addition, glass from broken windows, falling pictures and mirrors, the toppling of unsecured furniture, and other flying debris are safety hazards. For hurricanes, structures on the open coast must be of sufficiently sturdy construction that they can resist the direct impact of storm surf as well as the force of extremely high winds. However, both riverine flooding and hurricane storm surge also require the structure to have foundations anchored well enough to resist scouring by water currents that can undermine building foundations and cause structural collapse. Additional protection can be provided by expedient floodproofing that uses waterproof construction materials, sealing of cracks, provision of valves on sewer lines, steel bulkheads for lower-level openings, and sump pumps to eject seepage .

As with hurricane surge and riverine flooding, volcanic mudflows and floods present the challenge of maintaining the integrity of buildings and their foundation. However, flooding generated by volcanic eruption commonly contains a substantial volume of rock and ash, resulting in mudflows that have substantial carrying power. Moreover, as was found during the eruption of Mt. St. Helens, silt buildup can significantly raise the bed of the river channel.

Tsunami impact poses an even greater threat than inland flooding, surge from hurricanes and coastal storms, or volcanic mudflows. These seismic sea waves can threaten areas as much as 100 feet above sea level, so destruction is highly likely for most structures located very near the shoreline. However, properly designed steel-reinforced concrete structures located a short distance inland are likely to survive even the largest tsunamis.

Human Vulnerability to Inhalation Exposure

In the case of radiological or toxic materials, the principal public health hazard arises from inhalation of airborne materials that have an adverse health effect. Inhalation exposures can also result from the dispersion of airborne debris such as ash and gas from volcanic eruptions. Ideally, an enclosed space will provide a barrier if it can be closed tightly enough to keep out the hazardous material and has enough oxygen to sustain those within it until the danger has passed. Unfortunately, most structures are leaky, allowing contaminated air to infiltrate even when the doors and windows are closed. The rate of air exchange increases with the amount of leakage area, the wind speed, and the temperature differential between the indoor and outdoor air.

The rate at which indoor and outdoor air are exchanged is commonly measured in air changes per hour (ACH). However, emergency managers will find it more useful to think of air exchange in terms of *turnover time*, which the reciprocal of the air exchange rate, or t_B = 1/ACH, where ACH is the number of air changes per hour. As Wilson emphasizes, an infiltration rate of 1.0 ACH does not imply that all the clean air will be gone in one hour. Rather, the proportion of contaminated air gradually rises until at the end of 1.0 t_B hours, 63% of the original air has been replaced by contaminated air, while 95% of the original air has been replaced by the end of 3.0 t_B hours. Thus, for the case of 1.0 ACH, it will take over three hours (not just one hour) for the indoor air to become almost completely contaminated. This result is extremely important because it indicates that in-place sheltering is more effective than most people might infer from the apparent implication of the number of air changes per hour. The reason for the difference between the apparent result and the correct result can best be illustrated by examining the difference between the apparent, but incorrect, mechanism of air exchange and the actual mechanism. It would only take one hour to replace the clean air (the incorrect result) if the contaminated air somehow "pushed out" the clean air, but this is not what happens. Rather, the contaminated air that infiltrates into the structure mixes with the clean air rather than "pushing it out". Clearly, exfiltration of a mixture of clean air and contaminated air will take longer to exhaust the clean air in a structure than will exfiltration of ("pushing out") clean air alone. Consequently, sheltering in-place is at least three times as effective in reducing inhalation exposure as it first appears to be.

While this time lag effect is important, it is not the only mechanism by which sheltering in-place can reduce adverse health effects. It is also important to recognize the impact of a damping effect in reducing the fluctuations in plume concentrations. These fluctuations arise from irregularities in meteorological conditions and local terrain. One way of measuring peak concentration is by estimating the value that is exceeded approximately 1% of the time. Wilson reports that in the outdoor (contaminated) air, such 1% peak concentrations are 400% as large as the mean concentration. For indoor air, the equivalent peak concentration is only 50% larger than the mean. As he notes, even when the indoor concentration has risen after six hours to match the outdoor concentration, the indoor peaks would be expected to be approximately 150 ppm when the outdoor peaks would be 400 ppm. This is, of course, of considerable significance when peak concentrations are the principal health threats.

A major problem in assessing the effectiveness of sheltering in-place is uncertainty about whether indoor air concentrations will remain sufficiently low for a sufficiently long period of time. This can be answered definitively only if there is information about the hazardous material being released (especially the identity of the material released, and the rate and duration of the release), the meteorological data needed for a computerized plume dispersion model wind speed, wind direction, and atmospheric stability), and the air exchange rates for the structures in the hazard impact area. Data on the release and the meteorological conditions will not be available until an incident occurs, but data on the efficacy of sheltering in-place can be collected in advance. First, Rogers, et al. report that energy conservation research has shown air exchange in most US dwellings ranges from 0.5 to 1.5 ACH. Second, Wilson reports that the most important factor affecting leakage area is the presence of a vapor barrier in the walls and ceiling of a structure, a feature that is most common in houses built in cold climates after 1960. Thus, emergency managers could estimate the effectiveness of sheltering in-place by obtaining access to local data on the age of the housing stock within different neighborhoods within their jurisdiction. Finally, the fact that so much of the research and data on infiltration of hazardous materials has been developed from studies of energy conservation suggests that emergency planners consult with their local utilities to determine what information is available regarding the air exchange rates of different types of structures (e.g., residences, schools, and commercial buildings) in their communities. Special facilities, especially those such as hospitals that have low mobility residents, should be examined individually to assess their air exchange rates.

Human Vulnerability to Radiological Materials

Although both toxic and radiological materials present an inhalation hazard, a plume of radioactive material released from a nuclear power plant or during a transportation accident also can cause harm by means of external gamma radiation from the cloud and from ground contamination. Dense building materials such concrete, brick, and stone provide shielding from external gamma radiation and, thus, can provide a basis for in-place sheltering during radiological emergencies. The effectiveness of structures made from different types of building materials has been examined in studies by Burson and Profio, Anno and Dore, Aldrich, Ericson and Johnson, and Aldrich, et al.

These studies calculated the dose reduction factors (the ratio of the dose received while sheltering to the unprotected dose) for three exposure routes: external gamma radiation from the cloud, external gamma radiation from ground contamination, and inhalation of radioactive materials infiltrating into the structure. Burson and Profio found that sheltering in a wood frame dwelling provides little more protection from cloud and ground exposure than does "sheltering" in a vehicle while evacuating. Sheltering on the ground floor of a masonry home with no basement or in the basement of a wood frame home gave considerably higher levels of protection: about 50% of the unprotected exposure to the cloud and less than 20% of the unprotected exposure to ground. As one might expect, the basement of a masonry house was even more effective: 40% of the cloud exposure and 5% of the ground exposure. A large office building was the most effective shelter of all, reducing cloud exposure to about 20% and ground exposure to 1%.

The importance of the construction materials is underscored by Burson and Profio's work indicating it is the cloud exposure that produces most of the whole body radiation dose received by those sheltering in a home. Infiltration into the structure would account for only about 5% of the gamma radiation dose. Anno and Dore) calculated cloud dose reduction factors for single family dwellings and large structures. They considered 0.125 to 3 ACH to define the range of infiltration rates for single family dwellings and other structures that could be used as temporary public shelters. For single family dwellings, whole body dose reduction factors for low air exchange rates (0.125 ACH) were calculated to be 0.40-0.33 compared to 0.43 for more representative air change rates (3 ACH). For large structures, whole body dose reduction factors for low air change rates were calculated to be 0.08 compared to 0.17-0.11 for the more representative air change rates. These investigators also estimated thyroid (inhalation) dose reduction factors to be about 0.05 to 0.01 for low air change rates and from 0.25 to 0.10 for more representative air change rates for either single family dwellings or large structures.

Assessing Agricultural and Livestock Vulnerability

Assessing the physical vulnerability of crops and livestock is a task that is rarely considered to be the responsibility of emergency managers. One reason for giving minimal emphasis to the agricultural sector is that it accounts for a relatively small part of the total vulnerability in many jurisdictions. In those cases where the agricultural sector is a significant part of the local economy, emergency managers should consult agricultural experts such as those from the US Department of Agriculture because, as noted earlier, there is substantial variation among animal and plant species in their susceptibility to extreme environmental conditions. For example, fruit orchards can be devastated by wind speeds that have no impact whatsoever on rangeland. Moreover, the damage to many crops depends on the stage in growth cycle—with some crops having minimal susceptibility to wind damage until just before harvest.

Assessing Social Vulnerability

In contrast to physical vulnerability, which arises from the potential for environmental extremes to create adverse physiological changes, social vulnerability arises from the potential for these extreme events to cause changes in people's behavior. People can vary in their potential for injury to themselves and their families. They also vary in the potential for destruction of their homes and workplaces, as well as the destruction of the transportation systems and locations for shopping and recreation they use in their daily activities. The discussion below emphasizes census data but it also is important to examine other archival sources such as school records, immigration services, local aging agency, special needs registries, property tax records, facilities locations. In addition, consult local social service providers (government and NGO) and churches to identify vulnerable populations.

Assessing Psychosocial Vulnerability

One important component of psychological vulnerability is personal fragility—that is, a lack of *emotion-focused* coping skills. Another component of psychological vulnerability is rigidity—that is, a lack of *problem-focused* coping skills defined by an inability to develop adaptive strategies for responding to altered conditions. Ozer and Weiss's summary of research on post-traumatic stress disorder (PTSD) concluded the four categories of PTSD predictors were

— A person's pre-existing characteristics (e.g., intelligence, previous psychological trauma),
— The severity of the personal impact of the disaster,
— Psychological processes immediately after the impact, and
— Life stress and social support after the traumatic event.

Quite obviously, only the first of these categories can measure psychological vulnerability that exists before a disaster strikes and none of the variables in this category is routinely available through secondary sources such as Census data. Because direct measures of the incidence of PTSD predictors (e.g., through community surveys) are prohibitively expensive, psychological vulnerability must be measured indirectly.

A major concern is social isolation. Thus, vulnerability is also measured by the infrequency and superficiality of social contacts with peers such as kin (extended family), neighbors, and coworkers. Routine measures of social vulnerability are rarely available through surveys conducted using representative samples of community members. However, there are proxy variables that have statistically significant—although admittedly small—

correlations with social isolation. Suitable proxy variables that are routinely available through Census files include age, income, and ethnicity. Specifically, increasing age is associated with reduced levels of community participation (involvement in voluntary associations) and immersion in kin and friendship networks. By contrast, socioeconomic status is positively associated with participation in community organizations and minority ethnicity is positively associated with immersion in kin and friendship networks. Accordingly, the use of age, socioeconomic status, and ethnicity as proxy measures of psychosocial vulnerability will also be discussed below.

Assessing Demographic Vulnerability

Vulnerability to demographic changes follows from the demographic balancing equation discussed earlier. Until 2005, recent trends in disaster casualties had indicated the number of deaths would be relatively small for any North American disaster. It is unlikely that Hurricane Katrina marks a reversal of that trend because New Orleans is the only major coastal city with a significant portion of its land area (and, thus, its population) below sea level. In most disasters, it is the number of in-migrants and out-migrants cause significant changes in its demographic composition. Once again, census data can be used to provide indicators such as age, income, homeownership, and ethnicity. Older, more affluent homeowners are likely to have high levels of community bondedness and seek permanent housing in the community even if their homes have been destroyed. Similarly, ethnic minorities have tightly integrated kin networks that make them stay. However, even otherwise stable communities are likely to experience short term changes in their demographic composition if there are few rental vacancies after a disaster. This is because a local housing shortages would require residents to move farther away for temporary housing. Similarly, a community's demographic composition is likely to change if local businesses have high levels of physical vulnerability to disaster impacts. A declining local economy will make them financially vulnerable and, thus, more likely to cease operations altogether.

Assessing Economic Vulnerability

It is obvious that wealth is a major component of economic vulnerability, but the assets comprising wealth vary in their vulnerability to disasters. Tangible assets such as buildings, equipment, furniture, and vehicles that are located in the disaster impact area are more vulnerable than financial assets such as bank accounts, stocks, and bonds that are recorded electronically. Households and businesses both have tangible and financial assets, so both are vulnerable to the loss of their tangible assets and both have financial assets that can be used to support disaster recovery. Of course, there are substantial variations among households in their assets and the same is true for businesses.

One noteworthy difference between households and businesses is that the latter also have operational vulnerability arising from dependency upon those who supply its inputs (suppliers and labor) as well as those who purchase its outputs (distributors and customers). Evidence of businesses' operational vulnerability to input disruptions can be seen in data provided by Nigg, who reported that business managers' median estimate of the amount of time that they could continue to operate without infrastructure was 0 hours for electric power, 4 hours for telephones, 48 hours for water/sewer, and 120 hours for fuel. If this infrastructure support is unavailable for time periods longer than these, then businesses must suspend operations even if they have suffered no damage to their structures or contents.

Assessing Political Vulnerability

Political impacts of disasters often arise from conflicts over the management of the emergency response and disaster recovery. Accordingly, political vulnerability arises from inadequate emergency management interventions—which create situations that pit one group of stakeholders against another—and inadequate mechanisms for managing this conflict when it does arise. Government agencies that are believed to lack legitimacy, expertise, and adequate information for making decisions about the allocation of public resources will prove vulnerable in the aftermath of disaster. As is the case with psychological, demographic, and economic vulnerability, there currently are no direct measures of political vulnerability that are readily available for use by emergency managers.

Predicting Household Vulnerability

It is important to recognize that social vulnerability is not randomly distributed either demographically or geographically. In particular, the social vulnerability arising from a lack of psychological resilience, social network integration, economic assets, and political power vary across demographic groups. Some of these components of social vulnerability can be predicted by demographic characteristics such as gender, age, education, income, and ethnicity. Moreover, these demographic groups tend to be distributed relatively systematically across the landscape of each community. Even though there might not be sharp geographic lines of demarcation between the locations of different demographic groups within a community, there are variations in the concentration of these groups in different neighborhoods. Thus, GISs can be used to conduct disaggregated spatial analyses to identify the demographic segments most likely to be vulnerable to disaster impacts.

The demographic predictors of social vulnerability are frequently also associated with hazard exposure because the population segments with the fewest psychological, social, economic, and political resources often disproportionately occupy the most hazardous geographical areas. Similarly, demographic predictors of social vulnerability are often associated with structural vulnerability because those same population segments disproportionately occupy the oldest, most poorly maintained buildings. Thus, those who are most socially vulnerable are also likely to experience the greatest physical impacts such as casualties and property loss.

Because emergency managers rarely have access to direct measures of social vulnerability, geographic analyses of social vulnerability are conducted on Census data, preferably at the lowest possible level of aggregation. Recent research has shown these aggregated indicators of social vulnerability are strongly correlated, so it is advisable to use either a composite measure of social vulnerability or a subset of these indicators.

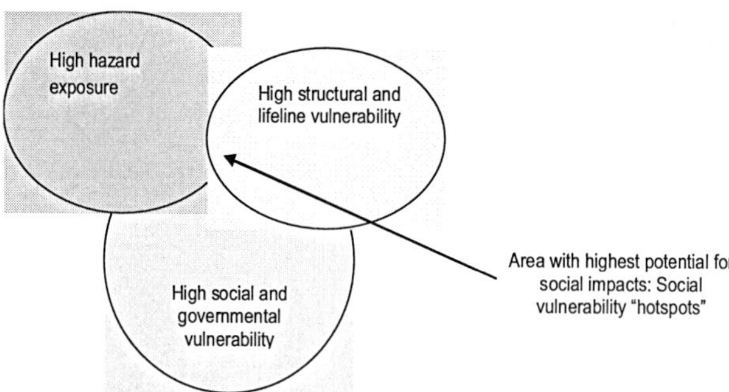

Figure 1. Disaster Impact Vulnerability Assessment Model

Based on the recognition, described above, that hazard exposure, structural vulnerability, and social vulnerability tend to be related, Prater and her colleagues advocated identifying *vulnerability hotspots*—the geographic areas occupied by demographic segments that are most vulnerable to disaster impacts. These vulnerability hotspots can be identified by using a GIS to either overlay or mathematically combine data on hazard exposure (e.g., ground motion and ground failure from earthquakes), structural vulnerability (e.g., due to dilapidated housing), and lifeline vulnerability.

Vulnerability Dynamics

A major challenge for emergency managers is to understand the processes by which communities increase or decrease their hazard exposure, physical vulnerability, and social vulnerability. According to economic theory, excessive hazard exposure and structural vulnerability arise from systemic complexities that can be characterized as *market failures* such as inadequate information, barriers to market entry and exit, and capital flow restrictions . An ideal pattern of economic development would be one in which risk area occupants purchase property on the basis of adequate information about hazard exposure and structural vulnerability.

Moreover, they would locate only where it was economically advantageous in the long term as well as in the short term, and would diversify their assets over other locations and other forms of financial (e.g., savings accounts, insurance, stocks/bonds) and social (e.g., extended family) recovery assistance. Finally, risk area occupants would adopt hazard adjustments to limit their losses if a disaster were to strike. These adjustments would include hazard mitigation (e.g., land use practices and building construction practices), emergency preparedness practices (e.g., detection and warning systems), and recovery preparedness practices (e.g., diversified investments and hazard insurance) to avoid casualties and property damage.

Actual patterns of development are significantly different from the ideal. In many cases, there is migration to hazard-prone areas because of beneficial land uses for agriculture, transportation, and recreation. This is compounded by a lack of accountability for investment decisions. Developers are at risk for only a short period of time before they pass an investment on to others who will ultimately experience the disaster impact. Such transactions can occur because many risk area residents are new arrivals who are unaware of the hazard. Even long-term residents of risk areas sometimes have little or no information about hazards and adjustments to those hazards because such information is suppressed by those with a major stake in the community's economic development.

Even when there is local knowledge about hazards, there often is a lack of hazard intrusiveness because events that are not recent or frequent tend not to be thought about or discussed. Moreover, many people ignore low probability events, think of them as occurring far in the future, or have an *optimistic bias* that the negative consequences of these events will not happen to them. In particular, politicians tend to ignore consequences that they expect to occur only after their term of office is over, so only frequent, recent, or major impacts lead to increased adoption of community-wide hazard adjustments such as land use controls or more stringent building codes. Even then, the *window of opportunity* for the adoption of these adjustments is open only temporarily.

Table 2. Indicators of Social Vulnerability

Vulnerable Groups	*Vulnerability Indicators*
Female headed households	Percent female headed households
Elderly	Percent individuals over 65 percent of elderly households
Low income/high poverty	Percent of households below poverty level
Renters	Percent of households residing in rental housingPercent of households residing in rental housing by type of dwelling units
Ethnic/racial/language minorities	Percent of individual from Black, Hispanic, and other minoritiesPercent of non-English speakers
Children/youth	Percent of population in selected age groupingsPercent of households with dependency ratios above a specified level
Social vulnerability hot spot analysis	Areas with combined social vulnera-bilities

Increased hazard exposure also is caused by displacement from safer areas due to population pressures. When this occurs, the demographic distribution of risk tends to be inequitable because geographical locations often are systematically related to their residents' demographic characteristics—especially their economic and political power to decrease hazard vulnerability. This pattern is very common in developing countries such as Brazil, where *favelas* are located in flood plains and on landslide-prone slopes because the residents cannot afford to purchase homes in safer areas.

There also are problems in the adoption of effective hazard adjustments. One of these arises from households' and businesses' concentration of hazard exposure. Diversification is an effective way of avoiding concentration of hazard vulnerability, but low-income households and small businesses often have so few physical or financial assets that they cannot afford to locate some of them in safer areas. Hazard insurance is problematic because it tends to suffer from *adverse selection*, which means that only those who are at the greatest risk are likely to purchase it. Moreover, the actions of one party can sometimes increase the vulnerability of another. In floodplains, upstream development cuts down trees and replaces it with hardscape, thus increasing the speed of rainfall runoff and downstream flooding. Technological protection works such as dams and levees can offset such increases in hazard exposure, but many risk area occupants overestimate the effectiveness of such hazard adjustments. This can cause further development of floodplains and, thus, increased hazard exposure that exceeds the risk reduction provided by the adjustment that was adopted.

References

Blaikie, P., T. Cannon, I. Davis & B. Wisner, (1994), *At Risk: Natural Hazards, Peoples' Vulnerability and Disasters*, London: Routledge.

Cannon, T. (1994). 'Vulnerability analysis and the explanation of "natural" disasters', in A. Varley (ed.) *Disasters, development and the environment*, Chichester: John Wiley.

Donald Hyndman, David Hyndman (2009). *Natural Hazards and Disasters*. Brooks/ Cole: Cengage Learning.

Graz, L. (1997), 'A question of vulnerability', *Red Cross, Red Crescent*, No.3, pp.2-7.

Keeney, J. (2007). *In Case of Emergency*. Sydney: Design Masters Press.

Varley (ed.), (1994), *Disasters, development and the environment*, Chichester: John Wiley.

3

Process of Disaster Management

Disaster management is a process or strategy that is implemented when any type of catastrophic event takes place. Sometimes referred to as disaster recovery management, the process may be initiated when anything threatens to disrupt normal operations or puts the lives of human beings at risk. Governments on all levels as well as many businesses create some sort of disaster plan that make it possible to overcome the catastrophe and return to normal function as quickly as possible.

One of the essential elements of disaster management involves defining the types of catastrophes that could possibly disrupt the day to day operation of a city, town, business, or country. Identifying those potential disasters makes it possible to create contingency plans, assemble supplies, and create procedures that can be initiated when and if a given disaster does come to pass. A truly comprehensive disaster management plan will encompass a wide range of possibilities that can easily be adapted in the event one disaster sets off a chain reaction of other types of disasters in its wake.

Because of the need to continue functioning in emergency situations, disaster management plans are often multi-layered and can address such issues as floods, hurricanes, fires, bombings, and even mass failures of utilities or the rapid spread of disease. The disaster plan is likely to address such as important matters as evacuating people from an impacted region, arranging temporary housing, food, and medical care. It is not unusual for the plan to also work toward containing and possibly neutralizing the root causes of the disaster if at all possible.

The process of disaster management will often address the issue of ongoing communication. Since many disasters can cause communication networks to fail, a competent disaster plan will include the quick setup of alternative communication capabilities that do not rely on the various switches, towers and hubs that are usually part of telephone and cellular communication networks. Often making use of short-wave transmissions that are supported with satellite technology, the communication flow can continue from the area impacted by the disaster to other points where aid can be extended when and as possible.

As part of the crisis management component of a disaster plan, it is not unusual for some type of disaster kit to be developed. The kit may include food and clothing for people who are evacuated from an area that has experienced flooding or extensive damage from a hurricane or tornado. Kits may also include basic medication to help with headaches, fevers, and other minor ailments. In some cases, the kits may include items such as sleeping bags or other necessities that will help displaced persons to cope with the after effects of the disaster.

Creating an effective disaster management plan is often easier said than done. As many nations have learned, what were thought to be comprehensive emergency plans turned out to be partially effective at best. In recent years, many government agencies stretching from the local to the national level have taken steps to revisit the structure of their disaster plans and run computer simulations to identify weaknesses in the plans, and refine them so they can operate with more speed and efficiency.

Phases of Disaster Management

The process of disaster management involves four phases:

1. Mitigation,
2. Preparedness,
3. Response,
4. Recovery,
5. Rehabilitation and reconstruction

Disaster management involves all levels of government. Nongovernmental and community-based organizations play a vital role in the process.

Modern disaster management goes beyond post-disaster assistance. It now includes pre-disaster planning and preparedness activities, organizational planning, training, information management, public relations and many other fields. Crisis management is important but is only a part of the responsibility of a disaster manager. The newer paradigm is the Total Risk Management (TRM) which takes a holistic approach to risk reduction.

The traditional approach was to provide immediate humanitarian aid as quickly as possible after the onset of a disaster. There has been a paradigm shift over the last decade. The modern view is that there must be pre-disaster mitigation measures to avoid or reduce impact of disasters.

Mitigation

Mitigation efforts attempt to prevent hazards from developing into disasters altogether, or to reduce the effects of disasters when they occur. The mitigation phase differs from the other phases because it focuses on long-term measures for reducing or eliminating risk.The implementation of mitigation strategies can be considered a part of the recovery process if applied after a disaster occurs. However, even if applied as part of recovery efforts, actions that reduce or eliminate risk over time are still considered mitigation efforts.

Mitigative measures can be structural or non-structural. Structural measures use technological solutions, like flood levees. Non-structural measures include legislation, land-use planning, and insurance e.g. the designation of nonessential land like parks to be used as flood zones. Mitigation is the most cost-efficient method for reducing the impact of hazards. However, mitigation is not always suitable and structural mitigation in particular may have adverse effects on the ecosystem.

A precursor activity to the mitigation is the identification of risks. Physical risk assessment refers to the process of identifying and evaluating hazards. In risk assessment, various hazards within a certain area are identified. Each hazard poses a risk to the population within the area assessed. The hazard-specific risk combines both the probability and the level of impact of a specific hazard. The equation below gives that the hazard times the populations' vulnerability to that hazard produce a risk. Catastrophe modeling tools are used to support the calculation. The higher the risk, the more urgent that the hazard specific vulnerabilities are targeted by mitigation and preparedness efforts. However, if there is no vulnerability there will be no risk, e.g. an earthquake occurring in a desert where nobody lives.

Non-structural personal mitigation is mainly about knowing and avoiding unnecessary risks. An example would be to avoid buying property that is exposed to hazards, e.g. in a flood plain, in areas of subsidence or landslides. Homeowners may not be aware of their home being exposed to a hazard until it strikes. Real-estate agents may not come forward with such information. However, specialists can be hired to conduct risk assessment surveys. Insurance covering the most prominent identified risks are a common measure.

Personal structural mitigation in earthquake prone areas include installation of an Earthquake Valve to instantly shut off the natural gas supply to your property, seismic retrofits of property and the securing of items inside the building to enhance household seismic safety such as the mounting of furniture, refrigerators, water heaters and breakables to the walls, and the addition of cabinet latches. In flood prone areas houses can be built on poles, like in much of southern Asia. In areas prone to prolonged electricity black-outs a generator would be an example of an optimal structural mitigation measure. The construction of storm cellars and fallout shelters are further examples of personal mitigative actions.

Preparedness

In the preparedness phase, emergency managers develop plans of action for when the disaster strikes. Common preparedness measures include the proper maintenance and training of emergency services, the development and exercise of emergency population warning methods combined with emergency shelters and evacuation plans, the stockpiling of supplies and equipment, and the development and practice of multi-agency coordination.

An efficient preparedness measure is an emergency operations center (EOC) combined with a practiced region-wide doctrine for managing emergencies. The purpose of the EOC is to coordinate the activities in the subsequent emergency response phase. Physically, the EOC may only be a couple of cabinets in a conference room combined with a significant group of professionals. The EOC have reliable external communications including access to civil and amateur radio networks.

On the contrary to mitigation activities which are aimed at preventing a disaster from occurring, personal preparedness are targeted on preparing activities to be taken when a disaster occurs, i.e. planning. Preparedness measures can take many forms. Examples include the construction of shelters, warning devices, back-up life-line services and rehearsing an evacuation plan. Two simple measures prepare you for either sitting out the event or evacuating. For evacuation, a disaster bag or knapsack should be prepared and for sheltering purposes a stockpile of supplies.

Response

The response phase includes the mobilization of the necessary emergency services and first responders in the disaster area, such as firefighters, police, volunteers, and non-governmental organizations (NGOs) such as Oxfam or the Caritas Network. A well rehearsed emergency plan developed as part of the preparedness phase enables efficient coordination of rescue efforts. Emergency plan rehearsal is essential to achieve optimal output with limited resources. In the response phase, medical assets will be used in accordance with the appropriate triage of the affected victims.

Where required, search and rescue efforts commence at an early stage. Depending on injuries sustained by the victim, outside temperature, and victim access to air and water, the vast majority of those affected by a disaster will die within 72 hours after impact.

Individuals are often compelled to volunteer directly after a disaster. Volunteers can be both a help and a hindrance to emergency management and other relief agencies. A spontaneous, unaffiliated volunteer is one type that can harm recovery efforts.

The response phase of an emergency may commence with a search and rescue phase. However in all cases the focus will be on fulfilling the basic needs of the affected population on a humanitarian basis. This assistance may be provided by national and/or international agencies and organisations. Effective coordination of disaster assistance is often crucial particularly when many organisations respond and local emergency management agency (LEMA) capacity may be over-stretched and diminished by the disaster itself.

On a personal level the response can take the shape either of a home confinement or an evacuation. In a home confinement scenario a family should be prepared to fend for themselves in their home for many days without any form of outside support. In an evacuation scenario, a family evacuates by an automobile (or other mode of transportation) with the maximum amount of supplies, including a tent for shelter. The scenario could also include equipment for evacuation on foot with at least three days of supplies and rain-tight bedding a tarpaulin and a bedroll of blankets is the minimum.

Recovery

The aim of the recovery phase is to restore the affected area to its previous state. It differs from the response phase in its focus; recovery efforts are concerned with issues and decisions that must be made after immediate needs are addressed. Recovery efforts are primarily concerned with actions that involve rebuilding destroyed property, re-employment, and the repair of other essential infrastructure. An important aspect of effective recovery efforts is taking advantage of a 'window of opportunity' for the implementation of mitigative measures that might otherwise be unpopular. Citizens of the affected area are more likely to accept more mitigative changes when a recent disaster is in fresh memory.

The recovery phase starts when the immediate threat to human life has subsided. In the reconstruction it is recommended to reconsider the location or construction material of the property. In long term disasters the most extreme home confinement scenarios like war, famine and severe epidemics last up to a year. In this situation the recovery will take place inside the home. Planners for these usually buy bulk foods and appropriate storage and preparation equipment, and eat the food as part of normal life. A simple balanced diet can be constructed from vitamin pills, whole-meal wheat, beans, dried milk, corn, and cooking oil. One should add vegetables, fruits, spices and meats, both prepared and fresh-gardened, when possible.

Rehabilitation and Reconstruction

The rehabilitation period involves the weeks and months after the disaster. The focus is to enable the area to start functioning again. This involves debris removal, restoration of public services and provision of temporary housing.

Reconstruction is a much longer-term activity. This phase involves permanent rebuilding, improved infrastructure and better disaster planning.

Both rehabilitation and reconstruction phases demand good management. Diversion of national and international aid prudently, prioritization of activities, proper coordination and monitoring as well as prevention of corruption and abuse of scarce funds become priorities.

The private insurance sector contributes important funding for natural disaster reconstruction in developed countries. But in developing countries, the social welfare arm of the government and the individual carry much of the cost of disasters.In developing countries the rising cost of disaster aid and insurance payouts are driving governments away from comprehensive insurance schemes.

Development funding is diverted for disaster relief in an ad-hoc manner, which postpones progress towards long-term economic and social improvement. Tools have to be developed to assist the very poor to more effectively manage disaster risk. This includes micro-finance mechanisms that can deal with covariate risk such as disasters.

Disaster Management planning

Disaster management planning is complex; the written plan is the result of a wide range of preliminary activities. The entire process is most efficient if it is formally assigned to one person who acts as the disaster planner for the institution and is perhaps assisted by a planning team or committee. The institution's director may play this primary role or may delegate the responsibility, but it is important to remember that the process must be supported at the highest level of the organisation if it is to be effective. The planner should establish a timetable for the project and should define the scope and goals of the plan, which will depend largely on the risks faced by the institution.

Identifying Risks

A prudent first step is to list geographic and climatic hazards and other risks that could jeopardise the building and collections. These might include the institution's susceptibility to hurricanes, tornadoes, flash flooding, earthquakes, or forest fires, and even the possibility of unusual hazards such as volcanic eruptions. Consider man-made disasters such as power outages, sprinkler discharges, fuel or water supply failures, chemical spills, arson, bomb threats, or other such problems. Take note of the environmental risks that surround your institution.

Chemical industries, shipping routes for hazardous materials, and adjacent construction projects all expose your institution to damage. While all institutions are not vulnerable to all disasters, any event that is a real possibility should be covered under your emergency plan. Look carefully at your building and site. Check the surrounding terrain. Is the building located on a slope? Is the basement above flood level? Are there large trees near the building? Are such things as utility poles and flagpoles secure? Is the roof flat? Does water accumulate? Do gutters and drains work properly? Are they cleaned regularly? Are windows and skylights well sealed? Is there a history of leaks or other building and structural problems?

Within the building, fire protection systems, electrical systems, plumbing, and environmental systems are of primary concern. Are there enough fire extinguishers, and are they regularly inspected? Does the building have fire alarms and a fire-suppression system? Are they well maintained? Are they monitored twenty-four hours a day? Are fire exits blocked? How old is the wiring? Is it overloaded? Are electrical appliances unplugged at night? Is auxiliary power available if needed? Are water pipes in good shape? Are there water detectors, and do they work? Are there any problems with the climate-control system? You may have already thought of many other questions, and you should create a risk-assessment checklist of your own.

It is also important to determine the vulnerability of the objects within the collections. What types of materials are included? Are they easily damaged? Are they particularly susceptible to certain types of damage such as moisture, fire, breakage, and the like? How and where are collections stored? Are they protected by boxes or other enclosures? Is shelving anchored to structural elements of the building? Is it stable? Are any artifacts stored directly on the floor where they could be damaged by leaks or flooding? All items should be raised at least four inches from the floor on waterproof shelves or pallets. Are materials stored under or near water sources? Analyse your security and housekeeping procedures. Do they expose collections to the dangers of theft, vandalism, or insect infestation?

Consider administrative vulnerabilities. Are your institution's collections insured? Is there a complete and accurate inventory? Is a duplicate of the inventory located at another site? Have collection priorities been set? In other words, do you know which collections should be salvaged first in the event of fire, water, or other emergency? Do you have a back-up priority list if you cannot reach the highest-priority objects due to building damage or the nature of the disaster?

While these questions may seem overwhelming, by the time you complete your survey, you will have a good idea of the significant risks your institution faces. Although there may be a wide range of disaster scenarios, the most common are water, fire, physical or chemical damage, or some combination of these. The specific procedures of a disaster plan focus on the prevention and mitigation of these types of damage.

Decreasing Risks

Once your institution's hazards are specified, the disaster planner should devise a programme with concrete goals, identifiable resources, and a schedule of activities for eliminating as many risks as possible. Geography and climate cannot be changed, but other vulnerabilities can be reduced. If building and collection conditions are regularly monitored, repaired and improved, many emergency situations will be eliminated. A regular programme of building inspection and maintenance should be a very high priority if one is not already in place.

It can prevent or reduce common emergencies resulting from burst pipes, defective climate-control equipment, worn electrical wiring, clogged drains, or other problems. If all improvements cannot be undertaken at once, make a schedule and follow it. If some items on your schedule prove impossible or are delayed, move on to the next goal and return to the earlier problem when it becomes more practical. Once building systems are in proper working order, devise a maintenance schedule.

Patchwork repairs and deferred maintenance only result in accelerated deterioration, leading to an increased risk of emergencies. Keep a log of building events like clogged drains, furnace cleaning, and equipment failures. The more you know about your building and its operation, the faster (and more economically) repairs can be made. While water damage is the most common form of disaster for museums, every institution with collections of enduring value needs a good fire-protection system.

Since most emergencies seem to happen outside normal working hours, reliable fire detection systems on professional, twenty-four-hour monitors are a wise investment. Wherever possible, collections should also be protected by a fire-suppression system. The use of halon is no longer recommended. Preservation professionals now recommend wet-pipe sprinklers for most libraries and archives. In addition, water misting suppression systems have become available within the last several years; these can provide fire suppression using much less water than conventional sprinkler systems.

Before choosing a fire-protection system, be sure to contact a preservation professional or a fire-protection consultant for information about the latest developments in fire protection and for advice appropriate to your collections and situation. All fire-protection systems should be designed and installed by professionals with experience in servicing museums, archives, and libraries, because the needs of these institutions differ from the needs for home protection. Talk to colleagues at other local institutions or a preservation professional in your region for recommendations, and always check references.

Other actions that reduce building and collection vulnerability include maintaining a collection inventory, improving collection storage, and following good security and housekeeping procedures. An inventory will provide a basic list of holdings to assist in assigning priorities for salvage, and will be essential for insurance purposes. Improved collection storage, such as boxing and raising materials above the floor level, will reduce or eliminate damage when emergencies occur. Comprehensive security and housekeeping procedures will ward off emergencies such as theft, vandalism, and insect infestation. They will also ensure that fire exits are kept clear and fire hazards eliminated.

Cooperative Plan

Disaster planning should not take place in a vacuum. To work effectively, it must be integrated into the routine operating procedures of the institution. In fact, you will probably find that in planning for disasters you will also be working toward the accomplishment of other goals. For example, a properly functioning climate-control system will prevent fluctuations in temperature and relative humidity, resulting in a better preservation environment and a longer life for all collections. At the same time, this prevents disasters such as water leaks from air-handling units.

Similarly, if an institution surveys its collections and creates an inventory for disaster planning, a corollary benefit is better access to the collections for researchers and staff. Remember three important characteristics of an effective disaster plan: comprehensiveness, simplicity, and flexibility. The plan needs to address all types of emergencies and disasters that your institution is likely to face. It should include plans for both immediate response and long-term salvage and recovery efforts.

The plan should also acknowledge that normal services may be disrupted. How will you proceed if there is no electrical power, no water, and no telephone? The plan must be easy to follow. People faced with a disaster often have trouble thinking clearly, so concise instructions and training are critical to the success of the plan. The key is to write in a clear, simple style without sacrificing comprehensiveness. Above all, remember that you cannot anticipate every detail, so be sure that while your plan provides basic instructions, it also allows for some on-the-spot creativity.

Decide who will be responsible for various activities when responding to an emergency. Who will be the senior decision-maker? Who will interact with fire officials, police, or civil defence authorities? Who will talk to the press? Who will serve as back-up if any of your team members are unable to get to the site? Identify a location for a central command post (if necessary), and space for drying collections. Set up a system for relaying information to members of the salvage team.

Because written information is less susceptible to misunder-standing, your communications strategy might include notes to be delivered by "runners." Good communication is essential to avoid confusion and duplication of effort in an emergency. Finally, if the planning process seems overwhelming, approach it in stages. Decide what type of disaster is most likely to occur in your institution, and begin to plan for it. The plan can always be expanded to include other scenarios.

Identifying Resources

Some important steps should be taken before you write your plan. First, identify sources of assistance in a disaster. Determine the supplies you will need for disaster response and salvage efforts for your specific collections. Basic supplies like polyethylene dropcloths, sponges, flashlights, and rubber gloves should be purchased and kept on hand. They should be kept in a clearly marked location, inventoried periodically, and, if necessary, replaced. If you choose to lock the cabinet containing the supplies, make sure the keys will be available in an emergency.

Keep a list of additional supplies that might be needed. This list should include suppliers' names, addresses, and phone numbers, and should provide backup sources for supplies. Arrangements should also be made for emergency cash or credit, because it is sometimes difficult to get money quickly in a disaster situation. In recent years, many disaster-planning guides have published lists of supplies and companies that provide disaster services as well as sources of technical assistance. Research these services thoroughly—it is an essential part of the planning process. If possible, invite local service providers to visit your institution to become familiar with your site plan and collections in advance of an emergency. It is also a good idea to plan for back-up companies to provide critical supplies and services in case there is a community-wide or regional disaster. Consider coordinating with other local institutions. The disaster planner should identify all appropriate disaster-response and recovery services. These can range from police, fire, and ambulance services to maintenance workers, insurance adjustors, and utility companies.

Several national companies provide disaster-recovery services such as dehumidification and vacuum freeze drying. Liaisons should be maintained with local emergency services so that they can respond appropriately in case of disaster. For example, you may want to provide the fire department with a list of high-priority areas to be protected from water if fire-fighting efforts permit. You may be able to arrange with the fire department to allow specific staff members from your institution to enter the building for evaluation or salvage if safety allows. It may be possible to rope off areas for arson investigation while allowing accessibility to other areas. All such arrangements must be prepared for in advance for efficient response.

Other valuable sources of assistance are local, state, or federal government agencies. While it is widely known that the Federal Emergency Management Agency (FEMA) provides disaster assistance programmes, institutions may not be aware that this can include support for recovery of art objects and cultural resources. An October 1991 policy change allows federal assistance to pay for conservation of objects that are damaged in a disaster. Conservation is defined by FEMA as “the minimum steps which are both necessary and feasible to place the items back on display without restoring them to their pre-disaster condition.” FEMA does not cover the replacement of destroyed items.

Disaster Priorities

The first priority in any disaster is human safety. Saving collections is never worth endangering the lives of staff or patrons. In a major event, the fire department, civil defence authorities, or other professionals may restrict access to the building until it can be fully evaluated. Once safety concerns are met, the next consideration will be records and equipment crucial to the operation of the institution, such as registrar’s records, inventories, and administrative files. Collections salvage and building rehabilitation will be the next priority.

Objects or collections of great importance to the institution must be identified ahead of time. If this is not done, valuable time may be wasted salvaging materials of little value or spent arguing about what should be saved first. Ideally, this step includes a floor plan that clearly states the priority of collections for salvage. This should be attached to the disaster plan, but the security of this type of information should be considered. It may be wise to allow only upper-level staff access to this part of the plan prior to an actual emergency.

Salvage priorities should be based not only on the value of objects, but on their vulnerability to the particular damage caused by the emergency. If you are not knowledgeable about the hazards for various materials, contact a conservator to help you incorporate these considerations into your salvage plan. Paper and textiles, for instance, are susceptible to mold when they are warm and damp.

Many metals will corrode rapidly under the same conditions. Salt water may accelerate this damage. Ivory, small wooden objects, and lacquer may swell and crack with rapid changes in moisture and temperature. Veneers and furniture may be constructed with water-soluble adhesives. Objects may become brittle after exposure to the temperatures of a fire. All categories of collections have special handling and salvage procedures developed by experienced professionals.

Writing the Plan

Once the necessary preliminary steps have been taken, writing the plan should be relatively straightforward. Although each plan will be different, a sample outline is given below:

- Introduction—stating the lines of authority and the possible events covered by the plan.
- Actions to be taken if advance warning is available.
- First response procedures, including who should be contacted first in each type of emergency, what immediate steps should be taken, and how staff or teams will be notified.
- Emergency procedures with sections devoted to each emergency event covered by the plan. This will include what is to be done during the event, and the appropriate salvage procedures to be followed once the first excitement is over. Include floor plans.

— Rehabilitation plans for getting the institution back to normal.

— Appendices, which may include evacuation/floor plans; listing of emergency services; listing of emergency response team members and responsibilities; telephone tree; location of keys; fire/intrusion alarm procedures; listing of collection priorities; arrangements for relocation of the collections; listing of in-house supplies; listing of outside suppliers and services; insurance information; listing of volunteers; prevention checklist; record-keeping forms for objects moved in salvage efforts; detailed salvage procedures.

Maintaining the Plan

No matter how much effort you have put into creating the perfect disaster plan, it will be largely ineffective if your staff is not aware of it, if it is outdated, or if you cannot find it during a disaster. A concentrated effort must be made to educate and train staff in emergency procedures. Each staff member should be made aware of his or her responsibilities, and regular drills should be conducted if possible. Keep several copies of the plan in various locations, including off-site (ideally in waterproof containers). Each copy of the plan should indicate where other copies may be found.

Most important, the disaster plan must be updated periodically. Names, addresses, phone numbers, and personnel change constantly. New collections are acquired, building changes are made, and new equipment is installed. If a plan is not kept completely up to date, it may not be able to assist you effectively in dealing with disasters. Disaster planning is essential for any institution to provide the best possible protection for its collections.

Disaster can strike at any time—on a small or a large scale—but if an institution is prepared, the damage may be decreased or avoided. A disaster plan must be considered a living document. Its risk-assessment checklist must be periodically reviewed, its lists must be updated, and its collection priorities revised as needed. An effective disaster plan will do its best to insure that historical collections in our cultural institutions are safeguarded for the future.

Role of Assessment in Disaster Management

Assessment is a crucial management task which contributes directly to effective decision-making, planning and control of the organised response. Assessment of needs and resources is required in all types of disasters, whatever the cause and whatever the speed of onset. Assessment will be needed during all the identifiable phases of a disaster, from the start of emergency life-saving, through the period of stabilisation and rehabilitation and into the long-term recovery, reconstruction and return to normalcy. The focus of assessment and the strategies for data collection and interpretation will need to change as the response evolves.

Assessments must be carefully planned and managed. A sequence of activities is involved and each must be planned in detail. The following activities typically constitute the assessment process:

1. Identify information needs and sources of reliable data
2. Collect data
3. Analyse and interpret data
4. Report conclusions, forecast and alternatives to appropriate planners and decision-makers

As the response actions begin to influence events, assessments become part of the monitoring and control loop, allowing those involved to monitor outcomes and attempt to correct the response. It becomes part of a continuing process of assessment, review and correction by which those managing the operation begin to restore the framework for survival and recovery.

Assessment and Decision-making

Assessment is the process by which decision-makers begin to bring order to the chaos that results from a disaster. Assessment activities provide data to emergency decision-makers and those involved in longer-term recovery planning. It is done for a specific user or group of users who must decide how best to allocate available and pledged resources for relief and recovery. The decision-making context varies greatly depending on the country involved, the disaster type and the phase of the emergency. Nonetheless, at least two aspects of the context, i.e. the cast of characters and the decision making scenario, are always present.

There is always a cluster of relief actors. They include:

1. The survivors
2. The government of the affected country-its ministries, agencies,
3. Political figures and civil servants
4. The United Nations agencies

5. Inter-governmental organisations
6. Donor governments and their local representatives
7. International and national NGO representatives
8. The national and international news media

Each of these will have different perceptions of the disaster and their role in the recovery effort. Each will have different information needs and will seek to meet these needs in different ways. Information that is meaningful and useful to one group may be wholly irrelevant to another. Many agencies will have a limited understanding of other group's requirements and resources. Increasingly, those participating in important decisions may not even be present within the country. With the emergence of sophisticated telecommunications, officials at centres thousands of miles from the affected area can be drawn quickly into the decision-process and can share much of the data that are available to national officials. With rapidly growing satellite coverage, relief actors are also now exposed to extensive live news coverage by highly mobile television crews from the international TV networks.

From the start of the emergency onwards, all the actors will be jointly or separately involved in a decision-making process which includes three stages:

1. Situation assessment
2. Choosing objectives and identifying alternative means of accomplishing them
3. Developing and implementing response plans

This process will be most intense and explicit during the emergency phase, but will continue in some form through all the phases of the recovery process.

Situation Assessment

Early in all emergencies, but especially in rapid onset disasters or sudden population influxes as a result of civil-conflict, there will be great uncertainty about what the problems actually are. These uncertainties include: the area affected, the numbers of people requiring immediate help, the levels of damage to services and "life-lines", the level of continuing or emerging threat and the possibilities for providing help.

In all kinds of emergencies decision-makers will need to start by building up a picture of where people are, what condition they are in, what their needs are, what services are still available and what resources have survived. A good system should pay particular attention to the emerging expressed priorities of the affected people themselves and identify the resources of the survivors an their coping levels. This overall picture is built up from assessment data collected by officials within the area, from survey teams on the ground, or from overflights. To a great extent, the quality and quantity of that data will reflect the level of prior planning.

Receipt and handling of data involves three distinct steps:

1. *Assessing the likely value of the data:* The reliability of the source and the likely accuracy of data
2. *Validating incoming data against "knowns"*: A validation check against existing baseline information
3. Incorporating data into a structured "picture" of the situation, which can be displayed graphically, or otherwise reported to those who will try to make sense of it.

Choosing Objectives

Initially, this stage requires interpretation of the data which highlights the risks to various populations, together with an attempt to define alternative means to reduce immediate risks. A detailed understanding of the general risk pattern in the particular type of emergency and how it may change is essential. Some general risks frequently present in the emergency phase are:

1. *Continuing presence of hazard agents*—secondary flooding, fire, landslides, extreme cold, chemical pollution, etc.
2. *Loss of "lifeline services"*—clean water, waste disposal, medical treatment
3. Inadequate supply of emergency clinical medical services Inadequate supply of essential foods
4. Effects of severe climatic conditions exacerbated by lack of shelter, warm clothing or heating fuel

Given adequate information, central decision-makers will also be able to gauge local response capacity and decide how best to use those existing resources over which they have some control for immediate relief.

A second important element of this stage of decision-making is forecasting—the attempt to develop a set of predictions of the relationship between needs and resources over time and, in particular, an attempt to judge whether resources can actually be made available in time to deal with particular problems before their importance fades Forecasting is particularly critical early on, when the pattern of need is changing very quickly. For example, decisions on emergency medical care and search and rescue during earthquakes are so time-sensitive that even a few hours delay in the organisation of support for a local response can lead to an almost total waste of resources.

Developing Response Plans

In the early phases of a disaster, assessment activities give decision-makers the information needed to set the objectives and policies for emergency assistance, to take account of the priorities of the affected people themselves and to decide how best to use the existing resources for relief and recovery. The third stage - response planning and implementation - involves allocating and scheduling resources including people, equipment and supplies, first to meet specific relief objectives and later to fulfil recovery and development goals. During this stage, assessment provides information on the progress of the recovery highlighting areas requiring further analysis and intervention.

Data Collection

Data are collected for a purpose: to improve emergency decisions and to provide more effective planning of relief and recovery. Data collection is ongoing. Bad or out of date data can lead to erroneous conclusions and wasted time and resources. Information must be found when it is needed. To achieve this, the frequency of data collection and reporting must match the rate of change in the situation being assessed.

A useful starting point in any data collection exercise is to seek advice from survey specialists, statisticians and epidemiologists at the planning stage. Proper design of sampling and survey methods can substantially increase the accuracy and usefulness of assessment data. Also, cultural attitudes and personal preferences can greatly influence the type of data that an individual or team will tend to focus on.

Consideration of local cultural and other social factors at this stage can help greatly in formulating interview methods and identifying useful sources of information and, also, in predicting how the people associated with the system are likely to behave.

There are a range of data collection methods, some of which are most useful during the emergency phase and others which depend on the development of more organised assessment procedures. A few can be applied effectively during all phases of a disaster and its aftermath. All data collection strategies are subject to problems of bias. Bias is the degree to which the conclusion drawn from a data observation deviates from the true situation. Sometimes bias results from asking the wrong question, sometimes from asking the wrong people and, sometimes, from the "biased" perception of the observer or reporter of data.

The following list outlines some of the more common ways of collecting assessment data in relation to the various phases of the disaster.

Impact and Emergency Phase

Automatic early self-assessment and local assessment by key elements in the system, e.g. staff of "lifeline" systems. This can involve pre-planned damage reporting by civil authorities and by military units in accordance with operational procedures established in the disaster preparedness plan.

Visual inspection and interviews by specialists. Methods can include overflight, actions by special point-assessment teams including visits anticipated in the disaster preparedness plan and sample surveys to achieve rapid appraisal of area damage.

Emergency Phase Onwards

Sentinel surveillance. This is a method used widely in emergency health monitoring, where professional staff establish a reporting system which detects early signs of particular problems at specific sites. The method can be applied to a variety of other problems where early warning is particularly important.

Surveying of specific characteristics of affected populations by specialist teams. Well-designed surveys drawn from reliable and systematic samples have a number of advantages, especially the relative confidence that may be attached to data collected using formal statistical sampling methods. Sampling allows researchers to survey a subset of an affected population and confidently generalise to the larger population from which the sample was drawn. There are several different types of sampling methods useful for conducting assessments:

1. *Simple random sampling.* One in which every member of the target population is equally likely to be selected and where the selection of a particular member of the target population has no effect on the other selections.

2. *Systematic random sampling.* Choosing, for example, every fifth, or tenth member on a numbered list. This may be wildly inaccurate if the lists are incomplete or structured in non-random ways.
3. *Stratified random sampling.* Divide the population into categories; then select members from each category by simple or systematic random sampling; finally combine these to give an overall sample.
4. *Cluster sampling*: This restricts the sample to a limited number of geographical areas, known as "clusters"; for each of the geographical areas chosen, select a sample by simple or random sampling; then combine these sub-samples to get an overall sample.

Detailed critical sector assessments by specialist staff. This involves technical inspections and assessments by experts. It is required in sectors such as water supply, electric power and other "lifeline" systems. Critical sector assessments may be compiled from reports by specialist staff of these systems or by visit by specialist teams from outside.

Interviews with key informants. In government and NGOs and within particular groups of affected people: local officials, local community leaders and, especially in food and displacement emergencies, with leaders of groups of displaced people.

Continuing surveillance by regular polling visits. This again is a technique which is well-developed in epidemiological surveillance of casualty care requirements and emergent health problems.

Rehabilitation Phase

As the situation develops, it will be especially useful if routine reporting systems can be adapted to develop a comprehensive picture of events. It is worth noting some special features of health surveillance. A major principle of health operations is to monitor continuously for the emergence of particular problems and then to focus precise interventions against demonstrated causes of these problems. A major component is reporting by medical staff (even in the first hours of sudden emergencies) through an established system, with simple procedures and an emphasis on easily detected diagnostic indicators of important problems This is combined with regular "polling" visits and detailed local investigation of reports by specialist professional staff.

Monitoring the Quality of Assessment Data

A both collectors and reviewers of assessment information, the disaster assessment staff need to have a clear set of standards for judging data collection systems and their products. At the preparedness stage, they may be in a position to offer useful advice and support to host government authorities in the design and implementation of data-collection and processing systems. During an emergency, they will be called upon to evaluate the accuracy and usefulness of data from official sources in-country.

Estimating accuracy depends on an understanding of data gathering methodologies and their limitations and a clear appreciation of how accuracy can be lost during transmission and processing. Estimating the usefulness of data requires an understanding of the ways in which patterns of risk and the corresponding relief priorities differ from place to place and how these risks change over time in different kinds of emergencies. It also requires an understanding of donor capabilities and the ways in which donors act upon incoming information.

Established NGOs with development programmes in the affected areas can often give valuable information on local situations even if they do not have nation-wide information. Churches and their missions often have extensive long-term local experience. While these sources of information often prove reliable, the limitations of many NGOs must also be recognised. The operations and knowledge of NGOs are highly localised geographically; some have limited numbers of personnel with varying degrees of competence. Not all have systematic and institutionalised data-gathering networks. The information provided is likely to be variable in quality and precision and should be evaluated in terms of the experience and proven competence of the organisation and individuals concerned.

Guidelines for Successful Disaster Assessments

A substantial body of knowledge has been developed over the last decade which provides guidance on the design and implementation of assessment systems in the aftermath of a disaster. The following general guidelines have been abstracted from those sources.

Planning and Systems Design Guidelines

1. Assessments are generally useful only if there is a system available to record and collate the data and to assess and disseminate its

implications. A pre-established assessment plan is crucial. It should specify who gathers what data, where and when, who reports what to whom, how the data can be analysed, how it can be presented, how assessments are disseminated and how the results are recorded.

2. The analyses of assessment data must take account of changes in needs and changes in resource availability over time. It is crucial to identify the likely needs at the time when resources will be available.
3. Planners need to pay close attention to the users of assessment information. Data should be collected to meet specific requirements by a specific, identified operational individual or unit. Assessments must teach them in a format they can use and at a time when it is relevant.
4. The government should designate a person who ensures coordinated collection and analysis of assessment data.
5. The qualifications of people chosen to do assessments-their skills and demonstrated capability to do the job are very important. This is especially vital where technical teams are chosen to assess "life-line" systems serving very large populations.
6. Specificity in data collection is an important objective. Assessments should be aimed to help match limited available resources to projected critical needs.
7. An important element of emergency assessment is the presence of background quality control checks on emergency plans and procedures and, when an emergency occurs, rapid quality checks on the collection, evaluation and dissemination of data.
8. Disaster survivors must be consulted and community social structures and coping mechanisms must be reviewed to assess a community's own response to the disaster. External resources should not supplant the community's own efforts but, rather, build on them.

Operational Data Collection

1. As a general rule, focus data collection on the most important areas of risk to the largest populations.
2. Assessment guidelines should be standardized wherever possible.
3. The barriers to access by assessment teams need to be identified early as well as means to get around them. This can help in assigning

priorities for access to high value transport resources and in scheduling these resources.

4. Existing information collection and reporting systems should be used as much as possible-especially the health reporting system.
5. A mix of specialists with appropriate skills and experience must be chosen. Multi-disciplinary teams often see more. It is often useful to assign an epidemiologist or survey statistician on each local assessment team from the outset.
6. Formal sampling and survey methods should be used whenever possible.
7. The source and method of collection, the team and the location, time and date-of-collection of all data should always be specified.
8. Data should be presented in the form rates and percentages not just absolute numbers.
9. Data recording and presentation techniques should be standardized where possible.

Routing, Analysing and Reporting Assessment Data

1. The communications system which survives the disaster will determine who actually gets what information. Pay particular attention in contingency plans to the ways in which assessment data will be routed back to the assessment centre and how to act quickly to improve communications where appropriate.
2. Incoming assessment data need to be structured to help with the following:
   a) Recognition of situations where decisions are required
   b) Formulation of the decision problem, in terms of the needs and objectives and identification of potential alternatives for action
   c) Analysis of the alternatives in terms of their likely impacts
   d) Evaluation and selection of a response, by comparing the alternatives in terms off their predicted outcome
3. All data arriving at an assessment center should be evaluated. In particular, stress the following procedures to staff of these centres and all other decision-makers:

a) Cross-check and compare reports from different sources
b) Avoid generalizing from data relating too only one area, one sector or one part of a population
c) Evaluate assessment data against a baseline, where possible.
d) Recognize that there will be underlying "normal" rates of specific problems which may continue throughout the emergency.
e) Remind analysts and decision makers that assessments may uncover and highlight problems that were already there, as well as those generated by the disaster
f) Question and check information that seems unreasonable
g) Seek information actively. Always check why no report has been received. Don't assume that no report means no problem
h) Update information continuously as needs and priorities change. Periodically reassess conditions in apparently stable areas.

4. During planning for assessment and reporting, establish desirable standards for emergency services-water supply, emergency medical care and other relief services. Situation assessments and reports can compare current conditions against these standards.
5. Information should still be relevant by the time it is processed and disseminated. This, in turn, means that the systems for collecting and communicating data must operate in real-time, i.e. while the need for decisions still exists and that the evaluation of the data must be done while the results are still likely to be meaningful.

Collecting Data for Future Operations

Some assessment data may be of more value after the emergency that during it. This is particulary the case for data on mortality rates and associated risk factors. This information has much less immediate operational value than data on injury patterns and health problems but may be invaluable later to shape future strategies for mitigation and preparedness. Ensure that data of this type is not lost and that its collection receives adequate support.

Guidelines on Assessment in Sudden onset Emergencies

In addition to the general guidelines described above, the unique attributes of specific types of hazards have significant implications for the assessment activities.

In sudden-impact disasters the key to effective life-saving relief is specific, precisely targeted interventions against demonstrated causes of death. There is sufficient scientific experience form previous emergencies to give a good indication of who is most likely to die, of what cause and when. It is clear that most of the effective interventions are time-critical and, hence, rely greatly on resources already present in the area and that most can be pre-planned. There will be insufficient time for extensive or detailed assessment and the organisation of large-scale external support. In earthquakes, in particular, search and rescue and early emergency medical care must rely substantially on local resources. To give any useful benefit, external help must involve delivery of very specific packages of aid to reinforce existing activity. The first external assessment teams should deliver additional emergency stocks of critical items. These may include hand-tools and gloves for local people engaged in search and rescue and specific medical support for local hospitals and clinics. Accurate and credible information telling decision-makers what is not needed can help to reduce the overall complexity of the logistical response, by excluding at least some useless materials from the impact area.

There are three general priorities for early assessments:

1. Determine location of problems
2. Determine the magnitude of problems
3. Determine the immediate priorities

When focusing on these priorities, it is important to have a systematic approach-assessments should be programmed to ensure that all sectors and all likely affected areas are covered. Sectors may include:

1. Emergency medical and health
2. Search and rescue
3. Damages to lifelines and critical facilities
4. Shelter and housing needs
5. Personal and household needs
6. Agricultural needs
7. Economic needs

Coordination is complicated by the need to ensure that the relationships among these sectors are identified. Activities in one sector will be affected substantially by damage in another. At every stage, assessments will have to be multi-sectoral in the sense that these linkages are explicitly taken into account.

Coordination of assessment in the very early hours will need effective scheduling of critical air transport resources. Emergency managers will need to allocate limited resources among competing demands-helicopters in particular may be needed early on for both assessment and casualty transport.

Scheduling of assessment resources is helped by having pre-existing "baseline" information on the affected region. This gives emergency coordinators the option to identify anticipated high loss zones and focus initial assessment activity on those areas where particular types off problem are predictable. For example, in tropical storms, maps off the following vulnerable areas will be important:

1. Urban low-income neighbourhoods
2. Coastal villages
3. Villages on flood plains
4. Villages on steep hillsides
5. Villages on low-lying river deltas
6. Villages on barrier islands.

Assessment Activities in the Impact and Emergency Phases of Sudden onset Disasters

While the precise approach will depend on the exact type of disaster agent, in all sudden emergencies a number of immediate actions are required to establish the framework for overall emergency assessments. High-value relief resources e.g. helicopters and mobile modern communications teams should be focused on the following activities during the first few hours.

1. Establish boundaries of the damage or disrupted zone and the location of any damage to major urban areas. Use air survey and/or radio communications with civilian authorities, police and military units.
2. Identify transportation blockages on main routes into the damaged area.
3. Identify major secondary threats to survivors-dam leakage, secondary flooding or landslides, damage to chemical plant or fuel storage fires. Encourage rapid initial assessment and reporting by operating staff or local units of police or armed forces. Use air surveys where appropriate.
4. Assess damage to broadcasting facilities and review additional coverage required and resources available for broadcasting recovery. Effective

communications with the public will be a major tool for mobilizing assistance and shaping the overall response.

5. Assess immediate and critical requirements for support to restore emergency telecommunications between police, military, fire services and hospitals in the most damaged areas.
6. Assign assessment teams first to areas from which no reports have been received.
7. Attempt to establish the status of hospitals and clinics in areas affected by sudden impact disasters which are likely to have large numbers of casualties e.g. in earthquakes: those that are close to the epicenter, high density of old, multistory structures, narrow streets, high fire risk or where there is evidence of secondary hazard. Assessments should follow standard guidelines, which generally cover:
    a. Access to the disaster site
    b. Damage to structure
    c. Availability of essential equipment-X ray, sterilisation, lighting
    d. Availability of essential stocks
    e. Availability of power and water supply
    f. Capacity of system to handle demands
    g. Personnel requirements and availability
8. Begin regional survey activity aimed at locating isolated and severely affected communities. Rapid identification of these communities will usually be needed if medical and other relief assistance is to be scheduled in time to be effective. Investigate the extent to which field medical teams are reaching injured people in isolated areas
9. Investigate the overall adequacy of treatment for injured people in these areas
10. Attempt to draw up a broad prioritisation of areas requiring early organised search and rescue and, later, intensive search and rescue.
    a. Establish the resources available for organised and intensive search and rescue in each area
    b. In floods, focus assessment resources particularly on high-density urban areas especially squatter and other low-income areas; also high flood-risk areas including deltas, off-shore islands and flashflood risk areas

c. In earthquakes, focus on urban low-income areas and other areas with high concentrations of old, multi-story domestic buildings Be aware that in search and rescue in earthquakes there is generally accepted to be a major drop in the survival prospects of trapped victims after about 24 hours.

11. Review the condition of data-assessment centres; restore or improve communications with individuals acting as coordinators; and reinforce the communications linkages which are operating.
12. Establish the level of damage to air-traffic control, airport runways, fuel storage, cargo-handling and link routes at airfields nearest to the impact area.
13. Identify ways of reinforcing the highest priority elements of the local administrations' response. As a general rule, the following criteria may assist in making a decision:
    a. Are local officials focusing on the highest priority problems first?
    b. Is action concentrated on things the public is not capable of doing for itself?
    c. Is priority given to restore the services and procedures that will help members of the public do what they want to do better?
    d. Are people receiving the material items they actually need?
14. Review the government's accessible stockpile of essential items.
15. Depending on the emergency, these may include plastic sheeting, building materials, boats and emergency storage facilities. This review will need accurate up-to-date information on the pre-impact location of critical resources, including large commercial stocks.
16. Shift priority form assessment of clinical medical requirements to support for specialists involved in assessment of public health requirements. Key factors off significance are large-scale population movements and water supply damage in urban areas.
17. Contact staff of lifeline services for assessment of lifeline system condition. The usual priority is:
    a. Communications
    b. Water supply
    c. Electric power

d. Road networks and potential points off blockage

e. Sewerage systems

18. Critically review requirements for temporary provision of shelter.

In-depth Assessment During the Rehabilitation

As conditions stabilise, usually after about one week, more in-depth assessments will be needed. Overall the aim should be to identify gaps and unmet and emerging needs and to develop more accurate estimates of the numbers off people requiring assistance and the amounts of materials and money required. Thereafter, as the disaster recovery continues, assessment will increasingly fulfil a programme monitoring function, providing feedback to planners on the extent to which detailed implementation targets are actually being met. The major activities during the rehabilitation phase include:

1. Restoration of "life-line" systems.
2. Safety of the basic infrastructure, hospitals, schools.
3. Critical and strategic industries.

Guidelines on Assessments in Slow Onset Emergencies

In food emergencies-where market instability, widespread loss of purchasing power or widespread failure of distribution leads to a collapse of household fool-security-and in the types of large-scale population displacements caused by war or famine, accurate and reliable assessment is also a crucial management tool. However, assessment requirements are shaped by a rather different set of factors:

Lead times for aid can be long. Donors may be unwilling to commit large amounts of assistance in response to ambiguous information. Reliable information is needed for forecasting and prediction at a very early stage, often before many of the problems are visible and this information must be reported to donor-staff who may be relatively unfamiliar with the affected area and its problems.

Efficient distribution of essential food and non-food items is usually a key factor early on. Matching food requirements to food supply flows along the transport chain is a crucial element. If the affected population is moving, the problems caused by population density and inadequate services at points of concentration will need to be addressed very quickly. Operationally, early assessments will have to place special emphasis on the needs for implementing rapid immunisation against childhood diseases, emergency water supply, nutritional monitoring, bulk food logistics and the administrative capacity for implementing fair registration and distribution systems. In food emergencies, including pre-famine conditions, the initial requirements are to establish the spatial distribution of the affected populations, review the condition of various categories of people within that population and identify groups at special risk. Data required will include:

1. Staple food availability in the areas affected and the prices of these foods.
2. The availability of alternative foods including wild food.
3. The current nutritional status of these populations.
4. Critical medical/health problems, particularly acute diarrhea disease and measles.
5. Indicators, where available, of significantly increased death rates among specific groups.
6. The condition of emergency logistics systems, including transport capacity, fuel availability and the location and capacity of storage facilities.
7. The condition of systems for delivering emergency health care, including measles immunisation and the associated cold-chain, and emergency water supply.
8. Options for income generating projects
9. Options for alternative projects for enhancing food security. Like the use of strategic food stocks as a tool for market-price stabilisation and the use of cash as a benefit.

Institutional Framework for Disaster Management

In this section, let us analyse the institutional framework for disaster management, taking the Indian case.Disaster management in India has evolved from an activity-based reactive setup to a proactive institutionalized structure; from single faculty domain to a multi-stakeholder setup; and from a relief-based approach to a 'multi-dimensional pro-active holistic approach for reducing risk'. The beginnings of an institutional structure for disaster management can be traced to the British period following the series of disasters such as famines of 1900, 1905, 1907 and 1943, and the Bihar-Nepal earthquake of 1937. Over the past century, the disaster management in India has undergone substantive changes in its composition, nature and policy.

During the British administration, relief departments were set up for emergencies during disasters. Such an activity-based setup with a reactive approach was functional only in the post-disaster scenarios. The policy was relief-oriented and activities included designing the relief codes and initialising food for work programmes. Post-Independence, the task for managing disasters continued to rest with the Relief Commissioners in each state, who functioned under the Central Relief Commissioner, with their role limited to delegation of relief material and money in the afected areas. Every five-year plan addressed flood disasters under "Irrigation, Command Area Development and Flood Control". Until this stage, the disaster management structure was activity-based, functioning under the Relief Departments.

Emergence of Institutional Arrangement

A permanent and institutionalised setup began in the decade of 1990s with set up of a disaster management cell under the Ministry of Agriculture, following the declaration of the decade of 1990 as the 'International Decade for Natural Disaster Reduction' (IDNDR) by the UN General Assembly. Following series of disasters such as Latur Earthquake, Malpa Landslide, Orissa Super Cyclone and Bhuj Earthquake, a high powered Committee under the Chairmanship of Mr. J.C. Pant, Secretary, Ministry of Agriculture was constituted for drawing up a systematic, comprehensive and holistic approach towards disasters.

There was a shift in policy from an approach of relief through financial aid to a holistic one for addressing disaster management. Consequently, the disaster management division was shifted under the Ministry of Home Affairs in 2002 vide Cabinet Secretariat's Notification No. DOC.CD-108/2002 dated 27/02/2002 and a hierarchical structure for disaster management evolved in India.

Organisation and Structure of Disaster Management

The Disaster Management Division is headed by Joint Secretary (DM) in MHA, who is assisted by three Directors, Under Secretaries, Section Officers, Technical Officer, Senior Economic Investigator consultants and other supporting staff. The upper echelon of the structure consists of Secretary (Border Management), Home Secretary, Minister of State in charge and the Home Minister.

Disaster Management Framework

Shifting from relief and response mode, disaster management in India started to address the issues of early warning systems, forecasting and monitoring setup for various weather related hazards. A structure for flow of information, in the form of warnings, alerts and updates about the oncoming hazard, also emerged within this framework. A multi-stakeholder High powered group was setup by involving representatives from different ministries and departments. Some of these ministries were also designated as the nodal authorities for specific disasters.

Present Structure for Disaster Management

The institutional structure for disaster management in India is in a state of transition. The new setup, following the implementation of the Act, is evolving; while the previous structure also continues. Thus, the two structures co-exist at present. The National Disaster Management Authority has been established at the centre, and the SDMA at state and district authorities at district level are gradually being formalized.

In addition to this, the National Crisis Management Committee, part of the earlier setup, also functions at the Centre. The nodal ministries, as identified for different disaster types of function under the overall guidance of the Ministry of Home Affairs. This makes the stakeholders interact at different levels within the disaster management framework.

Within this transitional and evolving setup, two distinct features of the institutional structure for disaster management may be noticed. Firstly, the structure is hierarchical and functions at four levels—centre, state, district and local. In both the setups—one that existed prior to the implementation of the Act, and other that is being formalized post-implementation of the Act, there have existed institutionalized structures at the centre, state, district and local levels.

Disaster Management Act, 2005

This Act provides for the effective management of disaster and for matters connected therewith or incidental thereto. It provides institutional mechanisms for drawing up and monitoring the implementation of the disaster management. The Act also ensures measures by the various wings of the Government for prevention and mitigation of disasters and prompt response to any disaster situation.

The Act provides for setting up of a National Disaster Management Authority (NDMA) under the Chairmanship of the Prime Minister, State Disaster Management Authorities (SDMAs) under the Chairmanship of the Chief Ministers, District Disaster Management Authorities (DDMAs) under the Chairmanship of Collectors/District Magistrates/Deputy Commissioners.

The Act further provides for the constitution of different Executive Committee at national and state levels. Under its aegis, the National Institute of Disaster Management (NIDM) for capacity building and National Disaster Response Force (NDRF) for response purpose have been set up. It also mandates the concerned Ministries and Departments to draw up their own plans in accordance with the National Plan.

The Act further contains the provisions for financial mechanisms such as creation of funds for response, National Disaster Mitigation Fund and similar funds at the state and district levels for the purpose of disaster management. The Act also provides specific roles to local bodies in disaster management.

Further the enactment of 73rd and 74th Amendments to the constitution and emergence of local self- government, both rural and urban, as important tiers of governance, the role of local authorities becomes very important. The DM Act, 2005 also envisages specific roles to be played by the local bodies in disaster management.

National Disaster Management Authority (NDMA)

The National Disaster Management Authority (NDMA) was initially constituted on May 30, 2005 under the Chairmanship of Prime Minister vide an executive order. Following enactment of the Disaster Management Act, 2005, the NDMA was formally constituted in accordance with Section-3(1) of the Act on 27th September, 2006 with Prime Minister as its Chairperson and nine other members, and one such member to be designated as Vice-Chairperson.

Mandate of NDMA

The NDMA has been mandated with laying down policies on disaster management and guidelines which would be followed by different Ministries, Departments of the Government of India and State Government in taking measures for disaster risk reduction. It has also to laid down guidelines to be followed by the State Authorities in drawing up the State Plans and to take such measures for the management of disasters, Details of these responsibilities are given as under :-

(a) Lay down policies on disaster management;

(b) Approve the National Plan;

(c) Approve plans prepared by the Ministries or Departments of the Government of India in accordance with the National Plan;

(d) Lay down guidelines to be followed by the State Authorities in drawing up the State Plan;

(e) Lay down guidelines to be followed by the different Ministries or Departments of the Government of India for the purpose of integrating the measures for prevention of disaster or the mitigation of its effects in their development plans and projects;

(f) Coordinate the enforcement and implementation of the policy and plan for disaster management;

(g) Recommend provision of funds for the purpose of mitigation;

(h) Provide such support to other countries afected by major disasters as may be determined by the Central Government;

(i) Take such other measures for the prevention of disaster, or the mitigation, or preparedness and capacity building for dealing with the threatening disaster situation or disaster as it may consider necessary;

(j) Lay down broad policies and guidelines for the functioning of the National Institute of Disaster Management.

Composition of NDMA

Besides the nine members nominated by the Prime Minister, Chairperson of the Authority, the Organisational structure consists of a Secretary and five Joint Secretaries including one Financial Advisor. There are 10 posts of Joint Advisors and Directors, 14 Assistant Advisors, Under Secretaries and Assistant Financial Advisor and Duty Officer along with supporting staff. Further, Recruitment Rules have been notified as

(a) National Disaster Management Authority, Group-'C' posts Recruitment Rules, 2009.

(b) National Disaster Management Authority (Group 'A') Recruitment Rules, 2009.

Under Section 7 (1) of DM Act an Advisory Committee with 12 Members has been constituted during 2007.

National Executive Committee (NEC)

A National Executive Committee is constituted under Section 8 of DM Act, 2005 to assist the National Authority in the performance of its functions. NEC consists of Home Secretary as its Chairperson, *ex-ofcio*, with other Secretaries to the Government of India in the Ministries or Departments having administrative control of the agriculture, atomic energy, defence, drinking water supply, environment and forest, finance (expenditure), health, power, rural development science and technology, space, telecommunication, urban development, water resources. The Chief of Integrated Defence Staff of the Chiefs of Staff Committee, *ex-ofcio,* is also its Members. NEC may as and when it considers necessary constitute one or more sub-committees for the efficient discharge of its functions. For the conduct of NEC, Disaster Management National Executive Committee Rules. NEC has been given the responsibility to act as the coordinating and monitoring body for disaster management, to prepare a National Plan, monitor the implementation of National Policy etc. vide section 10 of the DM Act.

State Disaster Management Authority (SDMA)

The DM Act, 2005 provides for constitution of SDMAs and DDMAs in all the states and UTs. As per the information received from the states and UTs, except Gujarat and Daman & Diu, all the rest have constituted SDMAs under the DM Act, 2005. Gujarat has constituted its SDMA under its Gujarat State Disaster Management Act, 2003. Daman & Diu have also established SDMAs prior to enactment of DM Act 2005.

State Executive Committee (SEC)

The Act envisages establishment of State Executive Committee under Section 20 of the Act, to be headed by Chief Secretary of the state Government with four other Secretaries of such departments as the state Government may think ft. It has the responsibility for coordinating and monitoring the implementation of the National Policy, the National Plan and the State Plan as provided under section 22 of the Act.

District Disaster Management Authority (DDMA)

Section 25 of the DM Act provides for constitution of DDMA for every district of a state. The District Magistrate/ District Collector/Deputy Commissioner heads the Authority as Chairperson besides an elected representative of the local authority as Co-Chairperson except in the tribal areas where the Chief Executive Member of the District Council of Autonomous District is designated as Co-Chairperson. Further in district, where Zila Parishad exist, its Chairperson shall be the Co-Chairperson of DDMA. Other members of this authority include the CEO of the District Authority, Superintendant of Police, Chief Medical Officer of the District and other two district level officers are designated by the state Government.

The District Authority is responsible for planning, coordination and implementation of disaster management and to take such measures for disaster management as provided in the guidelines. The District Authority also has the power to examine the construction in any area in the district to enforce the safety standards and also to arrange for relief measures and respond to the disaster at the district level.

Institutional Framework for Metropolitan Cities

In the larger cities, recommendation of second Administrative Reforms Commission has suggested that the Mayor, assisted by the Commissioner of the Municipal Corporation and the Police Commissioner to be directly responsible for Crisis Management. It has now been accepted by the Government.

Hierarchical Structure of Authority and Committee

In this structure, National Disaster Management Authority is the authority for formulation of policy and guidelines for all disaster management work in the country. The state authorities further lay down the guidelines for departments of the state and the districts falling in their respective jurisdictions. Similarly, district authorities direct the civil administration, departments and local authorities such as the municipalities, police department and civil administration. The State Executive Committees are responsible for execution of the tasks envisaged by the authorities.

National Institute of Disaster Management (NIDM)

Management Structure

The Union Home Minister is the President of the Institute, It was constituted on 23rd February, 2007 and has a general body of forty two members comprising of secretaries of various ministries, departments of the Union Government and heads of national level scientific, research and technical organizations.

In terms of Section 42(4) of the Disaster Management Act, 2005 vide order dated 3rd May, 2007.

Organizational Structure – NIDM is headed by an Executive Director along with the faculty and staff.

The Institute has four academic divisions

— Geo-Hazard Division
— Hydro-met Hazard Division
— Policy Planning and Cross Cutting Issues Division
— Response Division

Location and Facilities

Located centrally at the Indraprastha Estate on the Mahatma Gandhi Road, within the campus of the IIPA, the institute is equipped with state-of-the-art facilities of training and research on disaster management. It has fully air conditioned training and conference halls, a well stocked library, GIS laboratory, computer centre, and a video conference hall. The institute also provides Boarding and lodging facilities for participants of its programmes.

National Disaster Response Force (NDRF)

Constitution and Role of NDRF

The National Disaster Response Force (NDRF) has been constituted under Section 44 of the DM Act, 2005 by up-gradation/conversion of eight standard battalions of Central Para Military Forces i.e. two battalions each from Border Security Force (BSF), Indo-Tibetan Border Police (ITBP), Central Industrial Security Force (CISF) and Central Reserve Police Force (CRPF) to build them up as a specialist force to respond to disaster or disaster like situations.

The eight battalions of NDRF consist of 144 specialised teams trained in various types of natural, man made and non-natural disasters. 72 of such teams are designed to cater to the Chemical, Biological, Radiological and Nuclear (CBRN) calamities besides natural calamities. Each NDRF battalion consists of 1149 personnel organised in 18 teams comprising of 45 personnel, who are being equipped and trained for rendering effective response to any threatening disaster situation or disaster, both natural and man made. All these eight battalions are being trained in natural disasters while four of them are being additionally trained for handling CBRN disasters.

The Government of India has approved the raising of two additional battalions of National Disaster Response Force by upgradation and conversion of one battalion each of Border Security Force and Central Reserve Police Force to be located in the states of Bihar (Bihata, Patna) and Andhra Pradesh (Vijaywada) respectively. The administrative approval for raising the two battalions was issued on 13-10- 2010.

State Disaster Response Force (SDRF)

The states/UTs have also been advised to set up their own Specialist Response Force for responding to disasters on the lines of National Disaster Response Force vide Ministry of Home Affairs letter dated 26th July 2007 and 8th March, 2011. The Central Government is providing assistance for training of trainers. The state governments have been also advised to utilise 10 percent of their State Disaster Response Fund and Capacity Building Grant for the procurement of search and rescue equipment and for training purposes of the Response Force.

Civil Defence Policy

The Civil Defence Policy of the GoI until 1962 was confined to making the states and UTs conscious of the need of civil protection measures and to keep in readiness civil protection plans for major cities and towns under the Emergency Relief Organisation (ERO) scheme. The legislation on Civil Defence (CD) known as Civil Defence Act was enacted in 1968 which is in force throughout the country.

The Act defines CD and provides for the powers of Central Government to make rules for CD, spelling out various actions to be taken for CD measures. It further stipulates for constitution of CD corps, appointment of members and officers, functions of members etc. The Act has since been amended in 2010 to cater to the needs of disaster management so as to utilise the services of Civil Defence volunteers effectively for enhancement of public participation in disaster management related activities in the country.

The CD Organisation is raised only in such areas and zones which are considered vulnerable to enemy attacks. The revision and renewal of categorised CD towns is done at regular intervals, with the level of perceived threat or external aggression or hostile attacks by anti- national elements or terrorists to vital installations.

Compendium of Instructions

CD deals very briefly with all different aspects of CD in India and includes references to important policy letters including legal aspects. It was first published in February 1969. Subsequently, its scope was enlarged by including the Master Plan of Civil Defence, Civil Defence Act 1968, training courses conducted at NCDC, Nagpur, training syllabus of states.

Role of Civil Defence

During times of war and emergencies, the CD organisation has the vital role of guarding the hinterland, supporting the armed forces, mobilising the citizens and helping civil administration for saving life and property, minimising damage, maintaining continuity in production centres and raising public morale. The concept of CD over the years has shifted from management of damage against conventional weapons to also include threat perceptions against nuclear weapons, biological and chemical warfare and environmental disasters.

Three tier structure as given below has been created to formulate CD policy and for coordinating and supervising measures to implement it.

— Civil Defence Advisory Committee under the Chairmanship of Union Home Minister,

— Civil Defence Committee under the Chairmanship of Home Secretary and

— Civil Defence Joint Planning Staf Committee under the Chairmanship of Director General Civil Defence.

Directorate General of Civil Defence (DGCD)

DGCD was established in 1962 with its headquarters at New Delhi in the Ministry of Home Affairs to handle all policy and planning matters related to Civil Defence, Home Guards and Fire Services including the functioning of National Civil Defence College, and National Fire Service College, Nagpur. An IPS officer in the rank of Director General of Police heads the organisation. He has dual charge of D.G. National Disaster Response Force and Civil Defence (DG, NDRF & CD).

Civil Defence Setup in the States

The state government for the purpose of coordinating the activities of the Controllers of Civil Defence within the state appoints a Director of Civil

Defence and also may constitute, for any area within the state a body of a person to be called the Civil Defence Corps. Out of 225 towns from 35 states notified as CD towns, currently the CD organisations at only 130 towns have been activated. Each town has nucleus of four Permanent Staff along with 400 CD Volunteers for a two lakh population. It is expected that each state will have one CD Training Institute with permanent strength of 36 personnel, five vehicles and other equipments. The District Magistrate is designated as a Controller for CD Towns. The present strength of CD volunteers is 5.72 lakhs, out of which 5.11 lakhs are already trained. The target strength of CD volunteers has been fixed at 13 lakhs based on the population of CD towns as per 2001 census.

In accordance with the directions issued by Hon'ble Home Minister, one member high powered committee was constituted on 7th February, 2006 under the chairmanship of one of the member of NDMA to analyse the existing functions of Civil Defence Organisations and suggest changes required to enlarge its role to include Disaster Management.

Civil Defence at District Level

The state government may appoint a person, not being in its opinion, below the rank of a District Magistrate to be known as the "Controller". Under certain conditions, the state government may also appoint a Deputy Controller of Civil Defence in appropriate rank up to that of Deputy Collector, but not inferior to that of a Sub- Divisional Magistrate.

Fire Services

Fire services are mandate of the Municipal Bodies as estimated in item 7 of Schedule 12 under Article 243W of the constitution. The structure across is not uniform. Presently Fire prevention and Fire Fighting Services are organized by the concerned States and UTs. Ministry of Home Afairs, Govt. of India, renders technical advice to the States and UTs and Central Ministries on Fire Protection, Fire Prevention and Fire Legislation.

The Government of India in 1956, formed a "Standing Fire Advisory Committee" under the Ministry of Home Afairs. The mandate of the committee was to examine the technical problems relating to Fire Services and to advise the Government of India for speedy development and upgradation of Fire Services all over the country. This committee had representation from each State Fire Services, as well as the representation from Ministry of Home, Defence, Transport, Communication and Bureau of Indian Standards. This Committee was renamed as "Standing Fire Advisory Council" (SFAC) during the year 1980.

Fire Services in Gujarat, Chhatisgarh, Punjab, Maharashtra, Himachal Pradesh, Haryana and Madhya Pradesh excluding Indore are under the respective concerned Municipal Corporations. In other remaining States it is under the Home Department. While some States have enacted their own Fire Act, some others have not. As on today, there is no standardization with regard to the scaling of equipment, the type of equipment, or the training of their manpower. In each state it has grown according to the initiatives taken by the States and the funds provided for the Fire Services.

Presently the only Basic Life Line of Fire & Emergency Services which is fully committed to the common public, is the Municipal in some states and State Fire Services. The Airport Authority, Big Industrial Establishments, CISF and Armed Forces, however also have their own Fire Services and many a times in case of need rush in aid to the local Fire Services. Apart from the lack of being a proper government department with a complete developmental plan, State Fire Services have their own organizational structure, administrative setup, funding mechanism, training facilities and equipments.

Home Guard

The role of Home Guards is to serve as an auxiliary to the police in the maintenance of law and order, internal security and help the community in any kind of emergency such as air-raid, fire, cyclone, earthquake, epidemic etc. They are also expected to help the police in maintenance of communal harmony, assist the administration in protecting weaker sections, participate in socio-economic and welfare activities and perform Civil Defence duties.

Home Guards are of two types – rural and urban besides in Border States, Border Wing Home Guards Battalions at national level. Border Wing, Home Guard serve as an auxiliary to the Border Security Force. The total strength of Home Guards is 5, 73,793 against which the raised strength is 5,00,410. The organisation is spread over all states and UTs except in Kerala. Eighteen Border Wing Home Guards (BWHG) Battalions have been raised in the border states viz. Punjab (6 Bns.), Rajasthan (4 Bns.), Gujarat (4Bns.) and one of Bn each. for Assam, Meghalaya, Tripura and West Bengal to serve as an auxiliary to Border Security Force for preventing infiltration on the international border and coastal areas, guarding of vital Installations and lines of communication in vulnerable areas at the time of external aggression.

Statutory Mechanisms and Service Condition

Home Guards are raised under the Home Guards Act and Rules of the states and UTs. They are recruited from a cross section of the population such as doctors, engineers, lawyers, private sector organisations, college and university students, agricultural and industrial workers, etc. who give their spare time to the organisation for betterment of the community. Home Guards are provided free uniform, duty allowances and awards for gallantry, distinguished and meritorious services. Members of Home Guards with three year service in the organisation are trained to assist police in maintenance of law and order, prevention of crime, anti-decoity measures, border patrolling, prohibition, flood relief, fire-fighting, election duties and social welfare activities.

The Ministry of Home Afairs formulates the policy regarding role, target, raising, training, equipping, establishment and other important matters of Home Guards Organisation.

Interface between Ministries for disaster Management

The interface between stakeholders and the disaster management framework is permanent, backed by legislative measures, decisions, such as those taken for establishment of the bodies and committees for managing disasters and the government orders to execute these decisions. These decisions or measures direct the composition of the structure by identifying the stakeholders to be involved in the disaster management framework. The role to be performed by each stakeholder is in the evolving stage and needs to be defined within different SOPs.

The expertise based interfaces emerge when the stakeholders serve as 'service providers' to the disaster management framework. For instance, the institutions under Ministry of Earth Sciences and Ministry of Water Resources, that is, Indian Meteorological Department (IMD) and Central Water Commission (CWC) respectively, provide information on the weather and climatic parameters and the potential hazards and threats to the nodal management authority. Further, these organizations are involved with disaster planning activities – flood zonation and flood plain management in case of CWC, and hazard mapping and database generation in case of

IMD. The organizations and institutions under the Department of Space provide research and technical support by monitoring the weather elements and facilitating satellite based communication, and also undertaking activities such as land use mapping and hazard zoning.

The Disaster Risk Reduction (DRR) should be seen as on integral part of environment and development. The impending risk analysis should be done in the light of disasters and possible threat of high intensity disasters due to climate change. Accordingly, mitigation and adaptation programmes should be developed. The mitigation plan should address the issues of structural and non-structural interventions along with the fiscal and monetary tools for pre and post disaster planning. If this is main streamed, sustainable development can be attained and miseries of the people could be minimised. The top down and bottom up institutional linkages for policy formulation and programme execution would be interdependent with each other.

National Policy on Disaster Management (NPDM)

The National Policy on Disaster Management (NPDM) has been approved by the central government on October 22, 2009 and circulated to all concerned. The policy envisages a safe and disaster resilient India by developing a holistic, proactive, multi-disaster oriented and technology driven strategy through a culture of prevention, mitigation, preparedness and response. The policy covers all aspects of disaster management including institutional and legal arrangements, financial arrangements, disaster prevention, mitigation and preparedness, techno-legal regime, response, relief and rehabilitation, reconstruction and recovery, capacity development, knowledge management, research and development. It focuses on the areas where action is needed and the institutional mechanism through which such action can be channelised.

The NPDM addresses the concerns of all the sections of the society including differently abled persons, women, children and other disadvantaged groups in terms of granting relief and formulating measures for rehabilitation of the persons afected by disasters. The issue of equity and inclusiveness has been accorded due consideration. It aims to bring in transparency and accountability in all aspects of disaster management through involvement of community, community based organisations, Panchayati Raj Institutions (PRIs), local bodies and civil society.

National Plan on Disaster Management

An institutional mechanism for preparation of the National Plan has been put in place, which is under preparation in three parts namely:-

(i) National Response Plan,

(ii) National Mitigation Plan and

(iii) National Capacity Building Plan.

A Facilitation Committee under the Chairmanship of Secretary (Border Management) in the Ministry of Home Afairs and three sub-committees namely:

(i) National Response Plan Committee

(ii) National Mitigation Plan Committee and

(iii) National Capacity Building Plan Committee have been constituted for preparation of the National Plan on Disaster Management.

The National Mitigation Plans are under preparation by the concerned nodal ministries for disasters in respect of which the Nodal Ministries have been identified and designated. The Nodal Officers of the ministries concerned with the disasters are the conveners of the National Mitigation Plan Committees and are required to complete the Mitigation Plan in consultation with the members concerned with the respective disasters in NDMA.

Focus and Objectives of Guidelines

NDMA is engaged in the formulation of guidelines through a consultative process involving multiple stakeholders, including the government, non-government organisations, academic and scientific institutions, the corporate sector and community. Since its inception, NDMA has so far released various disaster specific and thematic guidelines. Salient features of the guidelines issued are as follows:-

Management of Landslide and Snow Avalanches

The objectives of these guidelines are to institutionalise the landslide hazard mitigation efforts, to make the society aware of the various aspects of landslide hazard in the country and to prepare the society to take suitable action to reduce both risks and costs associated with this hazard. The guidelines include regulatory and non-regulatory frameworks with defined time schedules for all activities.

Management of Cyclones

The guidelines aim to deal with the tropical cyclones by way of appropriate coping strategies and risk reduction plans along with greater public awareness. The guidelines call for proactive, participatory, fail safe, multi-disciplinary and multi-sector approach at various levels. An approach encompassing Early Warning System on cyclones, structural measures for preparedness and mitigation, covering cyclone shelters, buildings, road links, drains, embankments, communication/power transmission networks, and non-structural mitigation options, such as coastal zone management, coastal flood plain management, natural resources management, awareness generation related to CDM, hazard zoning and mapping, including the use of GIS tools, capacity development, etc.; and its implementation strategies are suggested.

Management of Earthquake

The guidelines emphasise that all new structures are built in compliance with earthquake resistant building codes. Town planning, bye-laws, structural safety audits of existing lifeline structures and other critical structures in earthquake prone areas, carrying out selective seismic strengthening and retroftting ought to be addressed.

Management of Floods

The guidelines aim at measures for preparedness, prevention, mitigation in the pre-flood stage and on prompt and effective response, relief and recovery during– and post flood stages. Importance on non-structural measures besides structural measures is emphasized in the guidelines. Setting of basin-wise organisations for flood management and also for setting up a National Flood Management Institute for training, education and research are suggested in the guideline.

Chemical Disasters (Industrial)

These guidelines call for a protective, participatory, well-structured, fail-safe, multi-disciplinary and multi-structural approach at various levels. On the basis of vulnerabilities and consequences of chemical accidents, the guidelines review the existing regulatory framework and practices and thus propose for a regulatory framework, code of practices, capacity development, institutional framework, etc. They further set out an approach for implementation of the guidelines.

Management of Chemical (Terrorism) Disasters

The guidelines focus on outlining the preparedness and efforts made for mitigating the chemical terrorism, the act of violence perpetrated to achieve professed aims, using chemical agents. While reviewing the existing legislations and regulatory framework, the guidelines identify the gaps and propose the measures required to fill the gaps in the legislative and regulatory frameworks. They also deal with the aspects of surveillance measures for strengthening the intelligence in order to prevent intentional use of chemical agents.

Preparation of State Disaster Management Plans

The aim of the state DM plan is to ensure that the components of DM are addressed to facilitate planning, preparedness, operational, coordination and community participation. The guideline suggests outlays for preparation of the plan to include the state profile, vulnerability assessment and risk analysis, prevention measures, mainstreaming DM concerns into developmental plan and programme projects, preparedness measures, response and partnership with the other stakeholders besides providing for financial arrangement.

Psycho-Social Support and Mental Health Services in Disasters

Disasters leave a trail of agony and affect the survivors' mental health. The guidelines on this subject outlay the entire gamut of psycho-social support and mental health services with a view to build the nation resilient to respond effectively in all types of disasters. The intent of these guidelines is to develop and integrate a holistic, coordinated and pro-active strategy for management of psycho-social support and mental health services after a disaster through a culture of prevention, mitigation and preparedness to generate a prompt and effective response.

Medical Preparedness and Mass Casualty Management

A Mass Casualty Event (MCE) is an incident resulting in a number of victims large enough to disrupt the normal course of emergency and health care services. The guidelines for MCE focus on all aspects of medical preparedness and mass casualty management with emphasis on prevention, mitigation preparedness, relief and medical response etc. They aim to develop a rigorous medical management framework to reduce the number of deaths during MCE.

Management of Nuclear and Radiological Emergencies

The overall objective of the guidelines is to implement the concept of prevention of nuclear and radiological emergencies. In rare cases of their occurrence due to factors beyond human control, the guidelines suggest the emergency should be managed through certain pre-planned and established structural and non-structural measures to minimise risks to health, life and the environment.

Incident Response System

These guidelines provide directions and guidelines to central ministries and the states for an effective and well coordinated response. They suggest a multi-disciplinary, and systematic approach to guide administrative mechanisms at all levels of the government with scope for participation of private sector, NGOs, PRIs and communities to work together seamlessly in the response activities. The guidelines are applicable to the management of all incidents—natural or human-made. The proposed methodology is expected to be equally useful for handling all kinds of incidents such as terrorism (Counter Insurgency), law and order situations, serial bomb blast, hijacking, air accidents, chemical, biological, radiological and nuclear (CBRN) disasters, mine disaster, port and harbour emergencies, forest fires, oil field fires and oil spills.

Strengthening of Safety and Security for Transportation of POL tankers

The guidelines envisage measures for prevention and for adoption of preparedness practices to a level that there is no chance of error. This calls for firming up the regulations, setting up of mechanisms of strict conformation, as well as fail proof functioning by each role player.

Management of Biological Disaster

The guidelines for management of biological disasters focus on all aspects of Biological Disaster Management (BDM) including Bio-terrorism (BT). It emphasises a preventive approach such as immunisation of first responders and stockpiles of medical countermeasures based upon risk reduction measures by developing a rigorous medical management framework to reduce the number of deaths during biological disasters, both intentional and accidental. These include the development of specialised measures pertaining to the management of biological disasters.

Management of Tsunami

The guidelines present an introductory overview on the tsunami risk and vulnerability in the country and the preparedness as a nation. It provides for structural mitigation measures and lay down strategies for protecting lifeline with the sea front besides laying down the guidance for developing the techno legal regime and giving an account of various tool kits for tsunami risk management.

Role of NGOs in Disaster Management

The guidelines discuss the role of NGOs in disaster preparedness, mitigation and response and spell out the institutional mechanism for improving the effectiveness of disaster management through effective coordination between NGOs and the government at different levels.

Urban Flooding

The guidelines aim to develop plans for the management of urban flooding with a view to guide the ministry and other government bodies for preparation of their disaster management plans on this aspect of disaster, recurrent in urban areas during monsoon. While reviewing the existing international and national practices for the design and maintenance of the urban drainage system, it addresses the issue of urban flood risk, vulnerability analysis and hazard mapping and provides for response action.

Management of Dead in the Aftermath of Disaster

These guidelines are aimed at institutionalising the standard procedure for proper management of dead bodies and animal carcasses in the aftermath of disasters.

Plan to Counter Threats to Municipal Water Supply and Water Reservoirs

The plan aims to counter any threat to municipal water supply and water reservoir in view of such a perception and taking into account the present water supply system and legislative framework. The plan suggests to framing a preparedness plan and also outlining the guidelines for a standard operating plan.

NDMA from time to time has also been organizing workshops on different issues related to disasters and publishing its reports for action by concerned Ministry or agency. Such reports are given as under

(i) *Training regime for disaster response:* The key to efficiency in disaster response does not lie in good equipment but in effective ongoing training of NDRF personnel.. The training regime so devised aims to help the process of capacity building of NDRF for efficient and effective discharge of its onerous responsibility.

(ii) *Pandemic preparedness:* The outcome of the workshop held on the subject on 21-22nd April, 2008 deals with the existing status of preparedness at different levels of the government and attached offices and inter-dependency of the sectors.

(iii) *Revamping of Civil Defence set up in the country:* The changing scenario, reducing changes and occurrence of traditional wars, an steadily and increasing threat from natural and man-made disasters, with large scale devastation of life and property, warrants a greater role on the part of Civil Defence from merely hostile act-centric responsibility to a holistic role in all the facets of disaster management in the country. It recommends revamping the existing structure of civil defence for enhancing its functional responsibilities in realistic and cost effective manner.

Management of Droughts

It suggests a system for drought management policy and programmes to be followed by the Government of India and state governments. It focuses on the general and common elements of drought management at the national level, while allowing the states to include their specific schemes and interventions. While classifying the droughts of different types and associated vulnerability, the guidelines suggests the measures for management of drought. The guidelines lay emphasis on risk management rather than following the traditional approach of crisis management as a reactive response measure. The vital components of drought management namely, drought intensity assessment, it's declaration, prioritisation of areas of drought management and implementation of drought management strategy are outlined in the guidelines.

National Action Plan on Climate Change

On June 30, 2008, Prime Minister Dr. Manmohan Singh released India's first National Action Plan on Climate Change (NAPCC), outlining existing and future policies and programs addressing climate mitigation and adaptation. The plan identifies eight core "national missions" running through 2017 and directs ministries to submit detailed implementation plans to the Prime Minister's Council on Climate Change by December 2008.

Emphasizing the overriding priority of maintaining high economic growth rates to raise living standards, the plan "identifies measures that promote our development objectives while also yielding co-benefts for addressing climate change effectively." It stipulates that these national measures would be more successful with assistance from developed countries, and pledges that India's per capita greenhouse gas emissions "will at no point exceed that of developed countries even as we pursue our development objectives." The plan can be visited on the website of Ministry of Environment and Forest (MOEF)

References

Carter, N. (1991).*Disaster Management, A disaster Manager's Handbook,* Asian Development Bank, Manilla.

Comfort, Louise K., ed. (1988). *Managing Disaster: Strategies and Policy Perspectives*, Durham: Duke University Press.

Haddow, George D. and Jane A. Bullock. (2003). *Introduction to Emergency Management*, Amsterdam: Butterworth-Heinemann.

Sharma, Vinod K. (ed.), (2001). *Disaster management*, New Delhi: National Centre for Disaster Management, Indian Institute of Public Administration.

4

Disaster Preparedness

Social scientists, emergency managers, and public policy makers generally organize both research and guidance around four phases of disaster loss reduction: mitigation, preparedness, response, and recovery. The core topics of hazards and disaster research include: hazards research, which focuses on pre-disaster hazard vulnerability analysis and mitigation; and disaster research, which focuses on post-disaster emergency response and recovery. Preparedness intersects with both of these two areas, serving as a temporal connector between the pre-impact and post-impact phases of a disaster event. Preparedness is typically understood as consisting of measures that enable different units of analysis—individuals, households, organizations, communities, and societies—to respond effectively and recover more quickly when disasters strike. Preparedness efforts also aim at ensuring that the resources necessary for responding effectively in the event of a disaster are in place, and that those faced with having to respond know how to use those resources. The activities that are commonly associated with disaster preparedness include developing planning processes to ensure readiness; formulating disaster plans; stockpiling resources necessary for effective response; and developing skills and competencies to ensure effective performance of disaster-related tasks.

The concept of disaster preparedness encompasses measures aimed at enhancing life safety when a disaster occurs, such as protective actions during an earthquake, hazardous materials spill, or terrorist attack. It also includes actions designed to enhance the ability to undertake emergency actions in order to protect property and contain disaster damage and disruption, as well as the ability to engage in post-disaster restoration and early recovery activities.

Preparedness is commonly viewed as consisting of activities aimed at improving response activities and coping capabilities. However, emphasis is increasingly being placed on *recovery preparedness*—that is, on planning not only in order to respond effectively during and immediately after disasters but also in order to successfully navigate challenges associated with short- and longer-term recovery.

The Capability Assessment for Readiness (CAR), which was developed by FEMA and the National Emergency Management Association (NEMA) identifies thirteen elements that should be addresses by states in their preparedness efforts. Those elements are:

- Laws and Authorities
- Hazard Identification and Risk Assessment
- Hazard Mitigation
- Resource Management
- Direction, Control, and Coordination
- Communications and Warning
- Operations and Procedures
- Logistics and Facilities
- Training
- Exercises, Evaluations, and Corrective Actions
- Crisis Communications, Public Education, and Information
- Finance and Administration

Mitigation and preparedness are sometimes conflated with one another (as they are in the list above), in part because they are intertwined in practice. Indeed, definitions contained in key resource documents reviewed for this project illustrate this conceptual blurring. For instance, the National Fire Protection Association (NFPA) defines preparedness as:

> activities, programs, and systems developed and implemented prior to a disaster/emergency that are used to support and enhance mitigation of, response to, and recovery from disaster/emergencies.

FEMA defines preparedness as:

> the leadership, training, readiness and exercise support, and technical and financial assistance to strengthen citizens, communities, state, local, and tribal governments, and professional emergency workers as they prepare for disasters, mitigate the effects of disasters, respond to community needs after a disaster, and launch effective recovery efforts.

Both these definitions make reference to mitigation, but disaster scholars and emergency management professionals generally define mitigation as actions that are taken well in advance of disasters that are designed either to avoid or reduce disaster-related damage. Mitigation measures include appropriate land-use and coastal zone management practices, mandatory and voluntary building codes, and other long-term loss reduction efforts. In some cases, mitigation can also include moving neighborhoods and communities to other locations in order to avoid future losses. Mitigation activities can take the form of specific projects, such as elevating homes for flood protection, as well as *process*-related activities, such as hazard and vulnerability analyses, that are designed to lead to future mitigative actions. However, some discussions, such as those cited above, also use the term "mitigation" to refer to actions taken *after an event occurs* that are designed to contain impacts so that they do not become more severe. In this sense, some would see efforts to contain an oil spill as a "mitigative" measure, even though spill containment is commonly thought of as an element in oil spill emergency response.

Providing additional clarification, the National Research Council report states that "hazard mitigation consists of practices that are implemented before impact and provide *passive* protection at the time impact occurs. In contrast, emergency preparedness practices involve the development of plans and procedures, the recruitment and training of staff, and the acquisition of facilities, equipment, and materials needed to provide *active* protection during emergency response".

Passive mitigation activities can be further separated into categories such as "process mitigation" or "indirect" activities that lead to policies, practices and projects that reduce risk. Such activities might also be referred to as "non-structural" mitigation activities. These include: efforts to assess hazards, vulnerability and risk; conduct planning to identify projects, policies and practices and set priorities; educate decision-makers and build constituencies and political will; efforts to facilitate the selection, design, funding and construction of projects; land-use planning to limit or prevent development in floodplains, building codes to reduce losses from earthquake and hurricanes and fires, and designing buildings to facilitate surveillance.

In contrast, "project mitigation" or "structural" mitigation activities include measures to avoid or reduce damage resulting from hazard events. They include projects to elevate, acquire and/or relocate buildings, lifelines and structures threatened by floods, strengthen buildings to resist earthquake or wind forces, and to improve drainage and land conditions and the building of dams and levees to prevent flooding.

The NRC report highlights the importance of both emergency preparedness and disaster recovery preparedness and emphasizes that response and recovery preparedness involve distinct sets of activities. Emergency preparedness provides short-term solutions during an emergency response that will support the longer term efforts of disaster recovery. Disaster recovery preparedness practices involve participating in activities and gathering materials needed "to provide rapid and equitable disaster recovery after an incident no longer poses an imminent threat to health and safety". Recognizing that the immediate post-disaster emergency period is not the time to begin developing disaster recovery strategies, the city of Los Angeles has included a "recovery and reconstruction" element in its emergency operations plan. One key resource for disaster recovery preparedness is "hazard insurance, designed to provide financial protection from economic losses caused by a disaster event".

There are a few activities discussed in the disaster literature that appear to span both mitigation and preparedness phases. One example is the development of warning systems, evacuation plans, disaster communications, and public education, which some sources view as mitigative because such practices must be implemented long before a hazardous event. As systems or plans, they serve as passive protection to support emergency response and recovery. At the same time, warning systems and plans can also be seen as a key element in disaster preparedness, since part of being prepared involves knowing how to respond when warnings are issued.

Emergency preparedness activities differ according to which social unit, (households, businesses, communities, public or governmental entities) is involved. For instance, for local emergency management agencies, disaster preparedness focuses on establishing authorities and responsibilities for emergency actions and resources to support those actions. Preparing for disasters includes leadership, training, readiness and exercise support as well as technical and financial assistance. For local emergency management agencies and other crisis-relevant organizations, preparedness means developing emergency operations plans and then training, exercising and testing in order to be ready to respond to a disaster, crisis, or other type of emergency situation. Other aspects of preparedness include the designing, equipping, and managing emergency operations centers (EOCs); developing partnerships with various community sectors (e.g., businesses, community-based organizations); and educating the public on disaster loss reduction.

Disaster preparedness for business organizations often focuses on activities designed to prevent physical damage and inventory loss, protect critical business records, and avoid downtime. Common preparedness measures center on information security and continuity of operations following a hazardous event. Business continuity planners conduct impact analyses to identify supply chain vulnerabilities and to establish backup resources in order to continue the flow of products to customers and clients. For households, disaster preparedness includes a range of measures and activities, including developing household disaster response plans, learning about evacuation routes and procedures, and knowing how to undertake expedient emergency measures, such as boarding up windows when a hurricane threatens or shutting off gas lines when an earthquake strikes.

Elements and Dimensions of Disaster Preparedness

The concept of preparedness has a variety of dimensions that are in turn supported by a number of activities. *Dimensions* of preparedness consist of the various goals or end-states that preparedness seeks to achieve. *Activities* are concrete actions that need to be taken in order to meet those goals. Sources vary in terms of how dimensions and activities are defined. Recommendations on public education campaigns for households emphasize four dimensions of preparedness; as noted above, FEMA's CAR specifies thirteen areas for targeted preparedness efforts; standards for business and industry focus on twelve different dimensions, while efforts to create accreditation standards for communities have highlighted fifteen, and the Department of Homeland Security (DHS) has identified 37 "target capabilities" for all-hazard preparedness.

Despite these differences, common themes appear both in research on preparedness and in guidance documents. In the following section, we will discuss key dimensions of preparedness and their associated activities, with an emphasis on dimensions and activities that cut across different units of analysis.

At the most general level, it is possible to identify eight dimensions or desired end-states for preparedness activities:

(1) hazard knowledge;

(2) management, direction, and co-ordination of emergency operations;

(3) formal and informal response agreements;

(4) resource acquisition aimed at ensuring that emergency functions can be carried out smoothly;

(5) life safety protection;

(6) property protection;

(7) emergency coping and restoration of key functions; and

(8) initiation of recovery activities. Descriptions that follow focus on each of these key dimensions and their associated activities.

Hazard Knowledge

All preparedness activities must be based on knowledge about hazards, the likelihood of different types of disaster events, and likely impacts on the natural and built environment, households, organizations, community institutions and communities. Types of information that provide a focus for preparedness activities include the potential for detrimental impacts of the hazards on health and safety, continuity of operations and government, critical facilities and infrastructure, delivery of services, the environment, economic and financial conditions, and regulatory and contractual obligations. Loss estimation tools such as HAZUS and HAZUS-MH were designed specifically to help communities envision the potential impacts of future disasters and mitigate and prepare for such events. Community-based disaster scenarios also provide a solid basis for preparedness efforts.

Community outreach and the development of plans for crisis communications and public information are vital for the continuity of operations in businesses and to ensure public trust within a community. Partnerships between public and private entities that have been established and maintained prior to a disaster event will influence the sharing of resources through mutual aid and enable a capability to deliver emergency public information through previously identified channels. Activities include the identification of publics that will be in need of information and developing communications plans and identifying private resources that can be used in service to the community for response and recovery.

Management, Direction, and Coordination (MDC)

This dimension of preparedness centers on strategies that make it possible for households, organizations, and other units of analysis to manage both preparatory activity and response processes. The MDC dimension includes identifying lines of authority and responsibility and specifying how resources will be managed, information analyzed, and decisions made. For example, guidance documents advise businesses to prepare for disaster by organizing an emergency management group that includes representation from the affected area, security, safety and health, environment, maintenance, human resources, planning and logistics, and public relations. Local emergency management agencies and crisis-relevant organizations must now adopt the National Incident Management System (NIMS) which requires the identification of organizational roles, titles, and responsibilities for each incident management function specified in the emergency operations and response plan.

The MDC dimension also includes activities that are designed to ensure that emergency operations will be carried out effectively when disaster strikes. These activities include training, drills and exercises, and educational activities for members of the public, households, and businesses.

MDC also includes developing policy, vision, and mission statements; developing and using enabling authorities; setting performance objectives; and assigning responsibilities in areas such as oversight and coordination.

Formal and Informal Response Agreements

This dimension of preparedness consists of activities targeting the development of disaster plans and other agreements. Such plans can be either informal or formal. Households, for example, can plan informally to address challenges such as evacuation, sheltering in place, and reunification of family members who are separated when disasters strike. A family disaster plan consists of elements such as communications between family members, identifying safe locations for shelter, determining evacuation routes and how to reconnect when separated from loved ones.

For organizations, multi-organizational response networks, and communities, preparedness activities center on the development and adoption of formal disaster plans, memoranda of understanding, mutual aid agreements, and other agreements that facilitate coordinated response activities. The concept of mutual aid, or the "sharing of personnel, equipment, and facilities…which occurs when local resources are inadequate to meet the needs of the disaster" is applicable across a wide spectrum of groups, organizations, and jurisdictional levels.

Also important are formal and informal arrangements that link households, community organizations, and businesses with broader and more comprehensive preparedness efforts. For households, this could include participation in CERT (Community Emergency Response Teams) teams, Citizens Corps, and volunteer networks. Non-profits and community-based organizations may link with broader VOAD (Volunteer Organizations Active in Disaster) networks. In the Bay Area, CARD (Collaborating Agencies Responding to Disaster) performs this linking function for local community agencies. Individual businesses can also establish linkages with private sector and industry-based partnership networks.

Supportive Resources

Management activities and preparedness agreements are of little use unless resources are available to support response activities. The goal of resource management is to identify and establish internal and external resources necessary for disaster response and recovery. Identifying resource needs, acquiring resources, and storing and distributing resources are thus key preparedness dimensions. The resource management dimension of preparedness is closely tied to the planning dimension in that plans commonly involve strategies for resource sharing, such as mutual aid agreements.

Included in the concept of resources are human, material, and informational sources of support. Skilled, well-trained personnel and staff constitute critical resources. Communications resources are critical for all response activities at all levels of analysis, although communications media can vary from low-tech to very high-tech. Disaster response tasks—such as evacuation and other self-protective measures, search and rescue, emergency medical care, fire suppression, debris removal, emergency transportation, security and credentialing, and response coordination—have specific resource and logistical requirements that must be taken into account during the planning process.

Included in the concept of resources are human, material, and informational sources of support. Skilled, well-trained personnel and staff constitute critical resources. Technologies to assist with important crisis-relevant tasks such as public warning are also critical for effective response. Communications and warning systems are essential to any business operation or community emergency response. They are needed to report emergencies, warn personnel of the danger, keep families and off-duty employees informed about what's happening at a facility or within a department, coordinate response actions, and keep in contact with customers and suppliers. Preparedness for communications and warning include the development of a communications plan, the establishment of a warning system including developing protocols and procedures, regular testing and support, and addressing the interoperability of multiple responding organizations and personnel.

The resource dimension also includes efforts designed at mobilizing resources to continue with operations when key resources are destroyed. Businesses and communities must prepare for the possibility that an alternate facility, in addition to the primary facility, will be needed for recovery and resumption of services following a disaster event. Emergency preparedness for a community may include an alternate emergency operations center, efforts to introduce redundancy into key response systems, and procedures to locate, acquire, store, and test back-up resources. Included in this dimension of preparedness are efforts directed at mobilizing resources to continue with operations when key resources are destroyed. Businesses and communities must prepare for the possibility that an alternate facility, in addition to the primary facility, will be needed for recovery and resumption of services following a disaster event. Emergency preparedness for a community may include an alternate emergency operations center, efforts to introduce redundancy into key response systems, and procedures to locate, acquire, store, and test back-up resources.

Life Safety Protection

Protecting the health and safety of family members, vulnerable populations, employees and customers, and community members is a top priority during an emergency or disaster. Preparing to take action includes the creation of a disaster supplies kit with items such as food, clothing, first aid supplies, tools, and key documents. It also includes the designation of evacuation routes and exits, shelter, training and information on safety procedures, incident stabilization, damage assessment, and the identification of resources needed to support response and recovery operations.

Property Protection

Property protection and hazard mitigation include preparedness activities to protect homes, buildings, facilities, equipment and vital records that are essential to restoring operations once an emergency has occurred. Activities include the use of applicable building construction standards; hazard avoidance through appropriate land-use practices; relocation, retrofitting, or removal of structures at risk; removal or elimination of the hazard; protection systems such as fire and smoke alarms or emergency power generation systems; records preservation; facility shutdown; and the establishment of hazard warning and communication procedures.

Emergency Coping and Restoration

At the organizational level, planning activities seek to develop strategies to address problems that are likely to develop when a disaster strikes, and training seeks to ensure that all those involved in the response are able to carry out their assigned duties. Household emergency plans seek to do the same thing at the household level. However, disasters almost invariably bring surprises, and for that reason preparedness activities must also focus on improving the ability to improvise, innovate, and think creatively. Preparing to improvise may seem like a contradiction, but in fact the two concepts are complementary. Preparations seeking to enhance adaptive capacity in disasters may include extensive "what if" explorations, various kinds of thought experiments, exercises in which players are required to assume others' roles, and discussions centering on potential worst cases. Although a family may have an evacuation plan, it is also useful to consider what would be done if the plan cannot be executed or if evacuation is impossible. What if help does not arrive in 72 hours, or if the wait for assistance is evenlonger? What if both main and back-up EOCs are unavailable, as was the case for New York City at the time of the terrorist attacks of September, 2001? What if an event is so severe that the local community is totally paralyzed, as New Orleans was following Hurricane Katrina? What if critical resources are unavailable? If recent disaster experiences have taught us anything it is that systems can and do fail and that disaster plans can provide wholly inadequate in the face of unexpected contingencies.

Emergency response activities also include measures to initiate restoration activities as soon as is feasible following a disaster. Restoration of critical services and facilities is essential, both to contain further losses and to serve as a basis for initial recovery activities. Utility restoration, for example, plays a key role in making dwellings habitable and containing business interruption losses. Transportation system restoration is crucial to ensure that needed supplies and personnel can reach the impact area.

Initiation of Early Recovery Activities

Business continuity planning focuses on avoiding costly downtime, lost revenue, and disaster-induced unemployment. Preparedness for business recovery includes such elements as making contractual arrangements with vendors for post-emergency services such as records preservation, equipment repair, and engineering inspection services. It also includes measures to get employees back to work as soon as possible—even if they must work at another location. Preparedness for recovery is also important for households and communities – especially with respect the purchase of hazard insurance designed to provide financial protection from disaster-related economic losses.

Communities must also plan in advance for recovery. Such planning should include the use of hazard and vulnerability analyses to determine which neighborhoods, groups of residents, and businesses will be especially hard-hit in future disasters, and then, based on this information, to decide what should be done following those events. Decisions must be made regarding emergency ordinances as well as new measures that may need to be undertaken to acquire vacant land for redevelopment and to ensure that mitigation issues are addressed during the recovery process. Community recovery planning also includes support that communities can provide to businesses and households to help ensure that they recover as rapidly as possible.

Disaster Preparedness Planning

Disaster preparedness involves the preparation of people and essential service providers in their communities for the actions that they will take in case of disasters. If this is the case, consideration must be given to the manner in which the formal responders prepare to respond to disasters. For example, the personnel in these response agencies may have to learn the use of new equipment, treatment methods for diseases or providing services to prevent the escalation of the effects of disasters that will further destroy lives and devastate property.

The International Federation of Red Cross and Red Crescent Societies states that disaster preparedness requires global, national, community and individual inputs. Disaster preparedness incorporates all activities that will enhance the efficiency, effectiveness and impact of disaster emergency response mechanisms in the local community and throughout the country. The following are of particular importance:

— Develop and test warning systems regularly and plan measures to be taken during a disaster alert period to minimize potential loss of life and physical damage.

— Educate and train officials and the population at risk to respond to the disaster.

— Train first-aid and emergency response teams.

— Establish emergency response policies, standards, organizational arrangements and operational plans to be followed by emergency workers and other response entities after a disaster.

Others feel that disaster preparedness should be one that is particularly "community-based" through national or international efforts that will provide for strengthening community-based disaster preparedness through educating, preparing and supporting local populations and communities in their everyday efforts to reduce risks and prepare their own local response mechanisms to address disaster emergency situations.

The following activities are essential to the development of a preparedness strategy. Although an implementation sequence for these activities is suggested, some activities may be undertaken simultaneously, or even in reverse order.

Vulnerability Assessment

In most instances, you can identify particular geographical areas or communities that are predictably under threat from a hazard. These may include traditionally drought-prone areas, or communities living near volcanos or in flood-prone areas. They could be squatter settlements in which housing structures are known to be vulnerable to hurricanes, or communities unprotected from industrial waste. However, vulnerability need not be tied to particular geographic locations or communities. Displaced people, forced to flee from conflict or collapsing economic conditions, represent a community of sorts that can fall within the purview of vulnerability assessments. Vulnerability assessments are valuable tools for establishing an essential disaster management plan.

Vulnerability analysis is a continuing, dynamic process of people and organisations assessing the hazards and risks they face and determining what they wish to do about them, if anything. Vulnerability assessment also includes a means of structured data collection geared towards understanding the levels of potential threats, needs and immediately available resources. Assessment includes two general categories of information. The first is relatively static infrastructure information that provides bases for determining the extent of development, types of physical advantages and disadvantages faced by communities residing in an area, and a "map" of available structures (such as roads and hospitals) that might be useful in times of emergencies. The other category includes relatively dynamic socioeconomic data indicating causes and levels of vulnerability, demographic shifts and types of economic activity.

There is nothing mysterious about the concept of vulnerability assessments. Their initial objective is to establish a data base that focuses upon the likely effects of potential hazards, relief needs and available resources. Vulnerability assessments should be linked with development interventions. When communities are determined to be vulnerable, development assistance may obviate the need for emergency assistance.

There are three main reasons why assessing vulnerability is critical for disaster preparedness. First, accurate vulnerability assessments serve as a means to inform decision-makers about the utility of national and local level approaches to disaster preparedness. Second, decision-makers are usually aware of disaster propensities within their own countries. However, until the dimensions of the disaster threat and levels of preparedness or unpreparedness are fully appreciated, there may not be an effective starting point upon which to construct an overall plan. Third, vulnerability assessments should serve as the basis for a more continuous "habit" of monitoring trends in physical, socioeconomic and infrastructure conditions of disaster-prone countries. In that sense, the initial effort of developing a data base through vulnerability assessments should become the basis for maintaining and updating an essential informational tool for development planning purposes.

On a technical level, vulnerability assessments serve as the starting point for determining the types of plans that should be developed as part of a national disaster preparedness strategy. For example, it is useful to know that people living on the deltaic coastline of Bangladesh are vulnerable to tropical storms. However, such information is of little use unless you also know the seasonal migration patterns of these people, whether or not those who till the land normally bring their families to the delta, and the number of two-story buildings in the area.

Planning

Planning is the theme of the whole disaster preparedness exercise. One objective is to have agreed-upon, implementable plans in place, for which commitment and resources are relatively assured. Planning for readiness includes working out agreements between people or agencies as to who will provide services in an emergency to ensure an effective, coordinated response.

These agreements might take various forms: memos of understanding, mutual aid agreements, or individual agency and master plans. The ultimate objective is not to write a plan but to stimulate on-going interactions between parties which may result in written, usable agreements. The written plan is a product, but not the main goal, of the planning process. There are four obvious points to be considered in any planning effort.

Four other aspects of planning should also be considered.

Clarity

Is this a "national disaster preparedness strategy" of a "contingency plan?" National disaster preparedness strategies include broad exercises which review the structure of all relevant institutions and their response capacities. It includes central and local levels of government in an attempt to prepare for disasters in the context of the "disaster continuum." It incorporates disaster preparedness within all disaster phases as well as within development programmes. Such strategies normally include disaster mitigation, preparedness, recovery and rehabilitation.

Disaster contingency plans normally focus on means to address particular hazards. This is not to say that a good contingency plan ignores the need for mitigation and recovery measures, but it usually is not concerned with the entire disaster continuum, such as rehabilitation and development linkages. The main focus is on ways to address a particular hazard (such as a flood), within a fairly finite period, such as from early warning and response to immediate recovery phases. An effective national strategy will usually generate various contingency plans to meet specific disaster conditions.

Disasters strike in different ways and at different times. For example, certain countries have to face persistent, slow-onset disasters that occur almost on an annual basis during a three to five year cycle, affecting substantial portions of a society, such as drought-related famines in the Horn of Africa. Other countries face chronic sudden-onset threats. For example, floods in Bangladesh may normally affect a predictable part of the population in a geographically well-defined area. There are other nations, including Mexico, which may suffer severely from natural disasters which are relatively rare in occurrence, spread out over much longer intervals.

Participation in the planning process

Of course, you can assume that the plan is designed for those most vulnerable to hazards. Determining who the plan is for reveals two standard planning dilemmas. The first involves determining who should be incorporated into the planning process. Experts often insist that local people and grassroots organisations should participate in the planning process. This advice is justifiable for anyone who has seen the effectiveness of local coping mechanisms in urban or rural communities. However, how best to do this often requires considerable institutional dexterity. Local participation can not only present a considerable logistically problem, but government officials may not be receptive to the input. The second point is the extent of centralisation or decentralisation, not only in the planning process but in the plan itself.

Planners

In the enthusiasm and commitment to develop a plan, international experts and institutions are frequently tempted to lead the planning process. This is a fundamental error. If this is done, it will result in a mound of paper that benefits few. The complexities for government of introducing such a plan might be considerable. Progress might be commensurately slow. The best leadership role for international experts is that of gently pushing the process from the back ranks.

Planning might best be seen as the coordination of the intentions and plans of each collaborating party. Planning is not simply the work of "experts." Rather, it includes such aspects as challenging shoe factory managers to decide how to protect and respond to threats to their employees and facilities; or asking farmers how they intend to protect their seedlings or animals. However, to identify central planners, define which ministries and agencies in the government might be directly or even indirectly involved in some aspect of the proposed plan. Do not assume that if a government structure has a designated disaster focal point, the field will be adequately covered by a representative from that focal point alone. Instead, cast a wide gaze over all government institutions that might feel left out if they were not represented. Suggest to the government authority responsible for developing the plan that full representation would ultimately derive greater commitment and more durable results.

National as well as international nongovernmental organisations (NGOs) which have a long-term commitment in vulnerable areas should be included in the process. Governments may not want NGOs directly involved in the planning process, but should be urged to link them into the overall objectives of the proposed plan. Similarly, bilateral donors should be kept informed about the planning process. Governments may not want them to play a direct role in the planning process; nor might the bilateral donors wish to become directly involved in the process. However, for any financial support which the eventual plan might require for implementation, a well-informed bilateral donor community can be a distinct advantage. Including UN staff in the planning process may also lead to successfully utilising their agencies' resources.

With all the potential participants that might become embroiled in the planning process, you might wonder if the planning process can ever be sustained and controlled. It can, if you think in terms of the variety of mechanisms in which participation can take place. For example, a national conference can set the overall tone for a wide range of ministries and relevant national and international institutions. A series of work groups asked to design specific components of the plan also distributes the load and may allow for greater participation. Workshops can bring together the various "subgroups" which inevitably will work under the guidance of a core steering group that can facilitate overall activities.

Planning Status

A variety of indicators will suggest if the plan is intended to be taken seriously. An obvious indication will be the level of commitment by participants to the planning process itself. An equally evident indicator is if the funds for implementing the plan are adequate. A clear sign of commitment on the part of government to the plan will be the enabling legislation that the plan may receive. A disaster preparedness plan has to be underwritten by the laws of the nation. Unless roles and responsibilities of ministries and individuals are reinforced by legal sanctions, implementation will be jeopardized.

With these various points in mind, you should now focus upon the contents of a disaster preparedness plan. Whether that plan is a contingency plan focusing on specific types of emergencies or on specific geographic areas, or a national disaster preparedness strategy, there are certain features common to all such endeavours. Generally speaking, all planning exercises will have to address various points which will eventually be incorporated into a planning document.

Institutional Structure and Systems

A coordinated disaster preparedness and response system is an essential condition of any disaster preparedness plan. There is no standard way of ensuring effective coordination. Each design will depend upon the traditions and governmental structure of the country under review. However, a plan will rapidly deteriorate unless there is "horizontal coordination" at central government and sub-national levels among ministries and specialised agencies and "vertical coordination" between central and local authorities. Avoid creating new organisations for disaster preparedness. Instead, work within established structures and systems. The emphasis must be upon strengthening existing institutions rather that devising additional layers of bureaucracy.

Disaster responses generally need the sanction of senior levels of government. For most disaster plans in the developing world, the approval of a president, prime minister or at least a deputy prime minister becomes the trigger mechanism for implementing a response. Consider the relationship between the senior level of government, ministerial levels and the functional disaster preparedness focal point.

An effective disaster preparedness plan will reflect an inter-ministerial response to disaster warnings and occurrences. These inter-ministerial committees, such as exist in India, should not be below the level of Permanent Secretary. This sort of committee will include a representative from the designated disaster preparedness focal point, and will keep appropriate senior government officials apprised on broad issues concerning preparedness and relief implementation.

A focal point should be designated to ensure effective disaster preparedness and to act as a coordination mechanism for disaster response. This focal point can be attached to or become a specialised agency, such as a Relief and Rehabilitation Commission. A focal point can also be developed within a ministry regarded as essential for certain types of disasters. For example, a Ministry of Agriculture might house the focal point if the nation's principal concern involves droughts which affect agricultural production. Finally, a focal point might be attached to the office of a senior level of government, as occurs in the Prime Minister's office in Jamaica. The need for a strong focal point is essential.

A variety of institutional options related to regional and community structures also exist. In the Ethiopian National Disaster Prevention and Preparedness Strategy, the government has decided to have parallel systems at regional and local levels. Representatives from relevant central government ministries are located at regional and local levels to work hand in hand with committees comprised of representatives from local peasant associations, as well as local and regional officials. In China and India, however, regional and state governments respectively determine most of the functional activities needed to develop preparedness activities and to implement plans.

Information Systems

Early warning systems are normally comprised of various elements. They can stem in part from information provided by meteorological offices, by a Ministry of Health, or by a Ministry of Agriculture. One major criterion for an effective plan is an established system to ensure the coordination of all these different inputs. An interministerial information committee can serve this purpose. This sort of committee has to have clear-cut guidelines, reporting formats and mechanisms as well as established reporting procedures. It is essential to link the disaster preparedness focal point to this committee. Perhaps the focal point might serve as the chair organisation for this interministerial information committee.

An added complication involves the combination of this information with grassroots information, the "early warning" information obtained from those most directly threatened, which is highly relevant and often ignored. Ensuring that appropriate information systems are in readiness includes stimulating information exchange systems within each agency in the emergency environment, between organisations and between the organisations and the public.

The most appropriate means of gathering and disseminating early warning information must be carefully assessed and well defined within the disaster preparedness plan. It is imperative that early warning messages be understood by the people for whom they are issued.

Vulnerability assessment updates and the coordinated approach to early warning should encompass all the standard features required of any monitoring system. This includes determining changes in patterns of disaster threats, numbers of vulnerable people, and preparations for response. Monitoring must include an overall disaster preparedness assessment process in which essential physical aspects of the plan are reviewed system-wide to ensure that when disaster strikes, all that the plan anticipates is in place. Monitoring must also include an assessment process after a disaster strikes. This is meant to ensure that the implementation of the plan is efficient, and that appropriate and timely relief is being distributed to targeted beneficiaries.

Resource Base

The requirements to meet disaster needs will depend upon the types of disasters the plan anticipates. Such needs should be made explicit, and should cover all aspects of disaster relief and recovery implementation. Specific arrangements should be established whereby each party to written agreements can secure goods and services as required. Critical issues include special internal arrangements for the acquisition and dispersement of funds; policies and agreements for the use of other's equipment and services; and emergency funding strategies. In assessing the resources required for a disaster preparedness plan, the following elements should be considered.

Emergency relief funding

It is important to establish an emergency contingency fund. There is often a need for items that cannot be easily stockpiled, such as medicines, or items that were not anticipated, such as alternative fuels. A special reserve fund is worth considering in your preparedness plan. Insurance is another form of creating reserves against potential future disasters.

Disaster preparedness funding

Solicit funds to pursue the activities of the planning process, including special studies, public awareness and training. Also seek funds to develop major inputs for the plan to function effectively.

Mechanism for aid coordination

Establish a means to ensure a coordinated, useful and timely response from the international community if and when its assistance is required. Not only should such a mechanism incorporate inputs from bilateral donors, but possible assistance from non-governmental organisations should also be brought into the coordinating mechanism.

Stockpiling

Consider the types and amounts of materials needed; whether they can be stockpiled, and where. This is not an easy task. In particularly disaster-prone countries, the very poverty that makes large segments of a society vulnerable to disasters means that stockpiling significant amounts of relief materials is a luxury. However, donors often are willing to make contributions to various forms of "stockpiling," such as food security reserves.

Warning systems

You must assume that functioning communications systems, such as telephones and telexes, may not be available in times of a major disaster. Begin to plan a warning system around that assumption. Consider what type of communications equipment will be needed and sustainable if power lines and receiving stations are destroyed. Preparedness plans should include provisions for access to alternative communication systems among police, military and government networks.

All too often, those for whom disaster warning systems are targeted have little faith in the warnings. This may be due to a human inclination to ignore what appears inconvenient at the time. It also reflects a general misunderstanding of the warning's message, or frustration with yet another false alarm. Planners of effective warnings take into account the public perceptions of warnings, training related to reacting to warnings, as well as local conditions, attitudes and experiences. Whenever possible, the international community should be forewarned about hazards that might lead to appeals for international assistance.

Response Mechanisms

There are a vast number of responses that ought to be considered. Each response depends upon the nature of the threat. Some of the broader categories of response for a variety of hazards include:

— evacuation procedures
— search and rescue
— security of affected areas
— assessment teams
— activating special installations
— activating distribution systems
— preparing emergency reception centres and shelters
— activating emergency programmes for airports, harbors and land transport

Once an effective disaster preparedness plan is in place, these response mechanisms should be familiar to potential beneficiaries or to those with the responsibilities of implementing such measures.

Public Education and Training

One emphasis of a disaster preparedness plan should be to anticipate the requirements for a disaster relief operation and the most effective ways of meeting those requirements. The planning process will only be effective if those who are the ultimate beneficiaries know what to do in times of disasters and know what to expect. For this reason, an essential part of a disaster preparedness plan is the education of those who may be threatened by disaster. Such education may take the following forms.

Public education in schools

Standardised curricula for children and young adults should include information about actions which should be taken in case of a disaster threat or occurrence.

Special training courses

Workshops should be designed for an adult population, either specifically or as an extra dimension of on-going programmes, such as literacy or cooperative training sites.

Extension programmes

Community of village-based outreach workers should be trained to provide relevant information.

Public information

Although television, radio and the printed media will never replace the impact of direct instruction, sensitively designed and projected messages can provide a useful supplement to the overall process. In establishing educational training, remember that education is often a two-way process in the field of disaster preparedness. For example, if a group does not fully comprehend the warning sequences in a tropical storm preparedness plan, it may be that the warning sequences need to be reworked.

Training of those who will implement portions of the disaster preparedness plan is essential. Those responsible for issuing warnings must be trained as well as those who will have direct relief functions. Training cannot be a one-time event. Refresher courses are essential. Training should be active in every way possible. Actual exercises should be performed, such as evacuation drills. An effective disaster preparedness plan will also give practical guidelines on its various components, such as organising reception camps and relief shelters.

Rehearsals

As with most simulations, disaster preparedness rehearsals cannot portray the full dynamics and chaos of a disaster relief operation. However, this is no excuse for avoiding the need to rehearse the disaster preparedness plan. Rehearsals will re-emphasise points made in separate training programmes, and test the system as a whole. Rehearsals invariably expose gaps that otherwise might be overlooked. Rehearsals must be conducted system-wide and taken seriously. Systemwide means that all the components which would be involved in a real disaster situation, from central to local authorities, should be rehearsed. Be forewarned that cynicism and halfheartedness may dog the rehearsal. You must persevere, because it is the nearest anyone will get, until disaster strikes, to seeing if the plan is effective. Rehearsals are also the only way to keep plans fresh, especially during extended periods without disasters.

Citizenry-based disaster preparedness

Because of their geographic location and physical environment, the citizens of the Philippines suffer from the effects of typhoons, storm surges, volcanic eruptions, floods, droughts, earthquakes, tsunamis and landslides, in addition to "red tide" infestations of seawater fishing areas. The country is situated on the western rim of the Pacific Ocean where 50% of the worlds tropical storms originate, and on the "ring of fire" where 80% of the world's earthquakes and volcanic eruptions occur. Another major factor contributing to vulnerability is increasing poverty levels: more than 70% of Filipinos live below the poverty line.

Description of events

Typhoons and floods are the main disaster events in the Philippines. According to government estimates, typhoons cause a average of 500 deaths per year and damages of US $ 128 million. Heavy rains accompanying typhoons, exacerbated by deforestation, soil erosion and siltation/clogging of waterways, cause extensive flooding and landslides. In the typhoon "Uring" disaster of November 1992, more than 8,000 people were killed in flashfloods, presumably brought about by uncontrolled logging.

A major earthquake has occurred in the Philippines once every six years. In 1990, a magnitude 7.7 earthquake killed 1,666 and caused US $ 440 million in damage. Of the 220 volcanoes in the country, 21 are considered active. In June of 1991, Mt. Pinatubo erupted resulting in US $ 400-600 million in damage, affecting 1.2 million people with ashfalls, mudflows and lahars and permanently altering the environment.

In addition to the "natural" hazards, human have created their own disasters by engaging in armed conflict for the past twenty years. Insurgent groups have established strongholds in many parts of the country where fighting occurs with government troops. Hundreds of thousands of persons have become uprooted or displaced from their homes, posing significant social and economic costs.

Government disaster mitigation and response

The Philippines loses about 2% of its GNP to disasters each year, has a population growth of 2.3% and a considerable foreign debt load. At least a five percent growth in GNP per year is required to maintain income levels. This growth level, however, was not achieved between 1986-91 and vulnerability to disasters has increased. Need to boost the GNP has led to exploitation of resources resulting in deforestation, erosion and pollution of water sources.

A national council was established in 1978 to oversee disaster mitigation as mainly an advisory and coordinating body, but it lacks funding and decision making power. Two national early warning systems agencies suffer the same shortages of funding and resources. A calamity fund which can be appropriated for relief and rehabilitation has been slow to respond in the past, and the result has been a high level of dependency on external relief assistance.

Citizen's Disaster Response Network

In the late 1980's, concerned citizens began to set up a nationwide network for disaster response called Citizens" Disaster Response Center (CDRC) which later became CDRN (network). The key concept behind the agency was the recognition that vulnerable sectors of the population should be the main actors in disaster response and not merely victims requiring outside assistance. This prompted preparedness and resource mobilisation efforts. CDRN tries to provide a framework for helping communities avoid or recover from disasters. It also seek to be development oriented in its approach to relief and rehabilitation operations.

Interagency Coordination

Operating from 19 centers, CDRN collaborates with municipal and village level disaster response committees, particularly in areas affected by the major disasters mentioned above. CDRN went on to establish relationships with other agencies on a national level and formed an interagency network composed of nine agencies including four NGOs. Each unit of the network can be activated to form an emergency structure composed of a disaster coordinator other staff dealing with information, local resource generation, finance and logistics and field officers. CDRN relies on peoples' organisations (POs) from local populations to mobilise disaster volunteers in sufficient numbers to perform different aspects of disaster management.

Planning

Agencies work together to avoid duplication in drawing up of a disaster operations plan.

The plan includes:

— *Analysis of vulnerabilities and capacities*: This includes summing up of the physical, social and motivational conditions of the communities, including coping mechanisms and responses. National data is verified through field visits.

— *Situation assessment*: Information gathering activities must be planned to be the basis for rapid implementation and to provide the direction for immediate interventions.

— *Adequate logistic support*: The importance of earmarking funds for emergency relief operations was underscored by the 1990 earthquake and 1991 eruptions. A stockpile of goods is needed for immediate access, and transport and communications networks should be pre-planned.

Training

CDRN has developed training modules relative to specific problems in the Philippines. Following the Mt. Pinatubo eruption of 1991, CDRN training included education inputs on volcanoes and volcanic eruptions, evacuation, and drills on relaying warning signals. First, the disaster response networks and the POs are given training and they, in turn, conduct education campaigns in the affected communities.

Formation of volunteer teams

The experience of CDRN in forming grassroots volunteer teams has shown that the teams lessen the impact of disasters and reduce costs of relief and rehabilitation. A programme has been set up for the communities which continue to be threatened by eruptions and lahars from Mt. Pinatubo. The functions of this programme, named the Barangay Disaster Response Unit, are:

— *Disaster Preparedness*: training in skills and operations related to disaster preparedness such as hazard mapping, disaster planning and community drills.

— *Mitigation*: implementing development projects to lessen the effects of disasters.

— *Social mobilisation*: enlisting support from the entire community and mobilising members to deal with issues and problems.

— *Networking*: linking with government agencies, the private sector, POs and NGOs.

Collaboration to solve problems: CDRN does not take the place of government agencies but rather cooperates with them to exchange information and services. Interaction with NGOs has facilitated mutual learning and understanding and, most importantly, the maximisation of resources. Both local and foreign donor agencies have much to contribute beyond providing funds, in terms of expertise, ideas and suggestions. Realising that certain issues affect vulnerability to disasters, CDRN also collaborates with NGOs and POs to seek solutions to the problems of foreign debt and environmental degradation. CDRN acts as an advocate for human rights and works toward finding a settlement to the armed conflict.

Disaster Planning

Disaster preparedness is achieved by planning, training, equipping, and exercising the Disaster response organization.

Disaster planning is most likely to be successful when it is viewed, either explicitly or implicitly, from a systems perspective. This entails an understanding of the goals of the disaster response, the resources of the community as a system, and the functional interactions of the different units within the system. The *primary goal* of the disaster response is to protect the health and safety of the disaster responders and the public. In addition, the disaster response should protect public and private property and the environment, as well as minimize the disruption of community activities. The *resources* of the community include trained personnel, and disaster relevant facilities, equipment, and materials. The *units of the system* are the elements that take action (households, governmental agencies, private organizations), while *organizational functions* are defined as the "most general, yet differentiable means whereby the system requirements are met, discharged or satisfied". In the case of disaster response organizations, the description of system functions can then be elaborated into operational event sequences and component processes that include the identification of job operations, together with personnel positions and their associated duties. In the conceptual design stage of a system, analysts define broad constraints that human limitations are likely to exert on system operation. As the system design develops in detail, the analysts develop correspondingly more detailed statements of the requirements for personnel qualifications and training, workgroup organization, workspace layout and equipment design, and job performance aids.

Such analyses are typically applied to the normal operations of complex technological systems such as high performance aircraft and the control rooms of nuclear power plants, but they also can be applied in similar form to the problems of community disaster planning. Whether a novel technological system is being developed for use in a normal environment or a novel social system such as an disaster response organization is being developed to respond to an unusually threatening physical environment, the rationale for systems analysis is the same—the opportunities for incremental adjustment through trial and error are extremely limited. The analysis of a social system conducted for an disaster management program must first identify the range of hazards to which a given community is vulnerable and the demands that the hazards would place upon the community.

The often expressed opinion "every disaster is unique" is true but the usual conclusion "we can improvise during an disaster rather than plan beforehand" does not follow. It is true that disaster responders must always improvise to meet the demands of a specific situation, but it is important to understand that there are different types of improvisation—reproductive, adaptive, and creative—that differ from *organizational continuity* (continuation of normal organizational routines) and *organizational contingency*. Specifically, *reproductive improvisation* responds to a deficiency (e.g., failure of a siren) by using a substitute (e.g., police officers going door-to-door) to achieve the same disaster response objective. *Adaptive improvisation* involves modifying normal routines or contingency plans to achieve operational goals. In this context, "adaptive" only means a change, not necessarily an improvement. *Creative improvisation* responds to an unanticipated disaster demand by developing a new course of action.

It is important to recognize that improvising and implementing response actions takes more time than implementing preplanned actions—and time is usually very limited in an disaster. Moreover, improvisations can impede or duplicate the response actions of other organizations. For example, Perry, et al. reported that firefighters fed and sheltered flood victims because neither they nor the victims knew about a mass care facility that had been activated not far away. Consequently, disaster managers should develop community Disaster preparedness so they can limit the amount of *unnecessary* improvisation even though they cannot eliminate improvisation altogether.

In fact, research has identified many regularities in the demands emergencies place upon response organizations. Disaster managers should identify the functions that must be performed to respond to these demands and the resources required to accomplish the response functions. The resources required for disaster response can then be compared with those maintained within the community. Any special actions required to ensure the continued availability of the disaster response resources can be made an integral part of the Disaster preparedness program.

One very important aspect of the systems assessment for disaster response operations arises from the environmental conditions that prevail during major disasters. At such times, response personnel often confront confusing and conflicting cues about the current status of hazard agent and its impacts, as well as major uncertainties about the future behavior of the hazard agent and impacts yet to come. During the 9 nuclear reactor accident at Three Mile Island and the chemical plant accidents in 4 at Bhopal, India, and in 5 at Institute, West Virginia, the inability of plant personnel to accurately assess the status of the disaster severely impeded their ability to communicate appropriate protective action recommendations to offsite agencies. A similar inability to conduct timely and accurate assessments on the Mt. St. Helens volcano led to casualties and property destruction. In all of these cases, the complexity of the situation—together with time pressure and the severity of the potential consequences—created conditions that were unforgiving of error and, thus, highly stressful for disaster response personnel.

To increase organizational effectiveness when there is enough time to respond, but not enough time to improvise a coordinated response plan, communities must engage in Disaster preparedness. A major component in Disaster preparedness is the development of preimpact EOPs that provide disaster responders with the resources they need to take prompt and effective response actions.

Preparedness is best thought of as a *process*—a continuing sequence of analyses, plan development, and the acquisition of individual and team performance skills achieved through training, drills, exercises, and critiques. The practice of disaster response planning varies considerably among communities. In some, the planning process is quite formal; there is a specific assignment of responsibility to an office having an identifiable budget. In other communities it is informal; responsibility is poorly defined and a limited budget is dispersed among many agencies. Moreover, the planning products might be either written or unwritten. To some extent, the disaster planning process correlates with the size of the community in which it takes place. Larger communities—characterized by an elaborate structure of governmental offices, many resources and personnel, and perhaps higher levels of staff turnover—tend to evolve formalized processes and rely more heavily upon written documentation and agreements. In smaller communities, the planning process might generate few written products and rely principally on informal relationships. Formalization of the planning process is also likely to vary with the frequency of hazard impact. In communities subject to frequent threats, disaster response may be a practiced skill rather than a hypothetical action. In one frequently flooded community, the fire department evacuates residents of the low lying areas when the flood water reaches a certain street.

Disaster planning is conducted in the face of apathy by some and resistance from others. A basic reason for apathy is that most people, citizens and public officials alike, don't like to think about their vulnerability to disasters. A common objection to planning is it consumes resources, that, at the moment, might seem like more pressing community issues—police patrols, road repairs, school expansion, and the like. Planning mandates help (for example, radiological disaster planning after the Three Mile Island nuclear power plant accident and chemical disaster planning under the Disaster Planning and Community Right to Know Act of 6—SARA Title III after Bhopal), but are insufficient to overcome such resistance. Consequently, the initiation of planning activities requires strong support from a jurisdiction's Chief Administrative Officer, an *issue champion* (or *policy entrepreneur*) who has the expertise and organizational legitimacy to promote disaster management, or a disaster planning committee that can mobilize a constituency in support of disaster management. However, acceptance of the need for disaster planning doesn't eliminate conflict. Organizations seek to preserve their autonomy, security, and prestige, so they resist collaborative activities that can threaten these objectives. Disaster planning involves the allocation of power and resources (especially personnel and budget), so every unit within an organization wants its "proper role" recognized and a budget allocation commensurate with that role.

The fundamental principles of community disaster planning can be summarised in the following points.

1. Disaster planners should anticipate both active and passive resistance to the planning process and develop strategies to manage these obstacles.
2. Pre-impact planning should address all hazards to which the community is exposed.
3. Pre-impact planning should elicit participation, commitment, and clearly defined agreement among all response organizations.
4. Pre-impact planning should be based upon accurate assumptions about the threat, typical human behavior in disasters, and likely support from external sources such as state and federal agencies.
5. Disaster planning should address the linkage of disaster response to disaster recovery and hazard mitigation.
6. Preimpact planning should provide for training and evaluating the disaster response organization at all levels—individual, team, department, and community.
7. Disaster planning should be recognized as a continuing process.

Adopt an All Hazards Approach

The disaster planning process should also integrate plans for each hazard agent into a multihazard Emergency Operations Plan (EOP). Disaster planners should use their community HVAs to identify the types of natural hazards (e.g., floods, tornadoes, hurricanes, earthquakes), technological accidents (e.g., toxic chemical releases, nuclear power plant accidents), and deliberate incidents (e.g., sabotage or terrorist attack involving hazardous materials) to which their communities are vulnerable. Following identification of these hazards, disaster planners should consider the extent to which different hazard agents make similar demands on the disaster response organization. When two hazard agents have similar characteristics, they are likely to require the same disaster response functions. Commonality of disaster response functions provides multiple use opportunities for personnel, procedures, facilities, and equipment—which, in turn, simplifies the EOP by reducing the number of functional annexes. In addition, it simplifies training and enhances the reliability of organizational performance during emergencies. Only when hazard agents have very different characteristics, and thus require distinctly different responses, will hazard-specific appendixes will be needed.

Promote Multiorganizational Participation

Disaster planning should promote interorganizational coordination by developing mechanisms that elicit participation, commitment, and clearly defined agreement among all response organizations. This obviously should include public safety agencies such as disaster management, fire, police, and disaster medical services. However, it also should include organizations that are potential hazard sources, such as hazardous materials facilities and hazardous materials transporters (pipeline, rail, truck, and barge) and organizations that must protect sensitive populations, such as schools, hospitals, and nursing homes. Coordination is required because disaster response organizations that differ in their capabilities must work in coordination to implement an effective disaster response. To perform their functions effectively, efficiently, and promptly requires members of the community disaster response organization to be aware of one another's missions, organizational structures and styles of operation, communication systems, and mechanisms (such as agreed upon priorities) for allocating scarce resources.

Rely on Accurate Assumptions

Disaster planning should be based upon accurate knowledge of community threats and likely human responses to those threats. Accurate knowledge of community threats comes from HVAs. Disaster managers must identify hazards to which their communities are vulnerable, determine which geographical areas are exposed to those hazards (e.g., year flood plains and toxic chemical facility Vulnerable Zones), and identify the facilities and population segments located in those risk areas. They also need to understand the basic characteristics of these hazards such as speed of onset, scope and duration of impact, and potential for producing casualties and property damage.

When identifying the hazards to which their community is exposed, planners and public officials frequently recognize the limits of their expertise. They recognize their lack of accurate knowledge about the behavior of geophysical, meteorological, or technological hazards and contact experts to obtain the information they need. Unfortunately, the same cannot usually be said about accurate knowledge about likely human behavior in a disaster. As a familiar saying goes, the problem is not so much that people don't know what is true, but that what they do "know" is false. Quarantelli and

Dynes and Wenger, et al. have described widespread myths regarding people's disaster response that persist despite research refuting them. Belief in disaster myths hampers the effectiveness of disaster planning by misdirecting resource allocation and information dissemination. For example, officials sometimes cite expectations of panic as a reason for giving the public incomplete information about an environmental threat or withholding information altogether. This response to the myth of panic is actually counterproductive because people are more willing to comply with recommended protective actions when they are provided with complete risk information. For these reasons, the planning process must be firmly grounded not only on the physical or biological science literature on the effects of hazard agents on human safety, health, and property, but also on the behavioral literature describing individual and organizational response in emergencies.

Finally, household, business, and government agency disaster plans must be based on accurate assumptions about aid from external sources. In major disasters, hospitals might be overloaded; destruction of telecommunication and transportation systems (highways, railroads, airports, and seaports) could prevent outside assistance from arriving for days; and restoration of disrupted water, sewer, electric power, and natural gas pipeline systems could take much longer. Consequently, all social units must be prepared to be self reliant for as much as a week.

Identify Appropriate Actions while Encouraging Improvisation

An effective preparedness process must balance planning and improvisation. The EOP establishes the disaster response organization's basic structure and broad strategies before a disaster strikes. In particular, it will document which organization is responsible for each disaster response function and, in general terms, how that function will be performed. Similarly, per-disaster training must explain how to perform any specific tactics and operational procedures that are likely to be needed during response operations. Even though disaster managers can forecast what types of disaster demands are likely to arise, there will always be some degree of uncertainty about the magnitude and location of those demands. For example, the disaster manager of a hurricane prone community should develop procedures for mass evacuation, but will be never be completely certain about how the population in each neighborhood will respond. The fact that people's response to warnings is reasonably well understood makes it foolish to improvise an evacuation plan as a hurricane is approaching.

Nonetheless, uncertainty about what proportion of the households in each neighborhood will begin an evacuation at each point in time makes it foolish to devise a rigid evacuation plan that has no provision for modification as an incident unfolds. An emphasis on specific detail can be problematic in at least four ways:

(1) the anticipation of all contingencies is simply impossible;

(2) very specific details tend to get out of date very quickly, demanding virtually constant updating of written products;

(3) very specific plans often contain so many details that the wide range of disaster functions appear to be of equal importance, causing response priorities to be unclear or confused; and

(4) the more detail incorporated into written planning documents, the larger and more complex they become.

This makes it more difficult to use the plan as a device for training personnel to understand how their roles fit into the overall disaster response and consequently makes it more difficult to implement the plan effectively when the need arises.

In summary, planning and training should identify the actions that are most likely to be appropriate, but also should emphasize flexibility so those involved in response operations can improvise in response to unexpected conditions. That is, planning and training should address *principles* of response in addition to providing detailed standard operating procedures (SOPs) and should encourage improvisation based on continuing assessment of disaster demands.

Disaster Response to Disaster Recovery and Hazard Mitigation

There will be an overlap between disaster response and disaster recovery because some portions of the community will be engaged in disaster response tasks while others will have moved on to disaster recovery tasks. Moreover, senior elected and appointed officials need to plan for the recovery while they are being inundated with policy decisions to implement the disaster response. Consequently, disaster managers should link preimpact disaster response planning to preimpact disaster recovery planning. Such integration will speed the process of disaster recovery and facilitate the integration of hazard mitigation into disaster recovery. The necessary coordination between preimpact disaster response planning and preimpact disaster recovery planning can be achieved by establishing organizational contacts, and perhaps overlapping membership, between the committees responsible for these two activities.

Conduct Thorough Training and Evaluation

Disaster planning should also provide a training and evaluation component. The first part of the training process involves explaining the provisions of the plan to the administrators and personnel of the departments that will be involved in the disaster response. Second, all those who have disaster response roles must be trained to perform their duties. Of course, this includes fire, police, and disaster medical services personnel, but there also should be training for personnel in hospitals, schools, nursing homes, and other facilities that might need to take protective action. Finally, the population at risk must be involved in the planning process so they can become aware that planning for community threats is underway, as well as what is expected of them under the plans. As noted previously, they need to know what is likely to happen in a disaster and what disaster organizations can *and cannot* do for them.

It is also essential that training include tests of the proposed response operations. As noted above, disaster drills and exercises provide a setting in which operational procedures can be tested. They also facilitate interorganizational contact, thus allowing individual members to better understand each other's professional capabilities and personal characteristics. Furthermore, multifunctional exercises constitute a simultaneous and comprehensive test of disaster plans and procedures, staffing levels, personnel training, facilities, equipment, and materials. Finally, multifunctional exercises produce publicity for the broader disaster management process, which informs community officials and the public that disaster planning is underway and preparedness is being enhanced.

Adopt a Continuous Planning Process

Finally, effective disaster planning is a continuing process. Hazard vulnerability, organizational staffing and structure, and disaster facilities and equipment change over time, so the disaster planning process must detect and respond to these changes. Unfortunately, this point is frequently not recognized. Wenger, et al. have found "there is a tendency on the part of officials to see disaster planning as a product, not a process", a misconception that confuses tangible products with the activities that produce them. Of course, planning does require written documentation, but *effective* planning is also made up of elements that are difficult to document on paper and are not realized in hardware. These include the development of disaster responders' knowledge about resources available from governmental and private organizations, the acquisition of knowledge about disaster demands and other agencies' capabilities, and the establishment of collaborative relationships across organizational boundaries. Tangible documents and hardware simply do not provide a sufficient representation of what the disaster planning process has produced. Furthermore, by treating written plans as final products, one risks creating the illusion of being prepared for an disaster when such is not the case. As time passes, the EOP sitting in a red three ring binder on the bookshelf looks just as thick and impressive as it did the day it was published despite the many changes that have taken place in the meantime. For example, new hazardous facilities might have been built and others decommissioned, new neighborhoods might exist where only open fields were found previously, and reorganization might have been taken place within different agencies responsible for disaster response.

Functional Capability Analysis

To ensure adequate disaster preparedness, disaster managers should analyze their disaster response organization's capability to perform its basic disaster response functions. Historically, these functions have been categorized as agent generated and response generated demands. The agent generated demands arise from the specific mechanisms by which a hazard agent causes casualties and damage, whereas response generated demands arise from organizing and implementing the disaster response. Lindell and Perry elaborated Quarantelli's typology by drawing on federal disaster planning guidance to define four basic disaster response functions. These are disaster assessment, hazard operations, and population protection (which are agent generated demands) and incident management (which encompasses the response generated demands). *Disaster assessment* consists of those diagnoses of past and present conditions and prognoses of future conditions that guide the disaster response. *Hazard operations* refers to expedient hazard mitigation actions that disaster personnel take to limit the magnitude or duration of disaster impact (e.g., sandbagging a flooding river or patching a leaking railroad tank car). *Population protection* refers to actions—such as sheltering in-place, evacuation, and mass immunization—that protect people from hazard agents. *Incident management* consists of the activities by which the human and physical resources used to respond to the disaster are mobilized and directed to accomplish the goals of the disaster response organization.

Preparedness for disaster assessment requires the disaster response organization to *detect and classify an environmental threat.* Some natural hazards—such as many flash floods and earthquakes—are detected and classified by local agencies. Other natural hazards—such as hurricanes, tornadoes, major floods, and tsunamis—are detected and classified by federal agencies. Moreover, incidents at fixed site facilities are usually detected and classified by plant personnel, whereas transportation incidents are detected by carrier personnel, local disaster responders (e.g., police and fire), and sometimes by passers-by.

The local disaster manager should review the community Hazard Vulnerability Analysis (HVA) to identify all hazards to which the community is exposed in order to determine how detection is likely to be achieved and transmitted to the appropriate authorities. Locally detected hazards require the disaster manager to ensure the necessary detection systems (e.g., stream and rain gauges for flash floods) are established and maintained. For hazards detected by other sources, the disaster manager must ensure that a report of hazard detection can be called in to a community warning point that is staffed around the clock, usually the jurisdiction's dispatch center.

Another important aspect of disaster assessment is *hazard monitoring*, which requires continuous awareness of the current status of the hazard agent as well as projections of its future status. The technology for performing hazard monitoring varies by hazard agent. In many cases, continuing information about the hazard agent is provided by the same source as the one that provided the initial hazard detection. For example, the National Hurricane Center provides hurricane updates every six hours. Similarly, plant personnel should provide continuing information about a hazardous materials release.

Environmental monitoring is also needed when the geographical areas at risk are determined by atmospheric processes. Toxic chemicals, radiological materials, and volcanic ash are carried downwind, so changes in wind direction, wind speed, and atmospheric stability must be monitored to determine if the area at risk will change over time. Thus, procedures must be established and equipment acquired to obtain current weather information and forecasts of future weather conditions. Environmental monitoring is also needed for hazmat spills into waterways because, for example, the speed and direction of ocean currents determine which sections of shoreline will be affected.

Moreover, *damage assessment* is needed to identify the boundaries of the risk area and initiate the process of requesting a Presidential Disaster Declaration. Here also, personnel, procedures, and equipment must be designated to perform this function. Finally, *population monitoring and assessment* is needed to identify the size of the population at risk if the number of people in the risk area varies over time . This requires disaster managers to maintain calendars of major events, such as festivals and athletic contests, that bring large numbers of people into their jurisdictions. It also necessitates working with schools, hospitals, and nursing home administrators to monitor the progress of special facility evacuations and with traffic engineers to monitor evacuation routes for risk area residents.

Hazard Operations

Preparedness actions for hazard operations vary significantly from one hazard agent to another. In some cases, hazard operations require equipment that is normally available within the community. For example, preparedness for structural fires, conflagrations, and wildfires mostly requires equipment that local fire departments use in routine methods of *hazard source control.* However, some hazard agents require special preparation. For example, chemical incidents might require special foams to suppress vapor generation. Area *protection works* are another type of hazard operations that is best illustrated by elevating levees during floods. The large number of sandbags needed for such operations also requires advance preparation. Moreover, some hazard agents such as earthquakes require special preparation for postimpact operations to implement *building construction practices* and *contents protection practices*. For example, heavy construction equipment is needed to stabilize buildings, extricate victims, and protect building contents from further damage.

Population Protection

Preparedness for population protection sometimes requires disaster managers to develop procedures for *protective action selection.* For some hazard agents, there is only one recommended protective action. People threatened by tornadoes or volcanic ashfall should shelter in-place whereas those threatened by lava flows, inland floods, storm surges, and tsunamis should evacuate. In other cases, such as toxic chemical and radiological releases, the appropriate protective action depends on the situation. Consequently, communities exposed to such hazards should develop procedures for protective action selection in advance.

Similarly, disaster managers should devise procedures to *warn* the risk area population about each of the hazards identified in the community HVA. In slow onset incidents, such as main stem floods, there is likely to be adequate time for mechanisms such as face-to-face warnings. However, rapid onset incidents such as toxic chemical releases might require the acquisition of siren systems. Disaster managers should also prepare for *search and rescue* by considering whether special training and equipment is needed for swiftwater rescue from floods, heavy rescue from buildings collapsed by earthquakes, and other specialized circumstances. *Impact zone access control/security, hazard exposure control,* and *disaster medical care* require special protective equipment for disaster responders in CBR hazards so disaster managers should prepare for these hazards as well.

Incident Management

Because incident management activities are directed toward the response generated demands of an incident, preparedness for this function varies relatively little from one hazard agent to another. *Agency notification and mobilization* requires the acquisition of equipment such as pagers and the development of procedures such as the designation of watch officers to ensure that key personnel are notified rapidly.

Mobilization of disaster facilities and equipment is achieved by acquiring critical documents (e.g., maps, plans, and procedures) and storing these in close proximity to the room that will be activated as the EOC (if the jurisdiction does not have a permanent installation). *Communication and documentation* are supported by the acquisition of radios, telephone systems, and personal computers as well as the establishment of procedures for message routing and recording.

Disaster managers prepare for many of the disaster response organization's specific activities such as *analysis/planning, internal direction and control, logistics, finance/administration,* and *external coordination* by identifying the ways in which personnel will perform tasks or have reporting relationships that differ from the ones they encounter in normal conditions.

The disaster manager can work with personnel assigned to the disaster response organization to devise organization charts, task checklists, telephone lists, and other job performance aids that will assist them in their disaster duties. Preparedness for *public information* can be facilitated by identifying a joint information center (JIC), providing extra phone lines for media personnel, and developing basic background information about the jurisdiction, its hazards, and the disaster response organization.

Collaboration for Preparedness

Disaster preparedness plans and their implementation are the responsibility of the government. The United Nations can facilitate and enhance government efforts, but the government must formally initiate and control the disaster preparedness and response processes. In spite of government primacy in the realm of disaster preparedness, most emergency situations of significant magnitude in the developing world require some form of collaborative assistance from the international community.

The terms "international community" and "international system" are largely abstractions. There are few manifestations of community or system when dealing with the various nations, international governmental and nongovernmental organisations that inhabit the globe. When discussing aspects of international involvement in disaster management, you will usually be dealing with a random assortment of governmental, nongovernmental and international institutions that form part of an adhoc network.

This perspective of the international community includes three obstacles that directly affect disaster preparedness at the country level. The first is that support for national disaster preparedness efforts by those who might be most able to assist, such as bilateral donors, is by no means a certainty. Their assistance is not guaranteed. Therefore, it is important from the outset to establish the type of support a government's disaster preparedness initiative might receive. This will entail not only establishing an effective means of interesting such donors in these activities, but also effective means to keep them interested.

Secondly, there are many reasons why governments are wary of including "outsiders" in the formulation of a disaster strategy or plan. One clear reason is that the planning process itself, if undertaken openly, exposes many of the inherent weaknesses of government perhaps resulting in embarrassing explanations about the causes of disaster vulnerabilities. These are insights that few governments wish to have paraded before the world. Yet, once a government accepts the rationale for a sound disaster preparedness plan, it will have to accept that the success of that plan may depend upon expertise, resources and technical assistance that may depend to some degree upon international contributions.

Finally, on some occasions, the inability of the United Nations "family" to work together towards a common country objective has proven disappointing. However, since much of the ability of U.N. Agencies familiar whith disaster management will be needed in the disaster preparedness formulation process, there exists an opportunity to advance effective collaboration.

Role of UN Agencies in Disaster Preparedness

The role of the United Nations in disaster management is rapidly changing. A variety of arrangements need to be agreed upon amongst the agencies themselves if these changes are to lead to more effective assistance to disaster-afflicted peoples. There are already various established agency roles and functions in the realm of disaster management.

The following international agencies have functions that support the practical implementation of disaster preparedness plans. UNDP, WFP, UNICEF and UNHCR have excellent manuals on disaster preparedness and management that should be incorporated into preparedness planning exercises. DHA-Geneva has a publication series on disaster prevention and mitigation that is another valuable resource.

As a means to strengthen the coordination of humanitarian emergency assistance, the Secretary-General has created a high level post of Emergency Relief Coordinator. This post will ensure better preparation for, as well as rapid and coherent response to natural disasters and other emergencies. Responsibilities of the Emergency Relief Coordinator include consolidated appeals, a register of stand-by capacities and a central emergency revolving fund. This US $ 50 million fund provides a cash-flow mechanism to ensure the rapid and coordinated response of the organisations of the U.N. System.

Advances to operational organisations of the system can be made with the understanding that they will reimburse the fund.

U.N. at Headquarters Level

In developing national disaster preparedness plans, there are at least four areas in which U.N. agencies can be of immediate assistance.

Disaster preparedness initiatives

It is important for agencies at the field level to know that disaster preparedness initiatives have the support of their respective headquarters. Beyond the intangible issue of moral support is the more practical matter of establishing the initiative as a recognised priority at the field level.

Short-term consultancies

Agencies at headquarters level should have better insight as to which experts might be available to support field level efforts, in both the planning and implementation stages. Agencies should compile rosters of available experts. These rosters should be exchanged with other agencies. Agencies should review hiring procedures to ensure the rapid fielding of experts. Wherever possible, agency workers should encourage government officials to discuss disaster preparedness measures at headquarters levels. These workers should take study tours to countries that have well established disaster preparedness plans. Such exchanges should be worked out between headquarters and the field office.

Emergency funding

More flexible systems will have to be developed among some of the agencies to improve the use of field office resources in times of emergencies, and to ensure additional resources for emergencies from headquarters. Such flexibility should be recognised as part of the anticipated resource base in the national disaster preparedness plan.

Procedures and scheduling

Through their field offices, agencies will have to make sure that the proposed disaster preparedness plan incorporates headquarters procedures and the scheduling necessary for an agency to respond effectively to various crisis scenarios.

U.N. at Field Level

At the field level, inter-agency collaboration can have a positive impact on devising and implementing a disaster preparedness plan. Four components of such collaboration are essential.

Interagency team

Each agency should designate an individual to become part of an interagency "Disaster Management Team" [UN DMT]. Because agencies increasingly have had field expertise in disaster management, the designated official would hopefully be an individual with such expertise. For example, where UNHCR is involved in relief management for refugees, a UNHCR representative should be invited to become a member of the UN DMT.

The UN DMT should be established as a permanent, functioning interagency body at the field level. Each member agency should have defined sectoral responsibilities. The chair of the DMT should be the Resident Coordinator. If agreed among the members of the DMT, the DMT's secretariat should be under the responsibility of UNDP's designated DMT participant, the "Disaster Focal Point." UN DMT meetings should be held at regularly-scheduled intervals. The frequency of meetings might be adjusted in times of known potential threats, such as during rainy seasons.

The DMT should be a forum in which information is exchanged on a variety of matters. Long-term risk reduction and preparedness arrangements within the country should be reviewed. Reviews of preparedness arrangements within the U.N. should include: mechanisms for the coordination of U.N. emergency assistance; inputs and operations between the government, bilateral donors and NGOs; location of personnel in the field when there is an immediate threat; and lists of resources available for specialised emergency activities. UN DMT members should discuss the analysis and interpretation of data derived from early warning systems, both from within the country and from outside. They should also review information requirements needed for reporting formats, such as U.N. Situation reports, to be disseminated either on preparedness or on relief activities.

The UN DMT should serve as the focal point for U.N. assistance in the preparation of national disaster preparedness plans. In collaboration with government counterparts, the DMT should review and comment upon proposals at their various stages. Representatives of the DMT should be on hand for expert advice during the policy formulation process. Where possible, these representatives should seek resources from individual agencies to bolster technical assistance and provide additional expertise.

The DMT should also look at disaster preparedness in a regional context. The activities of a neighbouring nation may directly affect those of another. Early warnings on locust infestation, for example, is but one practical issue in which regional cooperation should be incorporated into a disaster preparedness plan. While governments will know regional and international organisations relevant to their interests, the DMT might be useful in demonstrating specific ways that such organisations might be used to enhance particular disaster preparedness programmes.

The effectiveness of the UN DMT depends upon the leadership ability of the Resident Coordinator. To assist the disaster preparedness planning and implementation process, the Resident Coordinator, in close collaboration with sister agencies, will have to ensure that the UN DMT is established, and that regular meetings are organised in order to cover the types of issues listed above. The Resident Coordinator must also ensure that a secretariat is established for the UN DMT, with proper facilities and staffing to enable the general functioning of the secretariat. Key functions in this regard will include the collection and dissemination of information, reports and studies. The secretariat should serve as a focal point within the U.N. system for essential data on:

— National policies regarding acceptance and use of international assistance, including external teams or personnel; policies concerning the use of communications equipment; and policies concerning specific types of foods and medicines.

— Government structures, including relevant names, telephones/fax/telex numbers of key personnel within central, regional, and local authorities.

— Names and telephone/fax/telex numbers of institutions outside the country that could be of assistance in times of crises.

— Baseline data on each distinct disaster prone area, which should be part of the ongoing process for vulnerability assessments.

In close collaboration with the government and sister agencies, UNDP at the field level should review with the government the purpose and prospects for a disaster preparedness plan. If such a plan is already in place UNDP should review with the government ways that such a plan might be enhanced. UNDP should also discuss with the government ways to sensitise its authorities at local, regional and central levels to the needs of disaster preparedness. Finally, UNDP should promote specific projects concerning disaster preparedness and disaster preparedness planning. There are a range of activities that such projects might include, such as:

— Disaster preparedness planning projects, intended to launch the entire process of disaster preparedness. Features of such a project might include aspects of sensitisation, such as overseas study tours and conferences, technical assistance, and workshops to enable formulation of the proposed plan.
— Essential studies as part of an overall plan, such as a transport capacity study or vulnerability assessments.
— Institution-building projects, designed to strengthen already existing disaster preparedness focal points or to develop more effective early warning systems.
— Training projects that develop appropriate disaster planning courses within country. These projects might enable key personnel to take advantage of overseas courses.

U.N. Agencies and Projects

An essential role for U.N. agencies should be to review those projects that are within the Country Programme that might be linked with disaster preparedness planning. Present development projects should be reviewed in an effort to determine how these projects might be effectively linked to preparedness measures. Conversely, U.N. agency staff should consider how preparedness measures might enhance the development process. Through the UN DMT, other agencies might review their own projects along similar lines.

Well-established working relations with government authorities are essential if U.N. agencies are to provide effective assistance in the disaster preparedness planning process. The relations which U.N. agencies have with the nongovernmental and bilateral communities are equally important. UNDP, through the UN DMT, should seek wherever feasible and politic to support the NGO community. This may involve attending meetings when invited to discuss initiatives being undertaken by the U.N. system. If acceptable to sister agencies and the NGOs, other members of the U.N. system should attend such meetings to give briefings on their respective activities.

U.N. agencies should establish means to promote disaster preparedness activities proposed for the NGO community, such as workshops at training sites. If acceptable to government and NGOs, U.N. agencies should make every effort to incorporate the roles of NGOs into the formal structure of national disaster preparedness planning and implementation. Finally, U.N. agencies should ensure that the bilateral community is kept apprised of events in the disaster preparedness planning process. Regular meetings with donors are one means of establishing sound working relations. However, whether such meetings should be held under the auspices of the U.N. is an issue that may prove sensitive to the government as well as to bilateral donors. The appropriate mechanism for bilateral liaison will have to depend upon the conditions within each country.

Information dissemination if vitally important during a relief operation and only slightly less so in the disaster planning process period. It should be an essential responsibility of UNDP, in conjunction with the DMT, to devise appropriate public information formats. These formats should serve to provide a regular flow of information to the international community as well as members of the international community in-country and relevant government departments.

Information on relief assessments or preparedness measures, intended to be of benefit to the nation, can be regarded as highly sensitive. This is true not only for the government but also for sister agencies and NGOs. You must therefore think carefully about the contents of your various outputs. Two common types of information formats include situation reports and newsletters. Sitreps have become the standard source of information on emergency activities throughout the U.N. system. There is no rigid format for these reports. The message should include key activities related to preparedness, relief and needs assessments, noting requirements fulfilled and unfulfilled.

Implementation of Disaster Preparedness Plans

Many government officials will be skeptical about the benefits of disaster preparedness plans. Introducing the subject of disaster preparedness strategies or plans to government officials may elicit at least one of the following responses:

— *A tremendous idea*: This is just the answer all who are concerned with disaster management want to hear. In reality, the respondent may have little idea of what such a plan entails. Even if this person appreciates the broad principles that are involved, he or she may become wary when the full range of necessary measures begins to unfold.

— *We need development, not disaster preparedness*: A difficult argument to refute, particularly if an official assumes that the two are mutually exclusive. Ministries of finance and economic planning are often the most reluctant to dedicate time and funds to a proposal that seems tangential to their major concern of development. Focusing on development projects often reflects institutional success and generates considerable external assistance.

— *We already have one*: Excellent, but what does the official mean? The government may have a designated disaster relief office in some back ministerial corridor. That one room and one officer hardly constitute an effective disaster preparedness plan. It is not an easy task to suggest that efforts which the government has made to date are not adequate.

There is no trade-off between disaster preparedness and development. The two are closely linked, conceptually and practically. An effective disaster preparedness strategy or plan will:

— *Protect development.* Disasters delay, or, in the worst case, destroy progress that has been made to date. An effective disaster preparedness plan should be integrated into the development process so that the former can protect the latter.

— *Introduce disaster mitigation.* Disaster mitigation measures such as safer buildings, "off-the-shelf" food-for-work programmes or cash-forwork public works programmes not only protect people and their assets, but also speed up the development process if they are adequately designed.

— *Strengthen the local infrastructure.* For example, the institutional and communications structure required in disaster preparedness necessarily strengthens the overall local infrastructure.

— *Exert pressure of traditional aid donors.* This may affect the overall amounts these donors allot to development. Conversely, donors are increasingly interested in spending resources on disaster preparedness measures.

Reliable Information Base

The more disaster-prone a country, the less reliable the information base is likely to be. This point goes to the heart of what disaster vulnerability is all about: extensive poverty, weak infrastructure, and inadequate administration. Under such conditions, it is difficult to maintain a reliable information base. There is often a "data game" that is played before, during and after a disaster. Sometimes there are political reasons for governments to provide unreliable data. Certain demographic data might, for example, reflect an official's regional affiliation.

Infrastructural data might reflect the wishful thinking of a ministry that has not completed a project as well as it suggests. Agricultural data might reflect an optimistic forecast of the minister for agriculture. Such games are also played by international organisations. An agency might exaggerate the number of water projects it has completed, or assume that there are more primary health care facilities in a particular region than in fact is the case. At times agencies assume that food needs are greater than they are to avoid being accused of underestimating the extent of a possible crisis.

Even under the best of circumstances, baseline data and information systems cannot be perfect. Gathering sensible data and approximate information is a far more realistic information goal. It is highly recommended to implement the following information systems at the beginning of the planning process.

Vulnerability assessments

These assessments are particularly important for planning design purposes and for establishing a basis for information flows and updates. These assessments should be undertaken with the same rigor as any development project. With a team leader that knows a particular region well, sectoral experts from UN organisations should join with their national counterparts to undertake the sort of full-scale assessment.

Joint-information programmes

Joint data and information systems between the UN disaster preparedness focal point and this person's government counterpart are vital for both the planning process and the plan itself. The fact that the government is working from the same information base that the UN focal point is using will smooth debates that might arise. In project proposals relating to the disaster preparedness plan, be sure to allot funds for computer equipment, training, and whatever else the counterpart office might require to maintain an effective system.

Cross-checking

Even in the most disaster-prone country, lack of data is less often a problem than a plethora of conflicting data. Nongovernmental organisations often know more about particular areas than government offices. Some procedure should be established, in agreement with the government counterpart, to crosscheck information with other organisations, including other government ministries at central and regional levels.

Joint-assessment process

As part of the disaster preparedness plan, it should be formally agreed that in times of emergencies, a team or teams comprising agency representatives of the government focal point, the UN DMT, the government focal point and nongovernmental organisations familiar with the affected area assess the situation jointly. Such procedures should be formally adopted within the proposed disaster plan. Joint assessments can reduce duplication of efforts, promote a degree of consensus about damage and needs, and ensure that subsequent appeals have national as well as international endorsement.

Institutional Structures

A key feature of a disaster preparedness plan must be to ensure that line ministries have vested interests in the disaster preparedness proposal. This means that resources and responsibilities should be parcelled out amongst all those deemed important to the plan. The idea is not to take away the medical functions of a ministry of health, but rather to enhance its capabilities to respond in coordination with other ministries. That does not necessarily mean that a ministry of health would be responsible for the logistics of emergency medicines. It might mean that its responsibility for ensuring emergency medical provisions would be acknowledged, that its institutional strength at local levels would be enhanced, and that its commitment to the plan might be greater.

In a disaster situation, all responsible officials must have a clear idea of their roles and functions. This is what a disaster plan establishes and what rehearsals test. The effectiveness of implementation can be judged by an inter-ministerial committee and supported by the findings of a secretariat. It is advisable to have a secretariat to liaise with designated ministries: before implementation of a plan; during implementation periods; and after the first stages of implementation.

The roles and resources brought by nongovernmental organisations for disaster preparedness, mitigation, prevention and relief purposes should be incorporated into the information required by the inter-ministerial committee on disaster preparedness. The government should also have a mechanism to determine the amount and type of assistance provided by bilateral donors and international agencies. It is important to bring the planning process to the regional and local levels. This can be accomplished in a variety of ways. Having established a broad framework for the plan, take the plan and relevant officials to the field to work out the most effective ways to implement the proposal. The means of implementation should include attention to resources for preparedness at the family and local levels.

A national disaster preparedness strategy or plan should allow regional variations to meet the specific conditions of particular areas. This is essential for ensuring that the institutional structure of the plan has the support of regional and local officials. Establish local working groups to review the plans on a periodic basis and be sure that the substance of these reviews is considered. Where relevant, incorporate these reviews into updates of the overall plan. Such working groups are essential when it comes to warning systems, evacuation measures, and health or nutritional assessments.

Units of Analysis in Disaster Preparedness

Households

The household is the smallest unit of analysis for preparedness. A household may consist of an individual, a family of two or more, extended families, single parents with children, persons who are co-residing in a single residential unit, or even those who are transient. Just as "every disaster is local," preparedness begins in the home with some simple steps that can be taken to improve life safety, property protection, and survival from hazardous events.

Households vary in many ways that are important for understanding both disaster vulnerability and disaster preparedness. Particularly in the aftermath of Hurricane Katrina, it is clear that while many households are able to prepare for disasters, others lack the wherewithal and resources. For households, vulnerability is associated with income, education, ethnicity, age, and linguistic isolation. Factors such as income influence access to safe housing options and to insurance. Other axes of stratification play a role in making households either more or less vulnerable, better or less well prepared.

Businesses

All businesses operate for a profit, but an individual business may be organized as a corporation, partnership, or owner-operated entity. Businesses range from the very small to the extremely large; in the U. S., most businesses are small ones. Businesses inhabit a range of sectors and niches. Businesses may operate at single or multiple locations. A business may be part of a chain, part of a franchise, or a stand-alone operation. Like residential properties, business properties may be owned or rented, located in safe or dangerous places, or in vulnerable or disaster-resistant structures. A business may employ a team of business continuity and security experts, or have a single individual responsible for compliance with regulations on safety for hazards. These different business characteristics are associated with differential vulnerability to disasters.

Business preparedness is important not only because businesses are the engines of local, regional, and national economies, but also because many business entities become directly involved in crisis-relevant activities at the time of disasters. Businesses that perform critical services include for-profit hospitals and private utilities. Businesses may also be directly involved in disaster response through contracts and mutual aid agreements.

Communities and Organizations

A community is a social unit that may or may not be contiguous with a local political jurisdiction. The boundaries of a community may be represented by neighborhoods with common ethnicity, interest-based associations, or other social groups. However, for purposes of this discussion, the community is represented by the local political jurisdiction (municipal government, city government, county government) responsible for emergency preparedness, emergency alert and notification, emergency response and recovery. Communities range from small rural towns with limited governmental resources for public safety and emergency management to large municipalities with emergency operations boards and city-wide preparedness initiatives. With an increasing emphasis on regional preparedness, we also take into account regional collaboration and multi-jurisdictional planning.

Much of the discussion here looks as communities through the lens of public-sector organizations that play key roles in preparing for disasters. A partial list of such organizations includes local emergency management agencies, homeland security agencies, fire and police departments, utility service providers, offices of building and safety, public hospitals, public health systems, and departments of public works and transportation.

Also critical are the vast array of non-profit organizations that sustain communities during non-disaster times as well as during disasters. Such organizations include the Red Cross, United Way organizations, voluntary associations, community-based organizations, and other civil society institutions. Disaster preparedness is, of course, just as essential for organizations in the non-profit sector as it is for other organizations.

Principles Applicable to Disaster Preparedness

Research on preparedness has resulted in general principles of preparedness that are applicable to any unit of analysis, including households, businesses, public sector agencies, networks, communities, and intergovernmental alliances. Importantly, the same general principles apply *for all types of hazards*: natural hazards, technological hazards, and intentional attacks. As seen above, the concept of preparedness is multidimensional and includes elements such as hazard awareness and analysis, formal plans, mutual aid agreements, enduring social and institutional relationships, resource acquisition, training and education, drills and exercises, and methods for institutionalizing lessons learned. The following process-related principles are also fundamental to our understanding of what it means to be prepared for disaster.

1. Formal plans are only one element in comprehensive preparedness strategies.

Plans can be placed into a notebook and shelved until a disaster occurs and necessitates their use. "To assume that planning is complete when a written disaster plan is produced is to court trouble". Unless plans are trained, practiced, and improved upon, emergency response agencies, businesses, and households will not be ready for an emergency.

Also implicit in this guidance is the notion that households, businesses, and community agencies must continually find ways of improving their plans. Approaches for improving plans include identifying lessons learned from disaster events and adjusting plans accordingly; learning from the experiences of other communities; and seeking other sources of information, such as government and private sector guidance, that can be used to refine plans.

2. Plans mean little in the absence of other elements of preparedness.

Plans may be nothing more than "fantasy documents" designed to provide assurance that organizations or communities are ready for disasters or "wish lists" indicating what should happen when a major event occurs. Formal plans mean little unless resources exist to actually carry out planned activities and unless those assigned responsibility know what to do—and are able to do it—when disasters strike. One problem with the "paper plan syndrome" is that those involved may tend to think all potential problems are solved once the plan is formalized.

3. Preparedness is a process, not a product.

Obtaining a disaster supply kit, retrofitting a building, developing a business plan, or consulting with experts about potential hazards in the community are only steps in larger processes associated with preparedness. Effective planning can only take place when multiple agencies and stakeholders are directly involved on an ongoing basis in formulating plans and undertaking activities that ensure that plans can actually be carried out in a coordinated fashion. Effective response is based on prior knowledge of the capabilities and competencies of all entities designated as having tasks to perform when a disaster occurs. Such knowledge can only be developed through extensive engagement among partners. For businesses for example, site-based planning is a kcy process, but so is collaborating with supply-chain partners to ensure continuity in operations. One key objective of the planning process is to broaden and deepen both formal and informal connections among responding entities. Another is to identify and address gaps in preparedness and capability within and across partnership networks.

4. Preparedness efforts must be based on realistic assumptions concerning social behavior during crises.

Plans should be developed based upon what is likely to happen in a disaster, rather than on myths and misunderstandings about disaster behavior. For instance, based on research, it is known that public panic is not a problem during disasters, but also that public information-seeking will greatly increase. Factors associated with the receipt of warning information and with public warning responses are also well understood. It is important to plan, educate, train, and focus preparedness activities in ways that have a positive effect on influencing publics to take protective actions when warnings are given. Preparedness activities should not aim at controlling behavior, but rather on understanding and accommodating normal public responses during disasters. The disaster literature is replete with examples of misguided actions based on incorrect assumptions about disaster behavior. Officials have avoided issuing warnings for fear of causing panic and have allocated public safety resources based on erroneous fears of looting. It makes little sense to develop plans that attempt to discourage members of the public from volunteering to assist in disaster response activities, because the public will inevitably seek to be involved. Rather, plans should emphasize how to incorporate volunteers into the overall response effort. Similarly, rather than planning to deal with unruly and uncooperative disaster victims, officials should assume that members of the public will be cooperative and helpful when disasters strike.

5. Preparedness requires collaboration, not top-down direction – although clear guidance does help.

As in any other endeavor that seeks to enhance collaboration and cooperation, the disaster planning process must be carried out in ways that encourage "ownership" of the planning process. People are highly unlikely to feel that sense of ownership if plans are developed without the input of those who are supposed to carry them out. Guidance is essential for encouraging preparedness, but guidance should be sufficiently flexible that those who will be responsible for response and recovery activities can plan in ways that reflect their own distinctive local concerns. Overly specific, top-down directives will likely encourage a compliance-oriented rather than a collaborative mindset for those with planning responsibilities. Particularly now, when many preparedness activities are initiated at the federal government level, there is a strong need for preparedness strategies that are tied to place-specific hazard and vulnerability analyses and that are consistent with the needs of local communities, businesses, and households.

6. Planning activities should be guided by those who will actually carry out plans.

For individuals and organizations that are pressed for time and short on resources, there is a great temptation "borrow" disaster plans from other jurisdictions or hire an individual or a consulting company to write a plan.

This tendency has no doubt increased as regulations and requirements regarding extreme event planning have become more stringent. However, understanding planning as a process means also understanding that there are no short-cuts to effective preparedness. As noted in the section above, preparedness measures work best when they are collaboratively developed by those who will actually be involved in responding when disasters occur. Effective planning requires a sense of ownership of the planning process—something that is unlikely to develop if outsiders are given major responsibility for developing the plan. This is not to say that consultants should never be used in developing plans. Rather, this is an argument for using consultants and other outsiders as facilitators in a process that is owned by those who will ultimately be responsible for implementing plans.

7. Efforts should be comprehensive and inclusive, and should promote multi-organizational participation.

Disasters require inter-organizational coordination and cooperation for an effective response; therefore preparedness efforts should include all of the groups responsible for the various emergency management functions. Preparedness efforts should include representation from emergency management, law enforcement, fire, city management, public health, citizen and voluntary groups, schools, nursing homes, hospitals and health care organizations, the business community, and other sectors in order to create a network of organizations to support essential functions in a disaster event.

It is important to devise preparedness strategies that are intentionally broad in part because of the tendency for preparedness activities to be vertically integrated—or stovepiped—rather than horizontally integrated, across community organizations and sectors. Sector-based preparedness efforts are important. Law enforcement agencies, hospitals, and businesses need to plan extensively. However, effective planning efforts are those that span different organizations and sectors and that are guided by a common vision of community resilience in the face of disasters.

8. Preparedness advocates must overcome constraints, limitations, and sometimes outright opposition.

Emergency planning and preparedness efforts may face apathy from some and resistance from others. Reasons why support is generally lacking range from a resistance to thinking about disasters, to reluctance to allocate limited resources, to conflicts among organizations responsible for planning and preparedness activities. At a more general level, disaster-related issues must always compete with other concerns that are considered equally or more important. Household members who live in fear of crime and struggle daily to get by on low incomes may find it impossible spare time and resources for disaster preparedness, even if they are aware of its importance. More affluent community residents may be too busy juggling their varied responsibilities to pay much attention to a disaster that may or may not happen. Disaster preparedness may rank low on corporate and community agendas compared to pressing day-to-day problems. An enterprise that is struggling to stay afloat may not have the luxury of thinking about future disasters. Expenditures on disaster loss reduction must be weighed in light of other investments that may bring more immediate return. Planning horizons for both businesses and local governments may be short.

Preparedness efforts are quite often difficult to sustain over time. Public officials are educated and become advocates for disaster loss reduction, but then they leave office owing to term limits. If no disasters occur over a period of time, members of the public, officials, and business owners become less vigilant. Except in very unusual cases, disaster preparedness is typically "a policy without a public". What this means is that strong advocacy is required to sustain preparedness efforts. Advocates typically include scientists, engineers, individual activists and groups that focus specifically on hazards and disasters, and public officials who have decided to make loss reduction one of their key priorities. Disaster preparedness must always compete with other issues, including those that enjoy more widespread public, corporate, and government support.

9. Preparedness should be risk- and vulnerability-based, but should also consider low probability/high consequence events.

Implicit in many discussions in this section is the idea that preparedness activities should be geared to local concerns—which include scientifically-based assessments of what events are likely to occur in a given community, state, or other jurisdictional area. This perspective stands in contrast with current guidance that emphasizes the need for every community to prepare for terrorist attack. While it is of course conceivable that any community may become the target of terrorism—Oklahoma City is a case in point here—the fact remains that historical disasters to some extent predict future ones. Different regions of the country are zoned according to the likelihood of earthquake-induced damage because the historical record makes that kind of zoning possible. New flood plain maps should do a better job of indicating where future floods will be most severe. Efforts to assess long-term vulnerability by taking into account future development patterns may serve as a basis for mitigation and preparedness efforts. These are examples of the types of information communities need to take into account when undertaking their own preparedness efforts and communicating about vulnerability and preparedness with households and businesses.

At the same time, preparedness efforts must address all potential disaster events. Too many communities center their preparedness activities on the last disaster, rather than on those that are likely to occur in the future. Limited resources require communities to prioritize among the events for which they will plan, but at the same time communities should not neglect to plan for low probability events, including catastrophic and near-catastrophic disasters.

10. Preparedness efforts must be designed in ways that help responders and victims anticipate surprise – e.g. through fostering the ability to adapt, improvise, and innovate.

In earlier sections of this report, we emphasized the importance of systematic planning that recognizes that disasters always contain an element of surprise. Improvisation is one of the foundations of emergency management. The ability to adapt to an unfolding situation requires both flexibility within plans and broad permission to respond creatively to the unfolding of events that do not 'fit' well within existing planning frameworks.

Here again, Hurricane Katrina is a case in point. Many responding agencies, especially those at the state and federal levels, simply did not recognize until it was too late that Katrina was a catastrophe, rather than a garden-variety disaster. Adherence to bureaucratic rules and regulations slowed down response efforts, as key decision-makers simply refused to see that Katrina was not a disaster that could be managed through the use of standard emergency measures. Rather than encouraging creativity and improvisation, the preparedness strategies that were in place at the time Katrina struck appear to have instead discouraged decision-makers from seeking creative solutions— even though that was exactly what the situation called for.

11. Preparedness efforts should have an "all hazards" focus, while also incorporating special considerations associated with individual hazards. Preparedness activities should not be organized around specific perils.

It is well established in the disaster literature that preparedness efforts should focus on generic challenges associated with all disasters, rather than on the specific demands of different kinds of disaster events. The concept of all-hazard preparedness recognizes that, regardless of the agent causing the disaster, households, businesses, and community organizations must respond in roughly similar ways. This is not done by compartmentalizing various disaster agents and addressing each separately. Rather, the approach is to begin first by assessing what various agents have in common with respect to response demands, and only later focusing on specific contingencies. For example, responsibility for management, direction, and control (MDC) must be assumed no matter what type of disaster agent is involved. For businesses, challenges associated with business interruption are extremely important regardless of whether the source of disruption is a hurricane, an earthquake, or a technological disaster. For communities and crisis-relevant organizations, sheltering, feeding, and providing health care services to victims, restoring essential services, overcoming transportation system disruption, and removing debris are critical regardless of what type of disaster is involved. Depending on where they are located, families may need to develop evacuation plans for multiple hazards, ranging from floods to fires to nuclear plant accidents. Addressing the need for appropriate and sufficient resources is a generic preparedness task, even though specific resources needed to deal with different types of disasters vary. In cases in which hazard agents require distinctly different responses, hazard-specific planning, training, and resources are required.

References

Bohem, Hilda. (1978).*Disaster Prevention and Disaster Preparedness* . Berkeley: University of California.

Business Executives for National Security (BENS). "A Company Primer on Preparedness and Response Planning for Terrorist and Bioterrorist Attacks." BENS.

Genovese, Robert, Trish Taylor and Edward White. (1989). *Disaster Preparedness Manual*, Buffalo, N.Y.: W.S. Hein.

Waugh, William L. (2000). *Living with Hazards Dealing with Disasters: An Introduction to Emergency Management.* M.E. Sharpe: Armonk, New York.

5

Early Warning Systems

At a time of global changes, the world is striving to face and adapt to inevitable, possibly profound, alteration. Widening of droughts in southern Europe and sub-Saharan Africa, an increasing number of natural disasters severe and more frequent flooding that could imperil low-lying islands and the crowded river deltas of southern Asia, are already taking place and climate change will cause additional environmental stresses and societal crises in regions already vulnerable to natural hazards, poverty and conflicts.

A state-of-art assessment of existing monitoring/early warning systems (EWS) organized according to type of environmental threats is presented below. This report will focus on: air quality, wildland fires, nuclear and chemical accidents, geological hazards (earthquakes, tsunamis, volcanic eruptions, landslides), hydro-meteorological hazards (desertification, droughts, floods, impact of climate variability, severe weather, storms, and tropical cyclones), epidemics and food insecurity. Current gaps and needs are identified with the goal of laying out guidelines for developing a global multi-hazard early warning system.

Early Warning

Early warning (EW) is "the provision of timely and effective information, through identified institutions, that allows individuals exposed to hazard to take action to avoid or reduce their risk and prepare for effective response.", and is the integration of four main elements:

1. *Risk Knowledge*: Risk assessment provides essential information to set priorities for mitigation and prevention strategies and designing early warning systems.
2. *Monitoring and Predicting*: Systems with monitoring and predicting capabilities provide timely estimates of the potential risk faced by communities, economies and the environment.
3. *Disseminating Information*: Communication systems are needed for delivering warning messages to the potentially affected locations to alert local and regional governmental agencies. The messages need to be reliable, synthetic and simple to be understood by authorities and public.
4. *Response*: Coordination, good governance and appropriate action plans are a key point in effective early warning. Likewise, public awareness and education are critical aspects of disaster mitigation.

Failure of any part of the system will imply failure of the whole system.

For example, accurate warnings will have no impact if the population is not prepared or if the alerts are received but not disseminated by the agencies receiving the messages.

The basic idea behind early warning is that the earlier and more accurately we are able to predict short-and long-term potential risks associated with natural and human-induced hazards, the more likely we will be able to manage and mitigate disasters' impact on society, economies, and environment.

Operational Aspects

Early warning systems help to reduce economic losses and mitigate the number of injuries or deaths from a disaster, by providing information that allows individuals and communities to protect their lives and property. Early warning information empowers people to take action when a disaster close to happening. If well integrated with risk assessment studies and communication and action plans, early warning systems can lead to substantive benefits.

Is essential to note that "predictions are not useful, however, unless they are translated into a warning and action plan the public can understand and unless the information reaches the public in a timely manner". Effective early warning systems embrace all aspects of emergency management, such as: risk assessment analysis, which is one of early warning system's design requirements; monitoring and predicting location and intensity of the natural disaster waiting to happen; communicating alerts to authorities and to potentially affected; and responding to the disaster. All aspects have to be addressed by the early warning system. Commonly, early warning systems lack of one or more elements. In fact, the review of existing early warning systems shows that in most cases communication systems and adequate response plans are lacking.

Monitoring and predicting is only one part of the early warning process. This step provides the input information for the early warning process that needs to be disseminated to those whose responsibility is to respond. Monitoring and predicting systems, if associated with communication system and response plans, can then be considered early warning systems. Early warnings may be disseminated to targeted users (local early warning applications) or broadly to communities, regions or to media (regional or global early warning applications).

This information gives the possibility of taking action to initiate mitigation or security measures before a catastrophic event occurs. The main goal of early warning systems is to take action to protect or reduce loss of life or to mitigate damage and economic loss, before the disaster occurs.

Nevertheless, to be effective this warning must be *timely* so as to provide enough lead-time for responding, *reliable* so that those responsible for responding to the warning will feel confident taking action, and *simple* so as to be understood.

Timeliness is often in conflict with the desire to have reliable predictions, which become more accurate as more observations are collected from the monitoring system. There is therefore an inevitable trade-off between the amount of warning time available and the reliability of the predictions provided by the EWS. An initial alert signal may be sent to give the maximum amount of warning time when a minimum level of prediction accuracy has been reached. However, the prediction accuracy for the location and size of the event will continue to improve as more data is collected by the monitoring system part of the EWS network. It must be understood that every prediction, being a prediction, is associated with uncertainty. Because of the uncertainties associated with the predicted parameters that characterize the incoming disaster, it is possible that a wrong decision may be made. In making this decision, two kinds of wrong decisions may occur: Missed

Alarm (or False Negative) when the mitigation action is not taken when it should have been or False Alarm (or False Positive) when the mitigation action is taken when it should not have been.

Finally the message should at the same time communicate the level of uncertainty and expected cost of taking action but also be simple so as to be understood by those who receive it. Most often, there is a communication gap between EW specialists who use technical and engineering language and the EWS users, who are generally outside of the scientific community. To avoid this, these early warnings need to be reported concisely, in layman's terms and without scientific jargon.

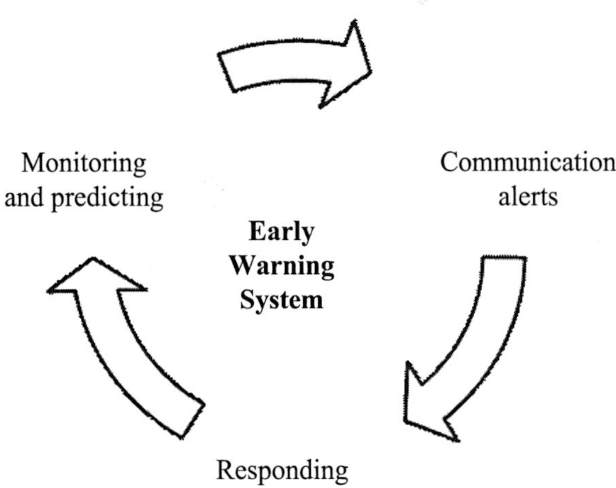

Figure 1. Early Warning System: Operational aspects

Communication of Early Warning Information

An effective early warning system needs an effective communication system.

Early warning communication systems are made of two main components (EWCII):

- communication infrastructure hardware that must be reliable and robust, especially during the natural disasters; and
- appropriate and effective interactions among the main actors of the early warning process such as the scientific community, stakeholders, decision makers, the public, and the media.

Many communication tools are currently available for warning dissemination such as Short Message Service (SMS) (cellular phone text messaging), email, radio, TV, and web service. Information and communication technology (ICT) is a key element in early warning. ICT plays an important role in disaster communication and dissemination of information to organizations in charge of responding to warnings and to the public during and after a disaster.

Redundancy of communication systems is essential for disaster management, while emergency power supplies and back-up systems are critical in order to avoid the collapse of communication systems after disasters occur.

In addition, in order to ensure reliable and effective operation of the communication systems during and after disaster occurrence, and to avoid network congestion, frequencies and channels must be reserved and dedicated to disaster relief operations.

Nowadays, an extreme decentralization of information and data through the World Wide Web makes it possible for millions of people worldwide to have easy, instantaneous access to a vast amount of diverse online information. This powerful communication medium has spread rapidly to interconnect our world, enabling near-real-time communications and data exchanges worldwide. According to the Internet World Stats database, as of November 2007, global documented Internet usage was 1.3 billion people. Thus, the Internet has become an important medium to access and deliver information worldwide in a very timely fashion.

In addition, remote sensing satellites now provide a continuous stream of data. They are capable of rapid and effective detection of hazards such as transboundary air pollutants, wildfires, deforestation, changes in water levels, and natural hazards. With rapid advances in data collection, analysis, visualization and dissemination, including technologies such as remote sensing, Geographical Information Systems (GIS), web mapping, sensor webs, telecommunications and ever growing Internet connectivity, it is now feasible to deliver relevant information on a regular basis to a worldwide audience relatively inexpensively. In recent years, commercial companies such as Google, Yahoo, and Microsoft have started incorporating maps and satellite imagery into their products and services, delivering compelling visualization and providing easy tools that everyone can use to add to their geographic knowledge.

Information is now available in a near-real-time mode from a variety of sources at global and local levels. In coming years, the multi-scaled global information network will greatly improve thanks to new technological advances facilitating the global distribution of data and information at all levels. Globalization and rapid communication provides an unprecedented opportunity to catalyze effective action at every level by rapidly providing authorities and general public with high-quality, scientifically credible information in a timely fashion.

Dissemination of warnings often follows a cascade process, which starts at international or national level and then moves outwards or downwards in the scale, reaching regional and community levels. Early warnings may activate other early warnings at different authoritative levels, flowing down in responsibility roles, but all are equally necessary for effective early warning.

Standard protocols play a fundamental role in addressing the challenge of effective coordination and data exchange among the actors in the early warning process and it aids in the the process for warning communication and dissemination. The Common Alerting Protocol (CAP), Really Simple Syndication (RSS) and Extensible Markup Language (XML) are examples of standard data interchange formats for structured information that can be applied to warning messages for a broad range of information management and warning dissemination systems.

The advantage of standard format alerts is that they are compatible with all information systems, warning systems, media, and most importantly, with new technologies such as web services.

CAP defines a single standard message format for all hazards, which can activate multiple warning systems at the same time and with a single input. This guarantees consistency of warning messages and would easily replace specific application-oriented messages with a single multi-hazard message format. CAP is compatible with all types of information systems and public alerting systems (including broadcast radio and television), public and private data networks, multi-lingual warning systems and emerging technologies such as Internet Web services, and existing systems such as the U.S. National Emergency Alert System and the National Oceanic and Atmospheric Organization (NOAA) Weather Radio. CAP uses Extensible Markup Language (XML) language. It contains information about the alert message, the specific hazard event, and appropriate responses, including urgency of action to be taken, severity of the event, and certainty of the information.

Early Warning Systems and Policy

For early warning systems to be effective, it is essential that they be integrated into policies for disaster mitigation.

Good governance priorities include protecting the public from disasters through the implementation of disaster risk reduction policies.

It is clear that natural phenomena cannot be prevented, but their human, socio-economic and environmental impacts can and should be minimized through appropriate measures, including risk and vulnerability reduction strategies, early warning, and appropriate action plans. Most often, these problems are given attention during or immediately after a disaster. Disaster risk reduction measures require long term plans and early warning should be seen as a strategy to effectively reduce the growing vulnerability of communities and assets.

The information provided by early warning systems enables authorities and institutions at various levels to immediately and effectively respond to a disaster.It is crucial that local government, local institutions, and communities be involved in the entire policy-making process, so they are fully aware and prepared to respond with short and long-term action plans.

The early warning process, as previously described, is composed of 4 main stages: risk assessment, monitoring and predicting, disseminating and communicating warnings, and response. Within this framework, the first phase, when short- and long-term actions plans are laid out based on risk assessment analysis, is the realm of institutional and political actors. Then EW acquires technical dimension in the monitoring and predicting phase, while in the communication phase EW involves both technical and institutional responsibility. The response phase then involves many more sectors, such as national and local institutions, non-governmental organizations, communities, and individuals.

Below is a summary of recommendations for effective decision-making within the early warning process:

— P*rediction is insufficient for effective decision-making*. Prediction efforts by the scientific community alone are insufficient for decision-making. The scientific community and policy-makers should outline the strategy for effective and timely decision-making by indicating what information is needed by decision-makers, how predictions will be used, how reliable the prediction must be to produce an effective response, and how to communicate this information and the tolerable prediction uncertainty so that the information can be received and understood by authorities and public. A miscommunicated or misused prediction can result in costs to the society. Prediction, communication, and use of the information are necessary factors in effective decision-making within the early warning process.

— *Develop effective communication strategies.* Wishing not to appear 'alarmist' or to avoid criticism, local and national governments have sometimes kept the public in the dark when receiving technical information regarding imminent threats. The lack of clear and easy-to-use information can sometimes confuse people and undermine their confidence in public officials. Conversely, there are quite a few cases where the public may have refused to respond to early warnings from authorities, and have therefore exposed themselves to danger or forced governments to impose removal measures. In any case, clear and balanced information is critical, even when some level of uncertainty remains. For this reason uncertainty level of the information must be communicated to users together with early warning.

— *Establish proper priorities.* Resources must be allocated wisely and priorities should be set, based on risk assessment analysis, for long- and short-term decision-making, such as investing in local early warning systems, education, or enhanced monitoring and observational systems. On the other hand, decision-makers need to be able to set priorities for timely and effective response to a disaster when it occurs based on the information received from the early warning system. Decision-makers should receive necessary training on how to use the information received when an alert is issued and what that information means.

— *Clarify responsibilities.* Institutional networks should be developed with clear responsibilities. Complex problems such as disaster mitigation and response require multi-disciplinary research, multi-sector policy and planning, multi-stakeholder participation, and networking involving all the participants of the process such as the scientific research community (including social sciences aspects), land use planning, environment, finance, development, education, health, energy, communications, transportation, labor, and social security as well as national defense. Decentralization in the decision making process could lead to optimal solutions by clarifying local government and community responsibilities.

— *Collaboration will improve efficiency, credibility, accountability, trust, and cost-effectiveness*. This collaboration consists of joint research projects, sharing information, and participatory strategic planning and programming.

— *Establish and strengthen legal frameworks*. Because there are numerous actors involved in early warning response plans (such as governing authorities, municipalities, townships, and local communities), the decision-making and legal framework of responsibilities should be set up in advance in order to be prepared when a disaster occurs. Hurricane Katrina in 2005 showed gaps in the legal frameworks and definition of responsibilities that lead to the disaster we all have witnessed. Such ineffective decision-making must be dealt with to avoid future disaster such as the one in New Orleans.

Importance of Early Warning Systems

Sudden natural disasters, such as hurricanes, floods, and earthquakes, can strike in minutes. Weather-related events are more frequent than geophysical events, and affect more people. Slow onset natural disasters (such as drought, famine, or extreme temperatures), which affect even more people, as their longer timescales do not demand such rapid communication of warnings and mobilisation of humanitarian aid resources. Rapid onset disasters have a high impact in a very short amount of time. For example, both the 1970 tropical cyclone in Bangladesh and the 2004 Indian Ocean tsunami killed more than 300,000 people in just hours to days. Although disasters cannot be prevented, some can be forecast. Their effects can be reduced if communities are warned and prepared.

Countries have long been concerned about the huge impacts that natural disasters have on society in developed and especially in developing countries. Unfortunately, societies have not adapted their frameworks of development to the natural environment surrounding them and the losses and costs associated with disasters of natural origin. On the contrary societal catastrophes are growing by the decade; global annual disaster costs of fifty billion US dollars are common. Between 1960 and 1990 the economic losses of disasters increased five times due to rising vulnerability. Our vulnerability to natural hazards is growing, because population increases and more people are living in risky places.

Nearly a million people have been killed over the last decade by disasters caused by storms, droughts, floods. While some material losses seem to be unavoidable, especially in the case of very large and infrequent events, in some cases the loss of human lives could have been avoided if the proper precautions and measures had been in place. This would have been the case for the December 26, 2004 Indian Ocean tsunami, which provoked fatalities surpassing a quarter of a million people.

In Sri Lanka, over 34,000 people lost their lives due to the lack of a tsunami early warning system. While there would have been sufficient time to warn some of the coastal population, the lack of awareness regarding tsunamis, the lack of an early warning system, and the lack of training to respond to a warning inhibited the authorities and the local population from executing the proper measures which would have significantly reduced the loss of lives.

The traditional framework of early warning systems is composed of three phases: monitoring of precursors, forecasting of a probable event, and the notification of a warning or an alert should an event of catastrophic proportions take place. An improved four-step framework being promoted by national emergency agencies and risk management institutions includes the additional fourth phase: the onset of emergency response activities once the warning has been issued. The purpose of this fourth element is to recognize the fact that there needs to be a response to the warning, where the initial responsibility relies on emergency response agencies.

Effective early warning systems require strong technical foundations and good knowledge of the risks. But they must be strongly people centred – with clear messages, dissemination systems that reach those at risk, and practiced and knowledgeable responses by risk managers and the public. Public awareness and education are critical; in addition, many sectors must be involved. Effective early warning systems must be embedded in an understandable manner and relevant to the communities which they serve.

For an early warning of a natural disaster to reach vulnerable populations, there must be bodies responsible for the following tasks:

— scientific monitoring, data processing, and event forecasting. Local knowledge can ensure that these activities are appropriately focused;

— translation of scientific information into public warnings that are meaningful to their targets;

— the widest possible dissemination of warnings to those who could be affected by the hazard.

For rapid onset events, warnings must reach people within minutes to hours of the event or its precursor being detected. It is thus important that all responsible agencies are on call 24 hours a day and that each task is carried out as quickly as possible. In particular, communication of data and warnings between agencies must be rapid. This requires established and regularly tested protocols for each stage of data transfer.

People-centred Early Warning Systems

A complete and effective, people-centred early warning system – EWS – comprises four inter-related elements, spanning knowledge of hazards and vulnerabilities through to preparedness and capacity to respond. A weakness or failure in any one of these elements could result in failure of the whole system.

Best practice EWS also have strong inter-linkages between all elements in the chain.While good governance and appropriate institutional arrangements are not specifically represented on the «four element diagram», they are critical to the development of effective early warning systems. Good governance is encouraged by robust legal and regulatory frameworks and supported by long term political commitment and integrated institutional arrangements. Major players concerned with the different elements should meet regularly to ensure that they understand all of the other components and what other parties need from them.

Risk Knowledge

Risks arise from both the hazards and the vulnerabilities that are present.What are the patterns and trends in these factors? Risk assessment and mapping will help to set priorities among early warning system needs and to guide preparations for response and disaster prevention activities. Risk assessment could be based on historic experience and human, social, economic and environmental vulnerabilities.

Warning Service

A sound scientific basis for predicting potentially catastrophic events is required. Constant monitoring of possible disaster precursors is necessary to generate accurate warnings on time. Approaches that address many hazards and involve various monitoring agencies are most effective.

Communication and Dissemination

Clear understandable warnings must reach those at risk. For people to understand the warnings they must contain clear, useful information that enables proper responses. Regional, national and community level communication channels must be identified in advance and one authoritative voice established.

Response Capability

It is essential that communities understand their risks; they must respect the warning service and should know how to react. Building up a prepared community requires the participation of formal and informal education sectors, addressing the broader concept of risk and vulnerability.

Models of Monitoring and Forecasting

If disasters arise from the concatenation of multiple factors, natural and social, then in principle at least, an early warning system should address all of the factors relevant to the particular risk. From this perspective it is desirable to monitor and provide early warning and foresight not only on the short-term precipitating hazards and geophysical conditions but also on the relevant longer-term factors such as declining environmental state, risk-raising development practices and projects, risk-altering policy changes, the status of social communications and capacities, trends in food markets, settlement trends and migration, conflict and health status. This involves a wide range of time frames, as illustrated in table 1, and diverse methodologies for monitoring and forecasting. Extending this line of thinking, one can argue that the citizen and the public risk manager is not so concerned with the specifics of particular hazards, but rather the package of risks faced and how to mitigate and prepare for them. This implies that an approach that addresses all relevant hazards in an integrated fashion, and not as separate unconnected systems, is more appropriate to the management of natural risks. Such a 'multi-hazard' or 'all-hazard' approach should provide synergies and cost-efficiencies, e.g. in data gathering and processing and in public preparedness efforts, and should assist in sustaining warning capabilities for the more infrequent hazards, such as tsunamis. It is important, however, not to gloss over the very specific characteristics of the different hazards. For example, tsunamis and storm surges both cause coastal inundation but the detection and monitoring methods, lead-time, duration of the hazard and response actions are very different. A multi-hazard approach should not be allowed to force generalities or centralised control upon warning systems, but must be tailored to the needs of each hazard and built upon the specific technical capabilities required and the available institutional capacities. The need is for a coordinated 'system of systems'.

Linear Paradigm of Model-based Early Warning Systems

The most common current view of early warning systems comprises a 'warning chain', a linear set of connections from observations through warning generation and transmittal to users. In the meteorological community the term 'end-to-end' warning system is often used. The end-to-end concept aims to make forecasts and warnings more relevant and useable to end-users, and has evolved partly in response to the commercialisation imperative in many national meteorological services, as well as through efforts to make better practical use of the probabilistic and weakly predictive seasonal forecasts of the ElNino phenomenon. It emphasizes the necessity to have all the links in the early warning chain in place and systematically connected.

Table 1. Illustration of factors of relevance to early warning systems and their time frames in seconds (S), minutes (M), days (D), weeks (W), months (M), years (Y) and decades (D).

factor	*time frame*						
	S	*M*	*D*	*W*	*M*	*Y*	*D*
Seismicity, tsunami	X	X	X				
Weather, oceans, floods		X	X	X	X		
Soils, reservoirs, snow pack, El Nio			X	X	X		
People exposed, conflict, migration			X	X	X	X	
Crop production, prices, reserves, food aid			X	X	X		
Environmental management and state				X	X	X	
Industry, urban, infrastructure design				X	X	X	
Land use planning, climate change						X	X

At the heart of all early warning systems is some sort of model that describes the relevant features of the hazard phenomenon and its impacts, particularly their time evolution. The model provides the means to make projections of what might happen in the future-and therefore what actions might be desirable in response. Models may be as elaborate as the physics-based global numerical weather prediction models, or as straightforward as 'common knowledge' mental models (e.g. that the noisy approaching tsunami wave will arrive in a few minutes). They may be slowly evolving, as in a drought model where the loss of soil moisture may occur over months, or very rapid, such as in an earthquake where the differential speed of electromagnetic signals relative to seismic waves can be used to automatically shut down a distant sensitive system a few seconds before damaging stresses occur.

Models also underlie the other parts of the warning system, such as the likely impacts of a hazard, the way warnings are communicated and acted on, and the dynamics of evacuation processes, but these vulnerability and response process models are generally much less developed than the geophysical process models.

All models are driven by a specification of an initial state, which must be obtained by observations (or from the output of an upstream observation-driven model). Observation systems can be expensive to install and operate and are often rather inadequate, especially in poorer countries. The initial state is, therefore, always imperfectly known, owing to imperfect spatial representation, instrument error and absence of data on some relevant factors.

These uncertainties of the initial state propagate through the models, and together with errors in the model physics and representations thereof and random noise factors, result in uncertainty in the model estimates of future conditions. Warnings are, therefore, inherently probabilistic, even if based on sound physics and presented in a categorical format. Of note are forecasts of seasonal climate anomalies, which are strongly affected by system noise and uncertainty, and can only be represented in probability terms, and where it must be left to the end-user to judge the possible impact consequences of the projected possible climate outcomes.

Currently, tsunami warnings mostly are based on simple statistical relationships with precursor seismic observations, but these latter observations do not allow accurate prediction of the oceanic response, and so the false warning rates are high and the probability characteristics are poorly known. Usually, the warnings are provided only in categorical forms that usually require immediate response action. However, developments in ocean observation systems and in ocean wave propagation and coastal inundation models are in place to improve this situation in the near future.

Limitations

Scientists and technologists are typically the core stakeholders in early warning systems, as they are the custodians of the geophysical and technical knowledge base upon which the warning system relies, and they are generally very motivated to use that knowledge for the good of society. As a result, early warning systems tend to be largely conceived as hazard-focused, linear, topdown, expert driven systems, with little or no engagement of end-users or their representatives. It can be noted, however, that people generally are not interested in early warning systems until some personally threatening event arises, and so most of the time are happy to leave the matter to the experts. While the prevailing end-to-end linear paradigm is an advance on previous techno-centric concepts it nevertheless retains a number of shortcomings, as follows:

(i) the focus still tends to remain on the hazard, with less emphasis on the vulnerabilities, risks and response capacities,

(ii) the different hazards are typically dealt with by separate independent technical institutions, with few synergies or mutual benefits being sought,

(iii) the dominance of the expert can lead to difficulties in user appreciation of such things as the meaning of a warning, warning uncertainty, the nature of false alarms and the necessary responses to different types of warnings,

(iv) the role of research and knowledge from outside the core area of expertise is often not acknowledged,

(v) there is little engagement or empowerment of those at risk in the design and operation of the warning system, and hence a tendency by users to lack any sense of ownership in the system and to mistrust the experts and authorities,

(vi) there are few systematic mechanisms to improve the system through the incorporation of the knowledge, experience and feedback from users and those at risk, and

(vii) weak public engagement and recognition tends to lead to weak political and budgetary support for the warning system.

The Hurricane Katrina disaster is a case in point where the meteorological warnings of wind speed, storm surge and rainfall were accurate and frequently communicated many hours in advance but the public and official engagement and responses to the warnings were inadequate. Similar experiences elsewhere have shown that to be effective, early warning systems must be both technically systematic and people-centred.

The 'people-centred' characteristic requires many systematic approaches and diverse activities spanning the four elements of early warning systems described above, such as: identifying target populations, especially the vulnerable and disadvantaged and interacting with them to determine needs and capacities; conducting town meetings and involving communities in exploring and mapping their risks and planning their responses; fostering the development by communities of monitoring and warning systems for local risks; generating public information tailored to target groups and making innovative use of the media and education systems; establishing people-focused benchmarks and performance standards for technical warning services; developing formal mechanisms for public representatives to monitor and oversee warning system design; using surveys to measure public awareness and satisfaction; creating monuments, publications, annual events and other anchors of public memory and learning; providing training on social factors for technical experts, authorities and communicators who operate the warning system; conducting research on factors that enhance or impede human understanding of and response to warnings; and providing exercises and simulations to enable people to experience and practice warning interpretation and responses.

It is important to recognise that these diverse activities cannot be undertaken or directed by any one organisation, but require the coordinated participation of many different types of organisations, bound by a consensus of commitment to the 'people-centred' concept, and to the idea of an integrated system that is measured by its performance-namely protecting those at risk. National platforms for disaster reduction, stakeholder roundtables or inter-departmental committees should be empowered or established to organise the required coordination. The core technical agencies can play a key role by demanding the establishment of such mechanisms and supporting them with specialised technical information.

Integrated Systems Model for Early Warning Systems

Early warning systems have evolved in line with the development and application of scientific knowledge. Four developmental stages can be distinguished:

(i) pre-science early warning systems. Warnings, if any, may be based on unrelated factors such as meteor occurrence, cloud shapes, plant flowering or fruiting performance, etc., but also may be based on indigenous observations of relevant factors such as the state of the oceans or visibility of the stars,

(ii) ad hoc science-based early warning systems. These are systems such as are often established on the initiative of scientists or community groups concerned with particular hazards, such as near-Earth space objects, a nearby volcano or a flood-prone river,

(iii) systematic end-to-end early warning systems. The best known and most developed are those of national meteorological services, for weather-related hazards. Typically these systems operate under a country-wide mandate and involve the organised, linear and largely uni-directional delivery by experts of warning products to users, and

(iv) integrated early warning systems. This concept, as proposed here and illustrated in figure 2, emphasizes the following characteristics: the linkages and interactions among all the elements necessary to effective early warning and response, the role of the human elements of the system and the management of risks rather than just warning of hazards.

The integrated model proposed in figure 1 includes the core warning system elements, but in addition contains two new key features. The first is the inclusion of actors that often are not recognised as part of the warning system, most notably the political-administrative supporting entities, the district and community actors and the research community.

The second feature is the explicit inclusion of multiple linkages and feedback paths, particularly from affected populations through their organisations to the political and technical actors. The model could be elaborated further for the particular circumstances of countries, e.g. to better specify the district-level and community-level elements or the collaborative roles of different discipline-based technical institutions (e.g. such as seismological, oceanographic and meteorological organisations in a tsunami early warning system).

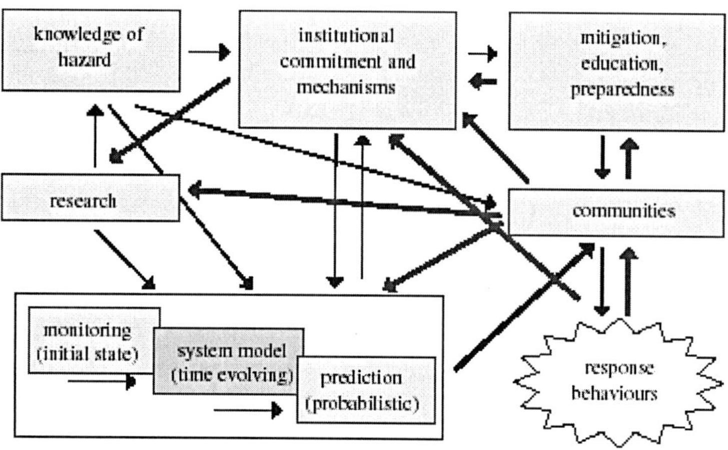

Figure 2. Integrated systems model of early warning system.

Figure 2 is largely conceived as a nationally based system, but it is worth noting that many warning systems depend on regional and international cooperation to secure the exchange of necessary data and warnings. This is not a simple matter to arrange, however, as sovereign states can view their data as having strategic or commercial value, and for these reasons can deny or limit its exchange. In the field of meteorology, many years of discussion under the auspices of the World Meteorological Organisation (WMO), a specialised technical agency of the United Nations, have led to formal agreements on the types of data that are routinely exchanged. Much remains to be done to achieve similar levels of agreement in other hazard fields, e.g. in respect to rainfall and river flow data required for flood warnings in shared river basins and seismic data for tsunami warnings. Underlying the integrated model is the important foundational assumption that we are dealing with a system, defined here as a set of elements and associated linkages designed to achieve a particular result-namely the reduction of risk for target populations and assets through early warning. The system is judged on its effectiveness at delivering the desired result, and can only be effective if the elements and the linkages are well-understood, well-designed and well-operated.

Modern Early Warning Systems

The December 2004 tsunami shone an intense spotlight on questions of early warning systems and preparedness, leading most notably to the call by United Nations Secretary General Koffi Annan in January 2005 for a global warning system for all hazards with no country left out. This was to be followed later in the year by his request to the International Strategy for Disaster Reduction (ISDR) secretariat to coordinate a global survey of early warning systems, with a view to identifying gaps and opportunities, as a basis for developing such global capacities.

Meanwhile, negotiations by states over 2004 culminated in a major international agreement on disaster risk reduction at the World Conference on Disaster Reduction in Kobe, Japan, 18-22 January 2005, namely the Hyogo Framework for Action 2005-2015: building the resilience of nations and communities to disasters. The topic of risk and early warning is one of its five priority areas for action.

Leading UN agencies announced at the conference the launch of an International Early Warning Programme (IEWP), as a vehicle to stimulate and coordinate cooperative initiatives to advance early warning methodology and to build early warning capacities. Shortly afterwards, Germany offered to host a third International Conference on Early Warning (EWC III) under UN auspices.

Rapid progress has been made on developing a tsunami warning system for the Indian Ocean, with strong support by the countries affected and by the international donor community, including through a multi-partner, multi-donor US $11 million project coordinated by the ISDR secretariat. This project has underwritten the important work of UNESCO's Intergovernmental Oceanographic Commission to upgrade regional seismic and oceanic observation systems, to assess national technical needs and to establish intergovernmental coordination mechanisms. It has also supported WMO efforts toward upgrading meteorological telecommunications networks to handle high-speed tsunami information transfers, as well as projects by United Nations organisations and Asian regional disaster organisations to improve public awareness and disaster preparedness.

The project seeks to link and integrate these various initiatives into a strategy to build long-term disaster risk reduction and risk management networks and policies. Separately, the IOC is building the necessary global institutional framework to support tsunami early warning systems in other at-risk regions such as the Mediterranean, Caribbean and Central America.

In early 2005, the British Government established a Natural Hazard Working Group under the guidance of the government chief scientist to advise on the mechanisms that could be established for the detection and early warning of global physical natural hazards, particularly those hazards that could have high global or regional impact, and including international mechanisms needed to enable the international science community to advise governments.

The Working Group recommended the establishment of an International Science Panel for Natural Hazard Assessment, within the UN disaster management framework, to enable the scientific community to provide authoritative information on potential natural hazards likely to have high global or regional impact, by addressing gaps in knowledge and advising on potential future threats and on how science and technology can be used to mitigate threats and reduce vulnerability.

The Working Group also noted that the wellestablished WMO international system operated by national meteorological services for weather data gathering and warning provision provided a potential basis for strengthening other less-developed hazard warning systems.

The Working Group's recommendations subsequently were taken up in part by the 2005 meeting of the G8 ministers, who noted that 'early warning systems for global geophysical events should be based on high quality and appropriate scientific advice that can be translated into effective action by policy makers and those most at risk at a local level'. While not explicitly referring to the British proposal for a new panel, the G8 stated 'We will support closer co-ordination on natural hazard assessment to enable the scientific community to advise on potential natural hazards likely to have high global or regional impact.'

Weather Warnings

Regional Specialised Meteorological Centres (RSMCs) are responsible for the detection, monitoring, tracking and intensity forecasting of tropical cyclones in their area. When a cyclone approaches, many nations will refine these forecasts for their own locality, before issuing official warnings. Risk assessments and local monitoring may then be used to issue local flood warnings. Although the standard of RSMCs varies, many NMSs know that ensuring that forecasts reach vulnerable communities is as important as improving the accuracy of the forecasts.

Volcano Warnings

Volcanoes differ from many other natural hazards in that their location is fixed and usually known before they erupt. Public warnings are extended to cover larger regions around the volcano as the perceived hazard increases. To issue meaningful and informative public warnings, assessments and forecasts of volcanic behaviour are combined with knowledge about:

— how topography and winds will affect flows, ashlouds, and fallout;

— how rainfall, unstable slopes, and water or ice bodies may cause secondary disasters.

The quality and completeness of this knowledge varies inifferent countries and at different volcanoes.

Tsunami Warnings

The Pacific is the ocean most prone to tsunamis, due to the major geological faults and volcanoes around its rim. It is the only ocean with an established tsunami warning system (TWS), coordinated by the Pacific Tsunami Warning Center (PTWC). When a large underwater earthquake is detected, nearby national agencies issue a local tsunami warning, while the PTWC issues a 'regional tsunami watch'. As these watches are based on earthquake information without sea level data, only 25% of them actually involve a tsunami. The timeline of the Indian Ocean tsunami shows that even such a local warning would have been too late for communities in the Andaman and Nicobar Islands, had a similar system been in place. Once the PTWC receives tsunami height information from ocean sensors, it either cancels the watch, or upgrades it to a regional or Pacific wide warning. This takes ~30 minutes, which in the Indian Ocean could have saved communities in Thailand, Sri Lanka, India, and further away. Although Thailand and Indonesia are part of the PTWS, they had no mechanisms for warning their Indian Ocean coasts. Coastal communities aware that earthquakes and receding seas are precursors of a tsunami may evacuate before an official warning is issued. This knowledge saved a few communities in the December 2004 Indian Ocean tsunami, and could have saved many more, if such basic geophysical knowledge were more widely appreciated.

International Transfer of Data and Warnings

The World Meteorological Organisation (WMO) coordinates the transfer of weather data and warnings through its Global Telecommunications System

(GTS). All nations can access data from each other This system allows all nations to exchange data without the need for any bilateral agreements or exchanges. Tsunami warnings for the Pacific are also transmitted through this system. This allows warnings for rare high impact events such as tsunamis to be transmitted through a system which is regularly tested with frequent weather warnings. It is planned that Indian Ocean tsunami warnings will be transmitted through the GTS.

Public Response to Early Warnings

EWs for rapid onset events do little to protect livelihoods and property. Furthermore, they save lives only if people respond to them. This is more likely if:

— there is an established response procedure, familiar to both the community and the body issuing warnings. This requires regular testing or use of the EW system;

— the community is aware of the effects of the hazard, and understand the warning and forecast information;

— the body issuing warnings is trusted. If a community is unfamiliar with EWs or those issuing them, it may be difficult to gain its trust. False alarms or inaccurate warnings may reduce credibility, so that warnings are not heeded.

Even with all these factors in place, some people will not respond to warnings due to other priorities, such as protecting their livelihoods. Many authorities are reluctant to issue warnings because of the potential loss of trust and the unpopularity of evacuations.

Although a country's level of development does not influence its likelihood of encountering a natural hazard, it can influence the scale of the disaster that results and its capacity for maintaining EW systems. Even if a scientific monitoring and warning service is supported by donor nations and organisations there can be problems with:

— warnings reaching remote or marginalised people. Few of these own phones, radios, or televisions, or have consistent power for these facilities;

— unclear institutional responsibilities. This can also be a problem in developed countries, but is often exacerbated by unstable governments in developing countries;

— People displaced due to conflict or food shortages. Evacuations to avoid such hazards may leave people exposed to another less familiar one.

Community-based early warning systems, which involve the local community in creating hazard maps, scientific monitoring and contingency planning, are often more effective than high tech systems.This involvement increases awareness and understanding of the impacts of natural hazards, but these systems offer shorter warning times than high tech systems. Integration of both types of system may allow warnings with a longer timescale to reach more communities in a form they understand.

REFERENCES

International Federation of Red Cross and Red Crescent Societies. (1984). *Prevention Better than Cure*. Geneva: IFRC.

Lopes, R. (1992). *Public Perception of Disaster Preparedness Presentations Using Disaster Damage Images*. Boulder, CO: Natural Hazard Research.

Mileti, Dennis S. and Paul W. O'Brien. (1992). "Warnings During Disaster: Normalizing Communicated Risk", *Social Problems*.

Twigg J., (2003). *Early Warning Systems for Natural Disasters Reduction*, Zschau J. and Kuppers A. Editors, Springer.

United Nations, (2006). *Global Survey of Early Warning Systems*, United Nations report.

World Meteorological Organization, (2006). *Drought Monitoring and Early Warning: Concepts, Progress and Future Challenges,* WMO Report No. 1006.

6

Recovery and Reconstruction

Disaster recovery (DR) is the process, policies and procedures related to preparing for recovery or continuation of technology infrastructure critical to an organization after a natural or human-induced disaster. Disaster recovery is a subset of business continuity. While business continuity involves planning for keeping all aspects of a business functioning in the midst of disruptive events, disaster recovery focuses on the IT or technology systems that support business functions.

Disaster recovery as a concept developed in the mid to late 1970s as computer center managers began to recognize the dependence of their organizations on their computer systems. At that time most systems were batch-oriented mainframes which in many cases could be down for a number of days before significant damage would be done to the organization.

As awareness of disaster recovery grew, an industry developed to provide backup computer centers, with Sun Information Systems (which later became Sungard Availability Systems) becoming the first major US commercial hot site vendor, established in 1978 in Philadelphia.

During the 1980s and 1990s, IT disaster recovery awareness and the disaster recovery industry grew rapidly, driven by the advent of open systems and real-time processing (which increased the dependence of organizations on their IT systems). Another driving force in the growth of the industry was increasing government regulations mandating business continuity and disaster recovery plans for organizations in various sectors of the economy.

With the rapid growth of the Internet through the late 1990s and into the 2000s, organizations of all sizes became further dependent on the continuous availability of their IT systems, with many organizations setting an objective of 99.999% availability of critical systems. This increasing dependence on IT systems, as well as increased awareness from large-scale disasters such as 9/11, contributed to the further growth of various disaster recovery related industries, from high-availability solutions to hot-site facilities.

Disasters can be classified in two broad categories. The first is natural disasters such as floods, hurricanes, tornadoes or earthquakes. While preventing a natural disaster is very difficult, measures such as good planning which includes mitigation measures can help reduce or avoid losses. The second category is man made disasters. These include hazardous material spills, infrastructure failure, or bio-terrorism. In these instances surveillance and mitigation planning are invaluable towards avoiding or lessening losses from these events.

As IT systems have become increasingly critical to the smooth operation of a company, and arguably the economy as a whole, the importance of ensuring the continued operation of those systems, and their rapid recovery, has increased. For example, of companies that had a major loss of business data, 43% never reopen and 29% close within two years. As a result, preparation for continuation or recovery of systems needs to be taken very seriously. This involves a significant investment of time and money with the aim of ensuring minimal losses in the event of a disruptive event.

Control measures are steps or mechanisms that can reduce or eliminate various threats for organizations. Different types of measures can be included in disaster recovery plan (DRP).

Disaster recovery planning is a subset of a larger process known as business continuity planning and includes planning for resumption of applications, data, hardware, electronic communications (such as networking) and other IT infrastructure. A business continuity plan (BCP) includes planning for non-IT related aspects such as key personnel, facilities, crisis communication and reputation protection, and should refer to the disaster recovery plan (DRP) for IT related infrastructure recovery / continuity.

IT disaster recovery control measures can be classified into the following three types:

1. Preventive measures - Controls aimed at preventing an event from occurring.
2. Detective measures - Controls aimed at detecting or discovering unwanted events.
3. Corrective measures - Controls aimed at correcting or restoring the system after a disaster or an event.

Good disaster recovery plan measures dictate that these three types of controls be documented and tested regularly.

Prior to selecting a disaster recovery strategy, a disaster recovery planner first refers to their organization's business continuity plan which should indicate the key metrics of recovery point objective (RPO) and recovery time objective (RTO) for various business processes (such as the process to run payroll, generate an order, etc.). The metrics specified for the business processes are then mapped to the underlying IT systems and infrastructure that support those processes.

Incomplete RTOs and RPOs can quickly derail a disaster recovery plan. Every item in the DR plan requires a defined recovery point and time objective, as failure to create them may lead to significant problems that can extend the disaster's impact. Once the RTO and RPO metrics have been mapped to IT infrastructure, the DR planner can determine the most suitable recovery strategy for each system. The organization ultimately sets the IT budget and therefore the RTO and RPO metrics need to fit with the available budget. While most business unit heads would like zero data loss and zero time loss, the cost associated with that level of protection may make the desired high availability solutions impractical. A cost-benefit analysis often dictates which disaster recovery measures are implemented.

Some of the most common strategies for data protection are (1) backups made to tape and sent off-site at regular intervals, (2) backups made to disk on-site and automatically copied to off-site disk, or made directly to off-site disk, (3) replication of data to an off-site location, which overcomes the need to restore the data (only the systems then need to be restored or synchronized), often making use of storage area network (SAN) technology, and (4) the use of high availability systems which keep both the data and system replicated off-site, enabling continuous access to systems and data, even after a disaster.In many cases, an organization may elect to use an outsourced disaster recovery provider to provide a stand-by site and systems rather than using their own remote facilities, increasingly via cloud computing.

In addition to preparing for the need to recover systems, organizations also implement precautionary measures with the objective of preventing a disaster in the first place. These may include (1) local mirrors of systems and/or data and use of disk protection technology such as RAID, (2)surge protectors — to minimize the effect of power surges on delicate electronic equipment, (3) use of an uninterruptible power supply (UPS) and/or backup generator to keep systems going in the event of a power failure, (4) fire prevention/mitigation systems such as alarms and fire extinguishers, and (5) anti-virus software and other security measures.

Nature of Disaster Recovery

The International Strategy for Disaster Reduction (ISDR) defines recovery as the "decisions and actions taken after a disaster with a view to restore or improve the pre-disaster living conditions of the stricken community, while encouraging and facilitating necessary adjustments to reduce disaster risk".

While emergency response is vital as it is aimed at saving human lives and providing relief, the ultimate objective of any crisis management is restoration of devastated livelihoods. Recovery eforts following rescue and relief in any disaster can be classified into short term and long term. The short term activities for recovery are debris clearance, providing semipermanent shelter and ensuring sanitation and restoring lifelines, while the long term activities involve building a safer and more sustainable livelihood.

The damage caused by foods, earthquakes and cyclones is on a much larger scale than other disasters and recovery after these disasters poses a challenge. In disasters like drought, the relief phase is prolonged and since there is no damage to the infrastructure and property, the rehabilitation is confined to restoration of livelihoods which can get subsumed in normal development programmes.

Recovery in case of epidemics is more in the form of sanitising the locality against any future recurrence and may also involve counselling of the victims. Industrial disasters being quite varied in nature, the rehabilitation in major ones like the 'Bhopal Gas Tragedy' could involve rehabilitation eforts spanning over a generation of victims apart from restoring livelihoods and providing social and psychological assistance.

Rehabilitation following disasters such as landslides and avalanches is localised and is of a similar nature as in earthquakes but on a smaller scale. Finding safer sites near such locations often poses challenges and resistance.

Assessment

The frst step after stabilizing the situation by providing sufficient relief is to assess the damage. A meticulously executed assessment exercise would provide an ideal base for the rehabilitation eforts. This exercise is best carried out through multi-disciplinary teams which go into all aspects of damage (social, economical, psychological) in participation with the local community. Based on the assessment of the damage and the needs, a recovery strategy has to be formulated. The strategy should include all interventions—economic, social, political and psychological. The resources should be identified and the roles and responsibilities of all concerned should be defined.

Co-ordination

Following any major disaster, a number of players arrive on the scene and as already stated, ensuring proper coordination amongst them thus becomes very important. Recovery activities are taken up by government agencies, local bodies, international agencies, voluntary organisations and others, through separate, overlapping and uncoordinated interventions. This leads to imbalances in the scale of operations, duplication of eforts in some areas, gaps in others and leakage and misuse of resources. Therefore establishing a framework for coordination is necessary for effective recovery. The role of voluntary organisations including international ones like the Red Cross is extremely useful for mitigating the impact of disaster.

The administration is also required to set up a voluntary organisations' coordination centre to coordinate the relief and rehabilitation activities of the multiple organisations so that they are not concentrated in a few pockets. It is often observed that post-disaster recovery eforts tend to focus on rapid and visible solutions to restore normalcy at the cost of sustainable development. The post-disaster recovery phase provides a 'window of opportunity' for disaster risk reduction. Risk reduction aspects should therefore be built into the redevelopment process.

Shelter

Shelter is one of the most visible and immediate needs in post-crisis settings. Relief eforts are often focused on providing shelter quickly, without taking into account the impact of short-term shelter strategies. Long-term shelter strategies help not only to focus on determination and implementation of realistic and permanent reconstruction plans for the afected communities, but are also concerned with rebuilding community confidence and support structure for civic responsibility and urban governance, through participatory planning of reconstruction. The development of disaster resistant housing is a major factor in reducing vulnerability to disasters. However, shelter issues in mitigation go beyond the structural aspects. Rights to ownership and security of tenure make an enormous difference to the maintenance, management and development of shelter, particularly in urban areas.

Sustainability in Recovery Process

Normally, it is seen that the recovery eforts have a tendency of tapering of with the passage of time. The Bureau for Crisis Prevention and Recovery of the UNDP has also observed "the general experience is that once the initial furry of activities of providing rescue and relief is over, the attention received by the recovery eforts goes on declining steadily over a period of time and 'business as usual' sets in". The sustainability component in recovery process therefore is important. This could be achieved by capability building of the community and awareness generation and preparing local crisis management plans.

Accountability

A system of accountability needs to be evolved during the relief and rehabilitation phase. This system should ensure that the relief material reaches the target groups and that the funds are being utilised efficiently and optimally. A grievance redressal mechanism should also be put in place.

Evaluation

After the recovery phase, it is necessary to conduct a detailed evaluation of all aspects of crisis management. This should bring out the strengths and weaknesses of the disaster management machinery and also provide the basis for future improvements. Such an evaluation should be carried out by an independent professional agency like the NIDM, in all major disasters. This assessment should also include a quick audit of the expenditure incurred.

Guidance Notes on Recovery

The International Recovery Platform (IRP) and United Nations Development Programme India have developed Guidance Notes on Recovery on nine sectors namely Shelter, Infrastructure, Gender, Livelihood, Environment, Governance, Climate Change, Health and Psychosocial support. These are initial steps in documenting, collecting and sharing disaster recovery experiences and lessons. This collection of the successes and failures of past experiences in disaster recovery is expected to help in the planning and implementation of future recovery initiatives. The aim of the guidance notes is not to recommend actions, but to place before the personnel involved in the risk-reducing recovery process a menu of options. The sector specifc Guidance Notes are primarily intended for use by policymakers, planners, and implementers of local, regional and national government bodies interested or engaged in facilitating a more responsive, sustainable, and risk reducing recovery process. Since the governments are not the sole actors in disaster recovery and IRP believes that the experiences collected in this document can benefit many other partners working together to build back better.

Indian Experiences of Disaster Recovery

Few experiences of post disaster recovery rehabilitation and reconstruction works are illustrated in the subsequent paras. This shows the experiences which country as a whole has gathered in course of its recovery process after the event of different kind of disasters whether human induced or natural.

Bhopal Gas Tragedy (1984)

6.12.1 The Bhopal Gas Tragedy is one of the world's worst industrial catastrophes. It occurred on the night of 2-3 December, 1984 at the Union Carbide India Limited (UCIL) Pesticide plant in Bhopal which was the Indian subsidiary of Union Carbide Corporation, USA. The accident occurred due to leakage of Methyl Iso Cynate (MIC) and other chemicals due to ingression of water and the resulting reaction afected a large number of persons. Approximately 2000 people are known to have died in the frst 72 hours and large proportion of the survivors suffered acute multi-system morbidities (eyes and lungs were the target organs). The ICMR estimated that approximately 62.58% of the total population in Bhopal suffered from inhalational toxicity. The people who resided in areas close to the carbide factory were exposed to higher concentration of potentially lethal toxic gases.A large proportion of population who survived this tragedy developed morbidity of varying degree over the last 25 years. As an immediate response, the state government of Madhya Pradesh provided financial support to the afected families and an amount of Rs.12.80 crore was distributed as immediate relief. Food items were also distributed to the afected population and compensation was paid for livestock loss. An amount of Rs 3.78 crore was spent to provide compensation to the families of a deceased.

During 1990 in the frst five year action plan a sum of Rs 258 Crore was sanctioned by the Central government and it got extended till 1999. This plan provided Rs 150.35 crore for medical rehabilitation in addition to economic rehabilitation (Rs 21.18 crore), social rehabilitation (Rs 49.72 crore) and environmental rehabilitation (Rs 23.76 crore). The present action plan for Rehabilitation of Government of Madhya Pradesh is given in Table: 1 includes the following features:

Table 1: Action Plan for Rehabilitation of Government of Madhya Pradesh

Item	*Amount (in Rs. Crore)*
Medical Rehabilitation	33.55
Social Rehabilitation	85.20
Economic Rehabilitation	104.00
Water Supply	50.00
Total	272.75

Committee of Group of Ministers

A 'Group of Ministers' has been constituted by GOI under the chairmanship of Home Minister to take decisions on all issues related to Bhopal Gas tragedy vide note 47/1/7/93-CAB dated 26/05/2010. There are 10 members in the Group of Ministers.

The 'Group of Ministers' have come out with the Rs. 982.75 crore work plan (75:25 sharing pattern) for Economic, Social, Medical and Environmental rehabilitation of victim of Bhopal Gas Tragedy. Central Government has sanctioned Rs. 272.75 crore to Madhya Pradesh Government.

Kutch Earthquake (2001)

The Kutch earthquake of 26th January, 2001 was one of the worst natural disasters to strike in Gujarat. It posed enormous challenges because of its magnitude, intensity and geographical spread for rescue, relief and rehabilitation. Were injured and over a million houses were damaged and destroyed. About 10,000 small and medium industrial units went out of production, affecting income and employment. Inspite of the immediate sense of shock, confusion, helplessness and grief, the government and the community rose to the occasion and quickly responded to the event. Soon after, a holistic and comprehensive reconstruction and rehabilitation programme was put in place. A new organization, the Gujarat State Disaster Management Authority was established. The Government of Gujarat also announced the Reconstruction and Rehabilitation Policy.

The Gujarat Earthquake Reconstruction Programme was designed to address the needs of the afected people comprehensively. It adopted a building back better approach, involved the community and encompassed a number of sectors such as housing physical infrastructure, social infrastructure (education and health), urban reconstruction, livelihood restoration, social rehabilitation and long term disaster risk reduction.

The reconstruction programme had the following objectives:

(i) Promoting sustainable recovery in disaster afected areas, and

(ii) Laying the foundation for sustainable disaster management capacity in Gujarat.

The phase-wise focus of the programme is summarised as follows:

(a) The short term focus of the reconstruction programme was to address the immediate needs such as temporary shelters before the onset of the monsoon, debris removal, repair of houses and public buildings and emergency repair of irrigation structures.

(b) The medium term objectives of the programme emphasised the repair and reconstruction of houses, public infrastructure, and social infrastructure and initiating eforts towards disaster mitigation and reduction.

(c) The long term objective of the reconstruction programme was further strengthening the capacity of government institutions and community towards disaster risk reduction (preparedness, response, mitigation and prevention) and implementation of risk transfer mechanism.

Some of the salient features of the Gujarat Reconstruction Programme are as follows:

(i) *Owner driven reconstruction:* The reconstruction of the houses was done by the owners themselves with technical assistance provided by the government. This involved minimum relocation and out of 215,255 houses that were reconstructed only 5720 houses were partially relocated. To provide technical guidance to the community and ensure that the newly built houses were hazard resistant, large number of engineers, architects and masons were trained and technical guidelines were developed. A third party audit mechanism was established to control quality.

(ii) *Housing insurance:* The Housing Insurance Programme was incorporated as a compulsory component for all G-5 houses and optional for houses of other categories. The insurance covered 14 types of risks for 10 years and the premium was fixed at Rs. 349.10 for an insured sum of Rs.1 lakh.

(iii) Urban reconstruction of all the four towns in Kutch ensured planning principles with improvement of basic services and urban environment.

(iv) A regulatory system for safe construction was strengthened and licensing of engineers and certification of masons were introduced.

(v) Mass awareness on disaster preparedness was undertaken to prepare the community to face similar future eventualities.

Tsunami (2004)

The Dec 26th 2004 Indian ocean tsunami caused extensive damage to the infrastructure including harbours, jetties, roads, bridges, power, telecom, hospitals, schools and other social sector buildings besides human loss of 9395 persons and 3,964 were missing after the disaster. The estimated loss in monetary terms including damage to property was reported at Rs. 11544.91 crore (Andhra Pradesh- Rs. 342.67 crore, Kerala- Rs. 2371.02 crore, Tamil Nadu- Rs. 4528.66 crore, Andman & Nicobar Islands Rs. 3836.56 and Puducherry – Rs. 466.00 crore).

In terms of housing, 86,688 houses were damaged, with 53,192 vulnerable to damage. Approximately 12000 hectares of agricultural land was damaged and 3000 hectares of land was rendered unusable due to salinity in the soil. A total 47 Fishing Landing Centres (FLC) got damaged and approximately 28000 boats were damaged. The loss assessed by respective state government may be seen at Table 2.

Table 2: Loss in Tsunami 2004, India

Items damaged	*TN*	*Kerala*	*AP*	*Puducherry*	*A&NI*	*Total*
Financial Loss						
(Rs. in crore)	4528.66	2371.02	342.67	466.00	3836.56	11544.91
Houses						
(i) Damaged	64976	3867	481	7567	9797	86688
(ii) Vulnerable	40248	11000	–	–	–	51248
Agricultural land (ha)	88451.72	2151	–	1145	8069	99816.72
Boats (nos.)	2727	3989	11394	7892	2065	28067
Roads (km)	1548.32	686	–	108	350.05	2692.37

It is not possible to prevent a tsunami. However, in some tsunami-prone countries, earthquake engineering measures have been taken to reduce the damage caused on shore.

(i) *Physical measures:* The State Governments and District Administration rose to the occasion in its search & rescue operation besides providing relief. The Central Government initiated relief operation by deploying 20,800 personnel of armed forces as well as Central Armed Police Forces in the afected States and UTs. It also send supports to Sri Lanka, Maldives and Indonesia. In all 881 relief camps were set-up and a total of 6,04,335 people were housed in these camps. About 12,735 tents were dispatched to the afected areas – mostly to A&N Islands. 64 special fights were operated between 27th Dec 2004 – 1st Jan 2005 to evacuate 6,318 stranded people including tourists in A&N Islands. In all 28,734 persons were rescued – 9950 in Kerala, 9284 in A&N Islands, and 9500 in TN including 1000 persons stranded at Vivekanand Memorial. 6.45 lakhs persons – Main Land (6.30 lakhs) and A&N Islands (0.15 lakhs) were moved to safer places.

(ii) *Financial measures:* Government of India made immediate release of Rs. 700 crore for the Tsunami afected States and UTs. An amount of Rs. 450 crore was released as an immediate assistance from the National Calamity Contingency Fund (NCCF) to the States of Tamil Nadu (Rs. 250 crore), Kerala (Rs. 100 crore) and Andhra Pradesh (Rs. 100 crore). In addition, an amount of ' 50 crore to Puducherry and Rs. 200 crore for Andaman & Nicobar Islands was also earmarked.

(iii) *Rajiv Gandhi rehabilitation package:* Government of India provided assistance to the Governments of Andhra Pradesh, Kerala, Tamil Nadu, and the Union Territories of Puducherry and Andaman & Nicobar Islands to implement the special package of ' 3644.05 crore named as "Rajiv Gandhi Rehabilitation Package for Tsunami afected areas" to provide assistance for immediate relief and response, revival of fishery and agriculture sectors, construction of temporary shelters and repair/ restoration of infrastructure. The amount of ' 700 crore released immediately from NCCF became a part of this 'Package'.

Long-Term Tsunami Reconstruction Programme (TRP)

After the completion of rescue and relief phase, the Government of India approved TRP at an estimated cost of Rs. 9870.25 crore which was to be implemented during 2005-06 to 2008-09. The GoI approved the revised TRP package, at an estimated cost of Rs. 9822.10 crore on 10.1.2007 comprising the following components:-

(i) Rs. 1776.62 crore under the Rajiv Gandhi Package.

(ii) Rs. 3332.43 crore through External Agencies viz World Bank, ADB and IFAD.

(iii) Rs. 4713.05 crore as Domestic Budgetary Support.

Status of rehabilitation measures taken up under TRP. The TRP includes reconstruction activities in five major sectors such as housing fisheries, agriculture and livelihoods, ports and jetties and roads and bridges, in addition to power, water and sewerage, social infrastructure and welfare, environmental and coastal protection and tourism. The prime objective of the Tsunami Rehabilitation Programme is to reconstruct damaged infrastructure with value addition and restore livelihood of the people. An amount of Rs. 4171.98 crore had been allocated for housing under TRP which is about 42.5% of the total outlay. The GoI while reviewing the progress of TRP on 11.2.2010 has further modified the outlay to Rs. 9381.96 crore (Rs. 6049.54 crore under ACA and Rs. 3332.42 crore under EAP). This includes an additional requirement of Rs. 108 crore for Puducherry and Rs. 138.30 crore for A&NI.

Kosi Calamity

The Kosi (known as "Kaushiki" in Sanskrit) is one of the most ancient rivers of India. The river is notorious for its vagaries and known to change its bed very often. During the last two centuries, the river has been changing its course in the westerly directions and it has laterally moved nearly 70 miles. On 18.08.2008 the Kosi river started eroding the spurs on the eastern efflux bundh 12 km. up stream of the Birpur barrage in Supaul district and breached the embankment. After the breach, the entire river spilled out and started flowing along a new course running straight down south. The course of the river was approximately 15 to 20 km wide and 150 km long north to south. The entire country side within this 3000 sq. kms. was totally devastated by the rapid surging flow of the river along its new course. Houses, schools, roads, dispensaries were all flooded and swept away. A total of 35 blocks, 407 panchayats and 980 villages in five districts with a total population of 33, 89, 000 fell along the new course of the river. Totally, 217 people and 868 cattle were killed and 3,38,986 houses were partly or fully damaged due to the catastrophe.

Immediate response

The afected areas had never experienced such a catastrophe and had not seen foods for the last 50 years, therefore they had inadequate arrangements to face the situation. The state administration deployed 1500 boats locally in addition to the 561 motor boats mobilised from NDRF, army, navy and other sources. About 12 helicopters carried out 314 sorties and air dropped about 1, 21, 892 packets of food, water and halogen tablets besides distribution of about 2, 39, 858 food packets by boats to the people in the afected areas.

The state government carried out one of the largest evacuation operations of about 9, 93, 992 persons ever organised in the country. About 5000 civilian personnel, 3500 police men, 35 columns of army, 4 columns of the navy, 850 personnel of NDRF, 1500 boats and 560 motor boats were deployed for the evacuation.

Mega Shelter Camps

The State Government set up 362 relief camps in the buildings of schools and colleges. At the peak of the disaster 4, 40,739 people were living in the camps. Self help groups were constituted to look after the preparation and distribution of meals. A special thrust was on women and newly born babies; clothes and utensils were given to each camp inmate as relief measures. Other features of the shelter are outlined below:

- A total of 3,750 temporary toilets constructed, 2,155 hand pumps installed in the camps, generators and solar lamps provided for lighting in the camps,
- Schools set up for the children in the camp and 56,304 children enrolled in these schools,
- Anganwadi Centres set up in each major camp,
- Skill development programmes initiated and training provided to willing persons in handicrafts and cottage industries,
- Health sub-centres set up in each camp with doctors on duty round the clock with provision for free medicines and camps were also covered by a mobile team. A total of 491 doctors and 1578 paramedical staff deployed on a daily basis. Maternity huts set up in relief camps and 183 deliveries reported in these maternity centres,
- A total of 108 ambulances were deployed.

Livestock

To cater to the afected livestock, 257 veterinary centres manned by 387 personnel were set up. As per the report 47,430 animals were kept in camps and 321630 animals were vaccinated.

Leh Cloudburst

A rare phenomenon, a rainfall of 12.8mm during the intervening night of 5/6th August 2010 coupled with cloud burst resulted in fash floods and mud slides causing havoc and large scale loss of life and public infrastructure/ private property particularly in Leh region. Besides the local population large numbers of tourists both Indian and foreign nationals, as well as labourers from outside the region who had gone there for earning a livelihood got trapped to face the most tragic and difficult circumstances.

Response

More than 6000 personnel of Army, Air Force, Border Roads Organization, National Disaster Response Force and Indo Tibetan Border Police were deployed along with rescue equipment to assist the civil administration in relief operations. Large quantities of relief material such as tents, blankets, tarpaulins, mattresses, food packets and bottled water were provided. Contributions from the charitable organisations and other sources were also sent. Apart from the medical teams available with army, CPMFs, state, etc.

one medical team consisting of 08 Doctors and 04 Nurses along with 10 quintals of emergent surgical/medical consumables were deployed in the afected area from Delhi. Additional medical supplies and medical equipments were sent to the afected areas. A total of 55 civil aircraft were operated and more than 8000 people were evacuated. The Air Force also carried out 226 sorties and airlifted 302 tonnes of relief material and equipments and 818 persons. Funds to the tune of ? 429.24 crore were available with the state government in their State Disaster Response Fund for undertaking immediate relief activities. The Prime Minister announced a rehabilitation package of? 125 crore.

Lesson Learnt

The gap in the response to the remote hilly area and the disaster being of unprecedented requires strengthening of the National Emergent Reserve and placing it at similar vulnerable areas for prompt relief. Besides there is an urgent need to strengthen the communication system i.e. multi modal system and create an awareness among people about the cloud burst and its consequences.

Mayapuri Radiation Exposure Delhi (2010)

The National Radiation Regulatory Authority, Atomic Energy Regulatory Board (AERB) received a message in the afternoon of 7th April, 2010 from Indraprastha Apollo Hospital, New Delhi that one person, aged 32 years, the owner of a scrap shop in Mayapuri Industrial Area, New Delhi had been admitted on 4th April, 2010 with symptoms of radiation exposure.

The Team of Atomic Energy Regulatory Board (AERB) visited the place immediately with radiation detection equipments and monitored the radiation levels at various positions near the scrap shop. They found that the particular shop as well as a couple of nearby shops had very high radiation fields. Next day, teams of Radiation Safety Experts from BARC, AERB & Narora Atomic Power Station were sent to Delhi with a wide range of radiation monitoring, detecting equipments and a lead fask to locate, identify, recover, safely secure and dispose radioactive sources.

The response team identified the radiation source as Cobalt-60, used mainly in industry for radiography and in teletherapy for cancer treatment. During the search operation, the team could locate, recover and secure eight sources of different intensities. These sources were placed in the lead shielded fask brought from Narora and sent for further examination and safe disposal. Subsequently the area was cleared for the public.

A radiation survey of scrap metal shops in neighbouring areas was carried out following the incident. It indicated elevated radiation levels in one more scrap shop about 500 m away from the ones where radiation sources were found earlier. A joint team consisting of AERB and National Disaster Response Force (NDRF) recovered two more radioactive sources from this shop. Both the sources were safely transferred to a shielding fask and transported back to Narora.

As a follow up to this incident, four joint teams of BARC, AERB and NDRF were formed and the surroundings of all remaining 800 shops in the market were scanned when the shops were closed on 14th April, 2010. The entire area was found to be free of elevated radiation fields except at the entrance of the market where the soil over a small patch was slightly contaminated. The contaminated soil showed Cobalt-60 contamination but of very low order. Subsequently, the contaminated soil up to a depth of few centimetres was removed to bring down the radiation field.

Constitution of a Working Group

In the backdrop of the discovery of radiation sources from the scrap in Mayapuri in New Delhi and also to minimise the possibility of such recurrences in future, NDMA constituted a working group headed by Shri B. Bhattacharjee, Member, NDMA to spell out the roles and responsibilities of various agencies in dealing with Radiological Emergencies.

REHABILITATION AND RECONSTRUCTION

Rehabilitation refers to the actions taken in the aftermath of a disaster to enable basic services to resume functioning, assist victims' self-help efforts to repair physical damage and community facilities, revive economic activities and provide support for the psychological and social well being of the survivors. It focuses on enabling the affected population to resume more-or-less normal (pre-disaster) patterns of life. It may be considered as a transitional phase between immediate relief and more major, long-term development.

Reconstruction refers to the full restoration of all services, and local infrastructure, replacement of damaged physical structures, the revitalisation of economy and the restoration of social and cultural life. Reconstruction must be fully integrated into long-term development plans, taking into account future disaster risks and possibilities to reduce such risks by incorporating appropriate measures. Damaged structures and services may not necessarily be restored in their previous form or location. It may include the replacement of any temporary arrangements established as part of emergency response or rehabilitation.

Sometimes, the term recovery is also used to embrace both activities. It should be remembered that rehabilitation and reconstruction actions do not always safeguard full recovery. It may take longer to return to 'normality' or, in some situations, recovery may never be possible. It is, therefore, not possible to suggest a 'model' time frame for rehabilitation, reconstruction or recovery as distinctive periods. The length of time required for rehabilitation and reconstruction depends on a large number of factors, including predisaster trends, the extent of damage, level of preparedness, availability of resources, administrative and legislative powers to act rapidly, and political stability and will to implement plans.

Furthermore, different sectors may vary in the time required to rehabilitate or reconstruct. For example, infrastructure requiring high levels of investment and sophisticated technology may take a very long time to fully rebuild to a higher standard. Similarly, economic setbacks due to a disaster can take time to recover from, and in some situations, a return to pre-disaster levels of production may never be possible. This will particularly apply where the disaster interrupted a key economic activity, thus allowing competitors (perhaps in other countries) the opportunity to intercept the market and hold onto it when recovery has been attained.

An example of this type of economic destruction could be where a cyclone has destroyed trees, such as coconut palms or banana trees that produce vital cash-crops It may take several years for them to grow again to pre-cyclone cropping levels. Thus authorities have to provide income support or alternative employment to the affected population during this period. The social and psychological recovery of the affected population are often assumed to be a community function and neglected in most post-disaster programmes.

Although this may be true for some societies, disasters can render some groups such as the elderly without an immediate family, orphans, single parents with young children more vulnerable due to a lack of adequate support. In the aftermath of a disaster family support systems can break down due to life losses, dislocation and migration of some members in search of work, food etc. These groups would need special social support to survive the impact of disaster. Similar to social disruption, the psychological trauma of losing relatives and friends, the shock of the disaster event can take much longer to heal than physical recovery.

It is, therefore, essential that social welfare and psychological support programmes are considered immediately after a disaster as an integral part of recovery programmes. This support should be provided not only for the affected public but also for the aid workers and the authorities operating in the disaster area as they can also become psychologically distressed from the event and working in difficult conditions.

Following are some important rehabilitation and reconstruction measures typically required for post-disaster situations:

Nature of the Disaster

Each disaster results in a different type of damage. However, on the basis of past events the sectors that will be at risk to a particular disaster can be predicted with some accuracy. For example, earthquakes often result in high physical damage to infrastructure and buildings and high winds can destroy both buildings and utilities above ground such as power lines. Floods, on the other hand, can be damaging for agricultural land and fisheries in rural areas which would not be affected by earthquake impact.

Planning for rehabilitation and reconstruction should therefore relate to the specific damage that results from a disaster and prioritise inputs to assist the rapid recovery of the affected population. For example, after a rural flood, replacing the lost livestock or seeds for the next planting season might be a higher priority for rural agriculturists than the rebuilding of their homes. Following the 1992 floods in Pakistan much of the government grants allocated for damaged houses were used by the communities to buy animals, fodder and seeds.

While physical damage may vary from one type of disaster to another, all major disasters have a psychological impact on the affected population as well as disrupting economic and social life of the survivors. In addition, all major disasters have significant political consequences which have sometimes resulted in the weakening of authorities, or the strengthening of weak ones as a result of their positive handling of the recovery process. Therefore, rehabilitation and reconstruction programmes should not only be seen as a way of replacing what is tangible but must be planned to strengthen what is not immediately visible, that is, the administrative, social and economic systems as well as the psychological well being of the people involved.

Damage Scale

The scale and location of the disaster damage are critical in understanding the type of inputs required for rehabilitation and reconstruction. The ratio of what is lost or damaged to what has survived influences the nature of recovery. A localised event which affects a relatively limited area in a country, for example an earthquake in a city, needs to be treated in a different manner than a situation where the whole country might be affected by a devastating event for example a hurricane which hits a small island.

In a large country it is likely that there will be adequate surviving material and human resources, and facilities to rehabilitate the situation whereas for a small country the same event may result in the loss of most facilities and resources that are needed for rehabilitation and reconstruction. A thorough evaluation of the local and national resources is essential before determining what is needed to be provided from outside.

Location

Location of a disaster is critical in understanding the sectors affected and the rehabilitation and reconstruction implications of the event. The sectors that are vulnerable to the same type of disaster vary from one area to another. While psychological needs may not vary greatly in relation to location for the same type of event, social, economic and physical damage can display a different pattern in urban and rural areas.

Rural areas are likely to have less infrastructure and concentration of administrative, commercial and industrial facilities but more agriculture and livestock than urban centers. The priorities for recovery and reconstruction inputs clearly need to reflect this difference. For example, replacing the livestock, agricultural tools and seeds after a rural flood will often be seen as vital for rapid recovery by the affected population. Whereas in an urban flood, rehabilitation of the damaged infrastructure will be essential for renewed functioning of the economy.

As most urban activities depend on the availability of power supplies, communication facilities and transport. However, it should be remembered that in rural areas if the few infrastructure and facilities such as a health post or a road are damaged, rehabilitation and reconstruction can be delayed since alternatives would not be readily available. Under such circumstances rehabilitation of the critical rural facilities should be considered as a high priority for the rapid recovery of the affected population.

For example, repair of access roads to markets or health posts might be a higher priority for the rural communities than reconstruction of their houses. The latter may be possible to rebuilt by their own resources but infrastructure will require investment, machinery etc. which are not easily available to rural communities. Special problems that may arise in some urban disasters, especially in developing countries, lie in the concentration of administrative, political, commercial and cultural facilities in the cities, often in the capital.

Heavy losses in a major city, therefore, can have a negative impact on the capacity for rapid decision making and long-term resources which are much needed for rapid recovery. Consequently, assessing the capacities of public and private institutions following a disaster and rebuilding or supporting them where they are inadequate should be considered before moving into other aspects of reconstruction planning.

Location of the disaster also determines the possibility of secondary effects. For example, heavy rainfall and earthquakes in areas with steep slopes can trigger land slides. Damage to dams, bridges and industrial plants by natural events may lead to future disasters. Reconstruction and relocation decisions need to incorporate such secondary risks that may arise from the possible location of the event These potential threats need to be evaluated especially in planning for physical rehabilitation and reconstruction projects. Failure to do so may result in reducing one risk at the cost of creating another one.

Another critical issue in relation to the location of a disaster is the limited attention that might be given to some affected areas vis-a-vis others which attract disproportionate support. This may be due to a number of factors. Sometimes selective media coverage shapes the nature of subsequent support. It is the big city in relation to small villages, or, the center of the event as opposed to the peripheries that receive the most attention even at times when there are only a few survivors.

The Armero volcanic mud-flow in Colombia is a classical example of this situation where the relocated town was built much larger than was needed for the very few survivors to benefit from the reconstruction. More often, however, it is the areas where ethnically, politically, economically or socially marginalised communities live that are overlooked. As these groups may not always be in a position to effectively articulate their needs, rehabilitation and reconstruction programmes can easily neglect them as beneficiaries.

Sectors Affected

Rehabilitation and especially reconstruction often refer to the repair and rebuilding of the physical damage. Authorities and donors focus on the provision of housing, clinics, schools and eventually rebuilding of the infrastructure.

The concentration on physical reconstruction is essential for a return to normality and is demanded by society. It is also an easily quantifiable and visible achievement for the authorities and donors. Social, psychological, cultural and even economic recovery is less tangible for government, agency or donor investment and is seen in most cases at the responsibility of the community. A comprehensive rehabilitation and reconstruction plan should take into consideration both physical and non-physical needs of the communities.

Failing to address reconstruction in its complexity can have adverse consequences-firstly it may result in large investment on buildings without the necessary inputs to help the victims to become psychologically fit, socially coherent and economically self-sustained. Secondly, it is important to recognise the links between physical and socio/psychological recovery. For example, the process of disaster victims being active in their own physical rebuilding can have an important economical and therapeutic value. Thus double dividends may result from their active involvement in physical rebuilding.

Rehabilitation and reconstruction programmes that encourage the affected population to act together in their own interest can also have psychological benefit as well as reducing dependency on external inputs. The sectors that need rehabilitation and reconstruction inputs relate to the disaster type and the elements that are at risk. A comprehensive correlation of these in the DMTP module, *Vulnerability and Risk Assessment*. The following list covers the sectors that can be vulnerable to disaster impact, and which, therefore, will require rehabilitation and reconstruction inputs.

— Buildings
— Infrastructure
— Economic assets (including formal and formal commercial sectors, industrial and agricultural activities etc.)
— Administrative and political
— Psychological
— Cultural
— Social
— Environmental

Losses

Damage and disruption to the above sectors will result in a number of tangible or direct and intangible or consequential losses. The aim of rehabilitation is initially to replace or normalise these losses and eventually to reconstruct them, if possible, to a higher standard than existed before.

Assessment of Needs

The assessment of needs that will arise from immediate and consequential losses will help to prioritise the rehabilitation and reconstruction actions. Initial assessment of a disaster naturally focuses on emergency needs, however, the losses that occur in each sector correspond to a wide range of needs to be met by the local communities, various ministries, local authority departments, NGOs and sometimes international donors and agencies. From the start of the emergency onwards, each of these groups will be making jointly, or separately, some assessment of the situation initially for relief response and eventually for rehabilitation and reconstruction decisions.

Conflict of opinions and difference of perceptions on what is needed in what priority will be all too common. Creating a clear picture of the situation for decision making involves collecting reliable information on each sector by experienced staff. It also requires consultation with the affected communities and their leaders in order to establish their perceptions and priorities. The critical issues which relate to rehabilitation and reconstruction are:

— Monitor the situation in order to make decisions for the long-term inputs which may sometimes be based on early, fragmentary assessment of the situation. Continuous monitoring of the changes as the situation develops is essential in order to revise the decisions. For example shelter needs may increase due to aftershocks, the long stay of flood water on the ground or by climatic changes such as the onset of monsoon rains. Equally, availability of building stock and migration to other areas can reduce this need.

— Balance psychological, social and economic needs with physical ones. High physical damage may distort the focus of attention to the neglect of other less tangible needs.

— Recognise that communities are not homogenous. Some groups such as the politically well-connected or the economically better off can be more vocal in voicing their needs. Additional assessment may be necessary to cover the specific needs of the disadvantaged groups: the elderly, children, single headed families, physical or mentally handicapped, the very poor, minorities etc. Generalised response targeting the average surviving family may leave out those most in need of support.

— Consider the less obvious needs. They may be essential in meeting the high investment inputs. For example, supporting administration, creating work for the disaster victims can speed up physical recovery.

— Distinguish needs from wants. Disasters can increase expectations at all levels: communities from the authorities, local government from the central government, national governments from the international donors. Rank the needs and prioritise the necessary inputs to improve the conditions for the worst affected and the least able groups Identify the capacities and resources of the affected population. Do not assume that they are passive victims and aim to strengthen what is available for increased self reliance. This also applies to the strengthening of the local authorities and the national bodies.

— Identify the un-met needs at each stage of decision making. As the situation develops conditions, problems and availability of resources change.

— Ensure that the needs in all sectors and affected areas are assessed. There is often a tendency to focus on the worst affected areas, the most tangible or easily quantifiable damage. Equally, the make up of the assessment team or the bias of an agency can create a distorted picture of needs by highlighting the selected sectors where they have expertise.

— Identify the critical needs upon which other sectors ma depend for recovery. Business and industry cannot function without communication, transport and energy facilities; provision of health facilities will be meaningless without available staff, medicine and equipment; physical reconstruction requires production of construction materials; rural areas depend on market centers and vice versa.

— Ensure that the assessment also covers what is not needed. Provisions that are not needed or are inappropriate can have an adverse effect on the recovery process. It is therefore essential that the assessment highlights what is locally available or manageable and hence should not be provided, as well as stating what will not be socially economically, or culturally appropriate.

Available Resources

Balancing needs with resources is critical at stages of post-disaster activities. While the relief period may attract large national and international inputs, rehabilitation and reconstruction may not benefit from such high levels of attention. Prioritisation of investment becomes critical where monetary resources are limited and sectoral needs are too many to meet. In disasters of considerable magnitude, not only various sectors but also a large number of counties, municipalities or settlements are often competing for the same funds and for the attention of the same authorities and expertise.

Strong community or administrative leadership is critical at this stage in marshaling national and international support. Local administrative preparedness plans and general capacity, together with technical mechanisms that are in place before the disaster, usually contribute significantly to expeditious recovery. Although some dependence on external resources (e.g. communities on local authorities, national governments on international donors) is to be expected after a large scale disaster, excessive dependence can cause loss of local control and delays in recovery.

Small communities that have sustained heavy damage are most likely to become dependent on external inputs of this kind. In such circumstances resources should be channelled to enhance local capacities to cope with the effects of disasters and to maximise community self-reliance. Efforts should not duplicate or provide what can be locally available or undertaken. Consultation with the local agencies and the affected population is essential in this process as the Donor's or the authorities perception of what is critical and essential may differ significantly from local perceptions.

In this respect, the role of external assistance should be to identify strengths and bottlenecks in order to mobilise the necessary resources that are not available and cannot be generated at the local or national level. The bottlenecks for speedy recovery vary greatly from country to country, area to area. On the basis of past examples, however, hold-ups may occur in the supply of:

Funds and the appropriate mechanisms for channelling them to the survivors and the necessary sectors. Large scales disasters often create inflation, balance of payment problems, fiscal expenditure increases and a decrease in monetary reserves. Interruption to economic activities, a decline in tourism in some countries, and delays to new development programmes are contributing factors. Public savings, private sector investment, credit and loans by commercial banks and government, international funds, special taxation will be necessary to resolve this bottleneck.

Revolving funds, grants and credit as opposed to gifts, income generating investments will be more appropriate forms of funding for long-term sustainability of programmes. Repayment capacity of the recipients and limitations of the very poor in benefiting from funds need special attention. Writing-off loans in agriculture, stock breeding and commerce in high damage areas can revitalise critical economies more rapidly.

Materials for construction of temporary as well as permanent buildings, infrastructure, health provisions etc. Need for vast quantities of construction material and sometimes for medicaments and equipment coupled with possible reduction in production and transportation problems can create the bottleneck. New safety standards in construction and infrastructure may also require materials that are not readily available in the affected area or country. Rehabilitation and reconstruction plans should consider the availability of material goods as an integral part of the assessment process.

Where possible, preference should be to use locally or regionally available materials. If necessary, loans and grants should be arranged for this purpose to boost local manufacturing capacity. This will not only reduce the cost of transport and possibly of the materials but also support economic recovery. In this option, management of production and distribution and quality control may become problematic and will require effective organisational arrangements. Introduction of new materials and imports from international markets should be limited to sophisticated construction or infrastructure as they may suppress national markets and, in the long term, create maintenance and supply problems. Supplies from external markets can sometimes be useful to control the increase in prices due to short supply or black-marketing.

Equipment and tools for the clearance of debris, repair and reconstruction, transportation of goods, revitalisation of health facilities, agriculture, industry, etc. Both simple and sophisticated equipment and tools will be in short supply throughout all sectors that suffer damage due to losses as well as increased demand to rehabilitate and reconstruct. Supply of simple tools for digging, cutting, cultivating etc., as well as credit to purchase them, will increase self-reliance at the local level.

A plan must be made to appraise availability of equipment in the hands of various ministries, local authorities and the private sector. Co-ordination and sharing of these resources and the Prioritisation of their use will improve effectiveness. Mandates for their acquisition and use during the reconstruction period must be integrated into preparedness plans.

Energy and power sources required for transport, communications, industrial production and functioning of the critical facilities. Damage to infrastructure and power plants can bring most sectors to a halt. Shortage of emergency and power supplies can greatly delay rehabilitation and reconstruction activities. For example, after the earthquake in Armenia a shortage of fuel created problems at all stages from airlift of relief goods to production and transport of construction materials.

Rapid restoration of power plants can partly alleviate the situation where such energy resources are available. If the problem is likely to extend over a long period of time, reliance on local materials and resources and facilitating production close to where it is needed will be the most realistic approach. Dependence on external support will be difficult to sustain throughout the reconstruction time.

Land to build on may not be available or may be too expensive. Land is likely to become a scarce resource where the affected communities were landless or were renters prior to the disaster. Land will also be scarce where usable land has been destroyed through landslides, volcanic eruption or flood erosion, where population density needs to be reduced in the damaged area as a mitigation measure or where relocation becomes inevitable due to the high risks involved. Often safe land may not be easily available. Such was the case in China after the floods in Anhui Province in 1991 and in Bangladesh following the cyclones of 1970 and 1989.

Building embankments and raising the level of ground can be solutions but they are labour intensive and, in the long run, may be rendered ineffective. Safeguarding land tenure and reducing population densities, especially in expensive urban areas, are politically contentious and often difficult to achieve. Releasing government and local public land, and providing emergency powers to expropriate private land can partly alleviate the pressure.

Human resources to plan, co-ordinate and implement rehabilitation or reconstruction. In large scale damaging events both administrative/ technical staff and skilled/unskilled labour will be in short supply. High casualties also play a role in this shortage. At the local level, loss of able bodied members of families may reduce the capacity to rebuild and recover. Casualties among the administrative and technical staff can delay decision-making and response. The volume of work can also be difficult to meet with existing human resources.

In Mexico City, rapid damage survey required large numbers of experienced technical staff which were not immediately available. As a result the quality of data collected varied greatly. External support of specialised technicians, health staff, etc., are often on offer during the rehabilitation phase. Reconstruction, on the other hand, takes a long time and if it goes slowly enough, skills can be developed internally through training and education. This was one reason why, after the war in Iran, some defended a more gradual process of reconstruction. As for many other aspects of rehabilitation and reconstruction, however, priority for utilising human resources should be given to the local population from the affected area and only the expertise where there are identified and essential gaps should be provided from other sources.

Adequate and relevant information to act upon. Reliable qualitative and quantitative information on damage, losses, needs, local national and international resources, futures risks, and development programmes are a prerequisite for decision making and planning. These will affect the scale, shape and timing of rehabilitation and reconstruction activities. While most information will be collected sector by sector, a sufficiently high level central system can improve quality control, co-ordination and dissemination of the data. Standardised formats for data collection and reporting, developing procedures and training for data collection and handling, creation of essential information bases will be a worthwhile investment in high risk areas.

Administrative structures and organisations to carry out rehabilitation and reconstruction activities. Local administrative and technical mechanisms, community groups and NGOs in place before the disaster contribute significantly to expeditious recovery. While disasters can act as a catalyst to create cohesion in some situations, communities and administrative systems that have been muddling along before the disaster hit are very much at a disadvantage in coping with massive disaster-related demands. Besides, most government departments are so rigidly staffed that undertaking extra post-disaster activities over an extended period of time may become difficult.

The shedding of some 'normal role' activities, and training and employment of extra staff can reduce the pressure. Arrangements with other government departments for staff support and sub-contracting the private sector can also be effective in pulling in extra human resources. NGOs and voluntary groups can equally complement or supplement public sector efforts and strengthen community self-reliance. However, it should be remembered that in most situations the bulk of long-term reconstruction inevitably falls on the public sector.

Pre-disaster plans to co-ordinate inter-agency and interorganisational relationships, creation of a centralised rehabilitation and reconstruction committee and integration of recovery planning into preparedness plans can improve effectiveness of rehabilitation and reconstruction response. Effective inter-agency and government collaboration has to be ensured and coordinated for the sharing of resources and avoiding duplication.

Political Commitment

Recovery from major disaster events necessitate large quantities of material and human resources and good organisational/institutional capacity. Although there may be various national and international organisations to support the local population in recovering from the impact of the event much of the responsibility for rehabilitation and reconstruction will fall on the government of the country concerned. Besides, effective recovery response very much depends on the authorities capacity to plan and coordinate the efforts of the various groups involved in this process.

Facilitating all these actions requires political commitment of the government for the benefit of the disaster stricken areas. However, channelling of funds, allocating resources of all kinds, providing services and opportunities for recovery often happens in a political context. Electoral pressures and local power structures may become instrumental in shaping the nature of reconstruction. While most governments in the immediate aftermath of a disaster declare their intentions of making up for all losses, with the progress of time, they can easily lose the initial momentum.

As media attention drops, the public loses faith in receiving support and the authorities shift their focus on other issues. Recovery will be delayed. In some situations such as civil conflict there may not be real commitment to begin with. The speed and effectiveness of recovery, therefore, is as much a political issue as it is a matter of resources. In this respect, the nature of rehabilitation and reconstruction planning will be greatly shaped by the level of political commitment and its sustainability throughout the process.

In terms of timing, Disaster Recovery relative to rehabilitation and reconstruction passes through five stages. The following matrix gives a rough indication of which actors might participate in a given stage. However, situations are all different. Therefore, those who plan recovery will need to develop their own 'role casting operation' to make certain that:

- all available 'actors' are involved,
- qualified 'actors' are given appropriate tasks,
- for each task there is clear definition of authority, resources, accountability,
- actors are co-ordinated by a designated focal point.

Mitigation into Reconstruction

Ideally, reconstruction should aim to build to a better standard than existed before. Any actions to improve the pre-disaster conditions can help to reduce disaster risk and mitigate the damage of future events. There are several structural and non-structural mitigation measures. Those that are likely to be implemented or improved in reconstruction are explained below.

- Construction codes to protect buildings and infrastructure are almost always introduced after major disasters. While post-disaster reconstruction may be a good period in which to establish codes, problems may arise in relation to their enforcement and the time taken to develop them. Full investigation of structural damage (and in the case of earthquakes, micro-zonation studies), can take a very long time and slow down reconstruction. Many people start rebuilding and repairing within weeks of the event. An interim emergency code and standard for repair can speed up the process and protect reconstruction and repair of damaged buildings until codes are revised for future construction. However, in some situations emergency codes may in the long-term become the norm.

Supervision and enforcement of codes in the long run can also be difficult. In most developing countries the system can easily be corrupted due to the loopholes in the legislation, lack of trained inspectors, the extra cost involved in protective measures and decline in public awareness of risk as the disaster fades from memory. Rural areas and unauthorised buildings such as squatter settlements often escape code enforcement since they may not come under the control of any jurisdiction. Codes alone will be of little use to ensure higher standards, unless they are supported by increased public awareness for self-control, incentives to implement them and the economic means to pay for improvements. Mitigation planning should therefore recognise this fact and develop measures that are affordable and achievable by the groups who have the least knowledge and the means.

— Land-use changes and zoning are easier to introduce where levels of damage are high. Reduction of densities and change of use during reconstruction in high risk areas can contribute to mitigation. In densely populated urban areas, clearance of damaged building for more open areas and parks, though expensive, can not only reduce future risks but provide areas for evacuation and erection of emergency shelters in a future disaster. Examples of such mitigation measures are; the building of schools on highest ground as evacuation centers during floods in Anhui Province of China in 1991, increasing park areas in Skopje after the 1963 earthquake in the most dangerous part of the city subject to river flooding and maximum seismic ground movement due to alluvial soil.

The replanning of Lisbon after the 1755 earthquake and Skopje in 1963 represent examples of major reconstruction efforts that incorporated many urban design principles for mitigation, including wide streets and increased open space. Obviously such grand change are not always possible or successful. Lack of political will, pressure groups with interest in land and public resistance to change can counteract these measures. Where damage is limited, pre-disaster land use plans will be more difficult to alter, even though the future risk may be high.

Property owners will fear that the value of their land or buildings will be reduced and that business will no longer be profitable. Authorities will also be more reluctant to divert resources into major alterations. Groups who live on marginalised land will benefit very little from any of the above measures even when they are implemented. As these groups lead their lives in very vulnerable conditions they are at highest risk from disasters and the least able to benefit from any mitigation measures that might be introduced after an event. Sometimes disasters can provide opportunities that should be utilised to the benefit of these groups.

Land reforms, tenure or title-deeds for land and property, grants and credit schemes may become possible in the post-disaster situation. Disaster mitigation for the marginalised, therefore, should be addressed in a political, economic and social context, otherwise such groups who do not have a voice themselves may be left out of any provisions.

- Decentralisation of facilities such as administration, health, industry, infrastructure and communications is more likely to be implemented during reconstruction after a major disaster. While this measure safeguards survival of some parts of any system if facilities are concentrated in a high risk area, the management practicality and cost of dispersed services have to be carefully balanced with their level of risk. Maintaining a diversity of locations in agriculture and food crops can also minimise the damage to rural economies. This has been put into practice at the local level in Fiji where farmers work land in more than one location.
- Diversification of economy during reconstruction of damaged industry and rehabilitation of agriculture can significantly mitigate losses and speed up recovery in future disasters. Reliance on one type of economy such as tourism, manufacturing, fishing or agriculture can create significant problems without alternatives to fall back on. Political will, public acceptance and international assistance will be more readily

available to achieve diversification during reconstruction than pre-disaster conditions.

Introduction of new seed types and plantation patterns can increase crop resistance and improve yields. In certain instances this may also help to alter plantation and harvest time to avoid damage from seasonal disaster, such as floods and hurricanes. Where applicable, activities such as stock breeding, poultry and beehive keeping, crafts etc., can provide an extra income if agriculture fails and cannot be restored rapidly.

Post-disaster reconstruction can influence development programmes both positively and negatively. Similarly, the pre-disaster level of development in a country will have a bearing upon the success of recovery and reconstruction. Past examples prove that in areas of low pre-disaster development, recovery will be slow or, sometimes, can never be achieved. Delays in reconstruction will also decrease public and private investments, divert resources away from development activities to sustaining rehabilitation over an extended period of time.

Productive capital takes a particularly long time to replace in the case of agriculture and stock breeding, which may result in migration from the disaster stricken area. Reduced industrial output, on the other hand, can lead to wage losses, unemployment and disruption of dependent economic activities. While loans and subsidies can act as emergency economic measures, reconstruction programmes need to be planned with close consideration of the likely developmental status of the affected area.

Since disasters often hit the least developed areas and the most disadvantaged groups hardest, rehabilitation and reconstruction programmes should also aim to change the vulnerable conditions for the high risk population through development programmes. These conditions can be much more deep rooted than they seem on the surface when revealed by disaster, such as lack of access to information, limited economic means to maintain safety, environmental degradation, lack of social networks or limited political power.

Conventional preparedness plans often include stockpiling of food, shelter, medicine, tools etc. for emergency and rehabilitation needs. Increasingly, however, the advantages of incorporating reconstruction needs into preparedness plans is becoming obvious. This has several implications that can improve the speed and effectiveness of rehabilitation and reconstruction efforts. These plans can include:

- Assessment of hazard, risks and vulnerability, including both physical and human, identification of possible future problems and anticipation of the location, scale and nature of rehabilitation and reconstruction needs.
- Improved standards and planning of data collection at the local level and dissemination of damage survey and needs assessment.
- Plans for evacuation and sheltering of affected people and accommodating health, educational and administrative facilities until reconstruction is completed.
- Resource inventories to meet rehabilitation and reconstruction needs, including community capacities and resources.
- Training and education to improve human resources, especially at the local level for rehabilitation and a registry of specialised personnel to be deployed, e.g. in health, psychological support, shelter, water, sanitation etc.
- Allocation of responsibilities for rehabilitation and reconstruction at all levels, definition of roles and responsibilities of the local and national organisations.
- Legislation for co-ordination of sectors, NGOs international assistance during rehabilitation and reconstruction; a clear structure for decision making.
- Legislation and decrees to expropriate land, change land use, generate and channel funds for reconstruction; codes, standards and procedures for repair, urban plans.
- Social and economic surveys to identify the community profile, living standards, repayment capacity, expected levels of local coping.
- Procedures and methods for the identification of beneficiaries.
- Strengthening of channels for local participation and self-reliance such as agricultural and housing co-operatives which may become useful institutions to operate through rehabilitation and reconstruction.

Emergency Relief

Although emergency relief is a distinctive stage of post-disaster activities, many of the actions and decisions of this period can influence later stages. Extended external relief assistance can undermine local and national coping capacity and create dependency. For example, food aid following a typhoon in Fiji might meet short term food needs, but if the traditional coping mechanisms are underestimated and under used the communities ability to feed itself may be damaged. Any relief assistance, therefore, should balance relieving of immediate pressure on the communities with support for local coping for rapid recovery.

Large scale damaging events, often with pressures from the media, result in large amounts of international relief which leaves limited resources for the long-term recovery and rehabilitation. Continuity of support by agencies and donor governments beyond relief needs to be considered at early stages of allocating funds and other resources in a more balanced way. Articulation of rehabilitation and reconstruction needs into relief appeals and ways of integrating relief and long-term assistance also need to be explored.

While assessment of damage, needs and resources need to be specific and prioritised for the task at hand, i.e. relief, often rehabilitation and reconstruction decisions are based on these early data. This is partly due to the cost and time it takes to collect data and to meet the public demand to act rapidly. Ideally, it is necessary to monitor the changing needs as the situation develops. However, this may not be the case after most disasters. This common pattern needs to be recognised. Therefore, the drawbacks of early disaster assessment and the need to maximise the initial data collection must be taken into account in the planning of rehabilitation and reconstruction.

During the early stages of disaster response it is important to plan the co-ordination of data collection, multi-disciplinary assessment teams, and data generation for later phases. This will improve the quality and effectiveness of early information for rapid rehabilitation and reconstruction decisions. However, it should be remembered that as conditions change, decisions need to be modified in light of updated information. For example, after a major earthquake the number of homeless is often calculated in relation to damaged or destroyed buildings.

However, due to the fear of after shocks, the public may refuse to go back to their surviving homes, which will increase the need for shelter provision beyond the initial assessment. While it is important to recognise patterns from early diagnostic indicators for rapid response, decisions to effect long-term actions should not be taken in the haste of relief operations. Decisions such as relocation or provision of temporary shelters require careful examination of their long-term implications and consultation with the communities. There are many examples of temporary shelter provision as a response to an early identified need which eventually became permanent at great cost and often in wrong locations. Similarly, medical programmes or food distribution should not be prolonged without monitoring of the changes at the local level.

Dilemmas and Alternatives

There are many dilemmas that decision makers face in planning for rehabilitation and reconstruction. Each set of actors involved in the process, such as the central government, local authorities, various sectors, a large variety of professionals, donors, NGOs and different segments of the community, is likely to have different priorities and perceptions and subsequently would like to act according to their own preferences. There are always alternatives, and before a decision is made on a course of action their short-comings, advantages and long-term implications need to be evaluated.

Failure to recognise these conflicts and alternatives can create resistance by one group or the other and can ultimately hinder the progress of decision making. Some of the likely dilemmas and alternatives in rehabilitation and reconstruction planning cover the following issues.

Rapid Damage Survey versus Accurate Technical Surveys: A rapid damage survey is essential in defining and prioritising the rehabilitation needs. It also helps to reduce eventual distortions that may occur in the scale of damage. However, initial surveys may not involve the necessary range of expertise to accurately define the losses. Consequential losses from damage to agriculture or business premises may require evaluation by economists; accurate definition of building damage require inspection by structural engineers.

Detailed damage assessment can also help to determine the causes of damage, and the sources of risks and vulnerability. As this level of information becomes available, planning tasks can be more precisely defined. The dilemmas concerning detailed technical surveys usually relate to the time it takes to complete the surveys, and the appropriateness of this information for the user.

Repairs versus Rebuilding: Restoration of services and lifelines through repairs after a major disaster is a high priority as rebuilding can be delayed considerably an requires high levels of investment, and sometimes technology. Quick repair of buildings, especially domestic buildings, on the other hand, is usually discouraged by the authorities who prefer detailed technical inspection, improved codes and identifying the safety of land. The dilemma is the trade off between rapid repair of rebuilding to higher standards, which may take longer to plan. Quick repairs, however, can alleviate some of the need for temporary housing and public facilities.

In fact, domestic repairs are often carried out by individuals if decisions are delayed. Training, technical and material support to families and builders can be effective in improving safety as mistakes are often carried over into repairs. This will be particularly useful in marginalised settlements and rural areas as they will have limited access to technical expertise. Rapid assessment of areas where repairs can move ahead without engineering evaluation, emergency codes and streamlined procedures to issue building permits, should be considered as alternatives to facilitate rapid reconstruction.

Safety Standards versus Rapid Reconstruction: Evaluation of the causes of losses, risks and vulnerabilities after a major disaster can be complicated, expensive and time consuming. Yet they are essential for improving the safety standards against future damaging events. Lack of safe land to build on and setting new safety standards can equally delay reconstruction decisions. Without security of land and tenure it will also be wrong to expect people to invest in safety. Pre-disaster planning for post-disaster reconstruction must address land use issues in advance.

Existing general information can be useful in identifying where reconstruction can begin without further studies. Phasing in decisions and prioritising areas for different safety standards can help to start reconstruction. For example, certain sectors or parts of a damaged settlement can be reconstructed more rapidly while others may need further investigation and planning. It should also be remembered that the speed of recovery is not solely a technical problem. Control of resources by influential local interest groups, limited institutional and economic capacity of the less powerful, political preferences of some authorities for some areas or groups may all result in different speeds of recovery, sometimes even in the same neighbourhood.

Relocation versus Reconstruction: This is a major dilemma that decision makers have to resolve after most disasters. The idea of starting afresh is assumed to resolve all the inherent problems attached to rebuilding in a vulnerable place and/or a damaged environment. However, past experiences reveal that there are several reasons why this option may not be desired by the communities or successful in the long run:

— Safer land is often unavailable.

— The vulnerable site may also be essential for the economic livelihood of the communities, such as flood plains or fertile volcanic ash areas; tourism or fishing etc. Proximity to work and markets can be critical for those with limited economic alternatives. In other words, the benefits of the original site may outweigh the risks.

— Cultural, symbolic and historical value of the damaged site to the nation or the inhabitants cannot be easily transferable to a new site.

— Attachment to the place, neighbors, friends may be more important than safety.

— Relocation requires substantial investment in infrastructure.

— Relocating a community or a settlement can affect local and regional balances negatively; for example, relocation of a market town may create problems of transport etc. for villages to sell their products.

Relocation may be desirable in some specific situations where:

— The proposed area is sufficiently close to the existing settlement to enable livelihood patterns to be retained.

— The original area is under frequent threat of damaging events with high losses.

— Risk reduction measures are too costly and difficult to implement for the area.

— Psychological impact of the event associated with the original site might be too strong on the community.

— The area has been under considerable decline before the disaster, for example, due to environmental degradation, pollution, economic changes etc.

Participation versus Rapid Response: Public participation is essential in planning for reconstruction. Often this is seen by the authorities as a lengthy process. Where this has happened, such as in the reconstruction after the Friuli and Mexico City earthquakes, it took time and organisational capacity, but the resulting reconstruction was widely accepted and successful. Rapid reconstruction at the expense of public participation may have an initial inertia but can result in delays in the process of rebuilding due to public opposition or apathy.

Planning for reconstruction and actual reconstruction may require international and central government support but ultimately they are local functions. Positive interactions among decision makers, local authorities and affected communities increase the chances that plans will be carried out.

Special Organisation versus Existing Organisation: A wide range of organisational structures for rehabilitation and reconstruction have been used after major disasters. Existing organisations often have the staff and resources but may not have the procedures to act rapidly. Emergency powers granted to existing institutions can expedite decisions concerning rapid rehabilitation. Reconstruction on the other hand can take a long time and requires a clear structure, resources and authority to oversee the work. Sometimes one agency, department or ministry can be designated with support from others. However, more often some new organisation is needed to plan and manage rebuilding.

The dilemma is that the existing organisations will have staff and other resources which a new organisation has to create. But the new organisation will have the special authority and power to handle reconstruction more independently and rapidly. A further problem with the creation of a new organisation is that pre-disaster collaboration and coordination of various groups and institutions for better rehabilitation and reconstruction preparedness will be limited. Ultimately, the choice will depend on the specific conditions in each country and in each situation.

The critical issues in any organisational structure will be the co-ordination of all relevant agencies and institutions and the mobilisation of resources. A high level Rehabilitation and Reconstruction Commission (e.g. in the Prime Minister's Office) can be effective. It should also be remembered that in some special situations such as conflict-induced disasters or where loss of life among the officials is high there may be a need for rebuilding the capacities of necessary institutions.

Public versus Private Investment: Public funds are usually available for rehabilitation and rebuilding of public facilities, but they can also extend into supporting rehabilitation of the economy and domestic losses such as buildings or assets. However, public investment alone is never sufficient to bring about full recovery nor does it necessarily help to develop an effective strategy for rebuilding. Private investment is more likely to happen in areas which are economically strong and are not perceived as high risk.

International and public inputs into economic recovery can create confidence for private investors to invest in rebuilding. Such funds can also be useful as loans to pay for reconstruction to be recovered eventually. Even in centrally controlled economies and with paternalistic governments, total reliance on public funds may delay recovery considerably. In fact, such situations may raise expectation, create dependency and bring private investment to a complete halt. Furthermore, heavy government or international assistance may delay or reduce the willingness to take self-help actions.

Physical Reconstruction versus Economic Rehabilitation: Governments face a dilemma following any disaster that causes extensive damage to both the local economy and to the physical environment. Both demands require immediate attention and the deployment of extensive resources. In a rich country the two sectors are likely to be fully addressed in parallel, but in a poor country the overwhelming financial and administrative burden may be such that choices have to be made about which should have priority attention and at what stage in the reconstruction process.

There is a growing awareness by many governments and international funders of the need to regenerate damaged economy—whether agricultural or industrial—as rapidly as possible. The logic is that if the damaged economy can get back on its feet rapidly then this can be one of the 'motors' to drive physical rebuilding. The mission recognised that the rehabilitation of the economy had to address both the flood impact as well as residual unemployment throughout the region. They also saw the need to divide the task into two stages:

- urgent, short-term employment for flood victims, particularly women who had suffered severe losses, and
- longer-term needs.

Local resources versus imported resources: Effective reconstruction requires skill, labour and materials. It also requires them in a vastly greater quantity than normal demand. Therefore, officials tend to look in all directions for the support they need. This is a natural and necessary response, but a dilemma remains whether to select local versus imported people or products. The advantage of local resources is the obvious need to strengthen the local economy which may have been significantly damaged or disrupted.

The use of local skills and labour can also provide vital employment and these may enhance local commitment to the recovery due to strong solidarity with their own wider community. However, local resources may be inadequate for the task, therefore external support may be essential to close the gap between needs and resources. It is also clear that some aspects of reconstruction require expert skills and knowledge which has to come from other parts of a country or from international sources.

Guiding Principles

Planning and management of rehabilitation and reconstruction are highly complex processes that cover a sequence of actions from data collection to assessment of needs, planning, implementation and evaluation. Recovery actions embrace numerous sectors of society and involve actions by individuals, communities, governments and international bodies. Although similarities exist between one recovery situation and another, each case has unique characteristics, diverse patterns of damage, different needs, varied constraints and levels of resources. Therefore, given such variables, only very general principles can be established. The following are some of the critical issues. Principles one to seven are processes to recognise while numbers eight to twelve relate to essential tools required to manage the recovery.

1. The planning of recovery needs to be broad in scope and fully integrated. Planning has to be wide ranging because the impact of disaster can be felt on all sectors requiring very detailed co-ordination. In addition, planning has to be integrated because each situation is complex, involving various actors risking a fragmented response.
2. A balance has to be achieved between the conflicting yet vital processes of reform and conservatism. In any major reconstruction process two powerful forces will exist; reformers, who recognise the opportunity to change administrative patterns, introduce new laws, modify urban

forms and conservationists, who resist all changes and want to return to what existed before the disaster. Wise officials will seek to balance these opposing forces. Both change and continuity are essential.

3. Reconstruction should not be delayed to await political, administrative or economic reform. Following major disasters there is a tendency for politicians to introduce reforms at various levels and in varied sectors. However, it is critically important that reconstruction not be delayed until laws are enacted since this will lose vital momentum for action. New legislation is normally essential, and reforms may be necessary, but they can be implemented in parallel with reconstruction to avoid costly delays.
4. Economic recovery should be regarded as a prerequisite for rapid physical recovery. Officials are faced with many options in recovery management. They could invest in rebuilding the economy or rebuilding structures. If they devote initial resources for economic regeneration this can stimulate physical recovery as well as addressing some of the root causes of vulnerability for the poor and the marginalised.
5. Reconstruction offers unique opportunities to introduce a range of measures to reduce future risks to persons and property. Reconstruction offers a unique opportunity for public officials wanting to improve the protection of people and property. This is due to the heightened public and political awareness following a major disaster, which stimulates a demand for safety.
6. The relocation of entire communities is usually not effective and is rarely feasible. Despite the risks of populations inhabiting dangerous sites, which can result in extensive casualties and property losses, relocation to safe sites is not normally feasible in social, cultural, developmental or economic terms.
7. Recovery actions can be regarded as a therapeutic process to assist individuals and their communities to rebuild their lives and livelihoods. If the victims of disaster become active participants in the recovery process as opposed to being mere spectators, they can play a valuable role in their emotional recovery. Psychological well being of the affected population and those who are engaged in helping them should be seen as an integral part of recovery process.

8. The basis of effective recovery is the availability and maintenance of an adequate flow of cash and credit throughout the entire process of recovery. The flow of finance through cash grants and loans is essential throughout the entire recovery process. A particular problem is that the initial political support after a disaster inevitably unlocks resources which decline over time when extensive finances are needed for reconstruction. Public, private and international funds need to be focused to support local level capacities for long lasting and sustainable impact.
9. Successful reconstruction is closely linked to the resolution of land ownership problems. Within urban areas suffering earthquake or floods there is often a serious pressure on available land, resulting in the occupation of unsafe sites. Governments will need to grasp the difficult issue of making safe land available with tenure for the occupants and enforcing land use planning controls within reconstruction planning. Although land can sometimes be more readily available in rural areas, it may be controlled by the few. Reforms to improve ownership and tenure of agricultural land can be relatively more feasible after a disaster.
10. To aid recovery it is preferable to maximise the use of local resources. Before planning for external support, it is vital for officials to check whether locally available expertise, labour and products are available in order to regenerate the local economy. It is preferable to use these resources rather than import skills and materials. Strengthening the capacities of affected people will increase self reliance, long-term sustainability of mitigation efforts as well as protect their dignity.
11. Physical recovery is dependent on the development of effective local institutions as well as training and leadership at all levels and in all sectors. Frequently, political leaders want to see rapid 'action on the ground' in response to public pressure for recovery. However, these actions depend on the development and maintenance of committed leadership, staff training and resilient institutions in each affected locality.
12. Political commitment is vital to ensure effective recovery. Political support is needed from the very highest level of government and right through the political system to ensure that integrated planning,

financing and implementation of recovery and reconstruction continue from inception to completion without interruption.

Recovery after disaster poses a challenge. It can easily become a series of lost opportunities: minimal advances in safety, protracted years, even decades of unfinished projects and an economy that has failed to reach pre-disaster levels of productivity. But, with careful planning, conscientious management and the full commitment of a society it can be regarded as a unique opportunity to bring many benefits which can lead to an improved natural and built environment.

References

Allen, E., (1994), 'Political responses to flood disaster: the example of Rio de Janeiro', in: A. Varley (ed.) *Disasters, development and the environment*, Chichester: John Wiley.

Anderson, M. B. & P. J. Woodrow, (1989), *Rising from the ashes: development strategies in times of disaster*, Boulder: Westview Press/London: Intermediate Technology Publications.

Bates, F. L. & W. G. Peacock, (1993), *Living conditions, disasters and development: an approach to cross-cultural comparisons*, Athens, USA: University of Georgia Press.

Cannon, T. (1997) 'What makes emergencies different? Inter-relations of disasters, environment and development' in: D Guha-Sapir (ed.) *Environmental impacts of sudden population displacements,* Brussels: European Commission Humanitarian Office (ECHO).

Hewitt, K.,(1997), *Regions of Risk: a geographical introduction to disasters*, Harlow: Addison Wesley Longman.

Maskrey, A., (1989), *Disaster mitigation: a community based approach*, Oxford: Oxfam.

7

Disaster Response Management

Disaster response is a phase of the disaster management cycle. Its preceding cycles aim to reduce the need for a disaster response, or to avoid it altogether.

The level of disaster response depends on a number of factors and particular situation awareness. Studies undertaken by Son, Aziz and Pen ~a-Mora shows that "initial work demand gradually spreads and increases based on a wide range of variables including scale of disaster, vulnerability of affected area which in turn is affected by population density, site-specific conditions (e.g. exposure to hazardous conditions) and effects of cascading disasters resulting from inter-dependence between elements of critical infrastructure".

Disasters impact on entire communities. The immediate effects include loss of life and damage to property and infrastructure, with the survivors (some of whom may have been injured in the disaster) traumatized by the experience, uncertain of the future and less able to provide for their own welfare, at least in the short term. More than likely, they are left without adequate shelter, food, water and other necessities to sustain life. Rapid action is required to prevent further loss of life.

The primary aims of disaster response are rescue from immediate danger and stabilization of the physical and emotional condition of survivors. These go hand in hand with the recovery of the dead and the restoration of essential services such as water and power. How long this takes varies according to the scale, type and context of the disaster but typically takes between one and six months and is composed of a search and rescue phase in the immediate aftermath of a disaster followed by a medium-term phase devoted to stabilizing the survivors' physical and emotional condition.

The social, economic and political consequences of disasters are frequently complex. For instance, the disaster may:

- disrupt vital community self-help networks, further increasing vulnerability;
- disrupt markets over a wide area, reducing the availability of food and opportunities for income generation;
- destroy essential health infrastructure such as hospitals, resulting in a lack of emergency and longer-term medical care for the affected population.

Moreover, the situation may be compounded by a secondary threat, such as earthquake aftershocks or epidemics. It is essential that disaster response activities do not make a bad situation worse by fostering dependency or destroying existing community-support mechanisms. Rather, they should lay the foundations for the subsequent recovery of the affected population. Disaster situations are highly fluid, evolve rapidly and therefore require a close degree of coordination and cooperation between those involved in the response, including the affected community itself.

Incident Response System

The Incident Response System (IRS) is an effective mechanism for reducing the scope for ad-hoc measures in response. It incorporates all the tasks that may be performed during DM irrespective of their level of complexity. If IRS is put in place and stakeholders trained and made aware of their roles, it will greatly help in reducing chaos and confusion during the response phase. Every one will know what needs to be done, who will do it and who is in command, etc.

The main purpose of these Guidelines is to lay down the roles and responsibilities of different functionaries and stakeholders, at State and District levels and how coordination with the multi-tiered institutional mechanisms at the National, State and District level will be done. It also emphasises the need for proper documentation of various activities for better planning, accountability and analysis. It will also help new responders to immediately get a comprehensive picture of the situation and go in for immediate action.

IRS Organisation

The IRS organisation functions through Incident Response Teams (IRTs) in the field. In line with administrative structure and DM Act 2005, Responsible Officers (ROs) have been designated at the State and District level as overall in charge of the incident response management. The RO may however delegate responsibilities to the Incident Commander (IC), who in turn will manage the incident through IRTs. The IRTs will be pre-designated at all levels; State, District, Sub-Division and Tehsil/Block. On receipt of Early Warning, the RO will activate them. In case a disaster occurs without any warning, the local IRT will respond and contact RO for further support, if required. A Nodal Officer (NO) has to be designated for proper coordination between the District, State and National level in activating air support for response. Apart from the RO and Nodal Officer (NO), the IRS has two main components; a) Command Staff and b) General Staff.

Command Staff

The Command Staff consists of Incident Commander (IC), Information & Media Officer (IMO), Safety Officer (SO) and Liaison Officer (LO). They report directly to the IC and may have assistants. The Command Staff may or may not have supporting organisations under them.

General Staff

The General Staff has three components which are as follows;

Operations Section (OS)

The OS is responsible for directing the required tactical actions to meet incident objectives. Management of disaster may not immediately require activation of Branch, Division and Group. Expansion of the OS depends on the enormity of the situation and number of different types and kinds of functional Groups required in the response management.

Planning Section (PS)

The PS is responsible for collection, evaluation and display of incident information, maintaining and tracking resources, preparing the Incident Action Plan (IAP) and other necessary incident related documentation. They will assess the requirement of additional resources, propose from where it can be mobilised and keep IC informed.

Logistics Section (LS)

The LS is responsible for providing facilities, services, materials, equipment and other resources in support of the incident response. In order to ensure prompt and smooth procurement and supply of resources as per financial rules, the Finance Branch has been included in the LS.

Features of IRS

Management by Objectives

Management by Objectives (MBO) covers four essential steps in IRS. These steps should be taken for the management of every incident regardless of its size or complexity:

a) Understand Government policy and directions including relief code, evacuation procedures etc.;
b) Establishment of incident objectives;
c) Selection of appropriate strategies; and
d) Performance of tactical moves.

Unity of Command and Chain of Command

Chain of Command means that there is an orderly line of authority within the ranks of the organization with a clear cut reporting pattern right from the lowest level to the highest. In the IRS, the Chain of Command is established through a prescribed organisational structure which consists of various layers such as Sections, Branches, Divisions, etc. This feature eliminates the possibility of receiving conflicting orders from various supervisors. Thus it increases accountability, prevents freelancing, improves the flow of information, and helps in smooth coordination in operational efforts.

Transfer of Command

The command of an incident initially is vested in the highest ranking authority in the area where the disaster occurs. The Transfer of Command in any incident may take place for the following reasons:

a) When an incident becomes overwhelming for the IC and IRT;
b) More qualified and experienced senior officers arrive at the scene;
c) The incident situation changes over time, where a jurisdictional or agency change in command is operationally required; and

d) Normal turnover of personnel in the case of long or extended incidents.

The various processes in IRS of briefing, debriefing, documentation through forms and formats, proves very useful during transfer of command. The IAP, assignment list, details of actions already taken, resources deployed, available, ordered etc. gives an immediate and comprehensive view of the incident status to the new comer.

Span of Control

Span of control refers to the number of elements that one supervisor can directly manage effectively. Ideally a supervisor should have five organisational elements under his control. However if the elements increase to more than five or are reduced to less than three, necessary changes in the IRS organisational structure should be carried out.

Area Command

Area Command is an expansion of the Incident Response function, primarily designed to manage a very large number of incidents that has multiple IRTs assigned or area being isolated because of geographical reasons. It is established for overseeing response and to ensure that conflicts, jurisdictional or otherwise, do not arise amongst deployed responding teams.

Unified Command (UC)

UC is a team effort that allows all agencies with jurisdictional responsibility for the incident, either geographical or functional, to manage an incident by establishing a common set of incident objectives and strategies under one commander. This is accomplished through the UC framework headed by Governor/Lt. Governor (LG)/Administrator/Chief Minister (CM) and assisted by Chief Secretary (CS) without losing or abdicating agency authority, responsibility or accountability.

Common Terminology

In IRS, common terminology is applied to Organisational Elements, Position Titles, Resources and Facilities which are as follows.

a) *Organisational elements:* There is a consistent pattern for designating each level of the organisation.

b) *Position titles*: Those charged with management or leadership responsibility in IRS are referred to by specific position titles such as Commander, Officer, Chief, Director, Supervisor, Leader, in-charge etc.

It provides a standardised nomenclature for requisitioning personnel to fill various levels of positions.

c) *Branch:* The organizational level having functional or geographic responsibility for major segments of incident operations.

d) *Division:* Divisions are used to divide an incident into geographical area of operations. It is positioned in the IRS organization between the Branch and Groups. Divisions are established when number of resources deployed exceeds the span of control of the Operations Sections Chief. It is also activated for closer supervision when an area is very distant or isolated.

e) *Group:* Group refers to only functional responsibilities for major segments of Incident operations. Group consists of different functional teams.

f) *Resources:* Resources are grouped into two categories: i) Primary and ii) Support. The Primary resources are meant for the responder and support resources are meant for the affected people. All resources are however designated according to the 'kind' and 'type'. 'Kind' would mean the overall description of the resource like Bus, Truck, Bulldozer, Medical Team. 'Type' would mean the performance capability of the resource which may be large, medium or small. This helps in ordering the exact and correct resource by the ordering unit. It also helps the deploying agencies to send the correct requirement.

g) *Facilities:* Different kinds of facilities have to be established to meet the specific needs of the incident. IRS tries to standardise them by using common terminology like Incident Command Post, Staging Area, Incident Base, Camp, Relief Camp, Helibase, Helipad, etc.

Accountability

In IRS, through a clear cut chain of command it is ensured that one individual or Group is not assigned to more than one Supervisor. Through other procedures and use of various forms, accountability of personnel and resources are ensured. It makes the response effort absolutely focused and leaves no room for unsupervised activity. It helps maintain a complete record of all activities performed and resources deployed. The various procedures and forms in the IRS are as follows.

a) *Incident Briefing*—Form 001 helps in briefing every one involved in the response activities. It also helps new responders to immediately get a complete view of status of response. It shows map of affected site, summary of current action, status of activated IRS organisation and resource summary.

b) *Incident Status Summary (ISS)*—Form 002 indicates the status of the tasks assigned, completed or still to be completed. It also has details of the weather conditions and other threats that may increase the severity of the incident.

c) *Unit Log*—Form 003 is a complete performance report of the IRT down to the different Sections, Branches, Groups indicating their locations and details of work assigned along with resources and the status of work done etc. The details of these information for the Unit Log will be obtained from the "Record of Performed Activities—Form 004".

d) *Record of performed activities*—Form 004 will be available with every responder under different Sections and will be a complete account of the activities performed during the concerned operational period. The information collected through this form will be compiled by OS and maintained in the Unit Log—Form 003.

e) *Organisation assignment list*—Form 005 helps in performing the task in a focused manner. After preparation of the IAP in the briefing meeting, the IC and the different Section Chiefs will ensure that the activities required to be performed is listed in the form 005 and circulated among all the concerned responders and supervisory Staff of different Sections respectively. It will be like a check list in a particular operational period that helps responders to respond in a comprehensive and focused manner.

f) *Incident Check-in and Deployment List*—Form 006 helps to keep track of resources received at different facilities and despatched to various incident site for response. This list will be maintained by the managers/in-charges of all the facilities that are set up for response.

g) *On Duty Officers List*—Form 007 The list contains details of the officers who have been deployed. It will be maintained at the Section level and sent to the RO through the IC. The list will help the RO and IC to easily locate officers and issue directions to them.

h) *Medical Plan*—Form 008 will be prepared by Medical Unit of the LS in accordance with IAP. This will contain the number of medical aid camps activated in various locations of affected sites, resources available; i) medical officer, ii) paramedics, iii) other volunteers, iv) life saving drugs, v) medicines/appliances, vi) list of referral services and blood banks, vii) availability and mobilisation of ambulance services and viii) list of Government and private establishments for further support, etc.

i) *Incident Communication Plan*—Form 009 helps to provide a complete picture of the already existing, available communication facilities and where new facilities have to be setup for disaster response. It gives details of the type of communications available, the source of their power supply and whether alternative arrangements are available or not. The plan will also have a design for networking of inter organisation communications facilities of the Police, NDRF, Armed Forces, Irrigation Department etc. keeping in mind the conflicting codes that may be in use. Because of the large number and variety of sets and possibility of heavy communication traffic, a number of nets may have to be established like command net, operational net, logistics net and ground to air net. It will also help in working out the requirement of supervision, maintenance, replacement, repair and transportation for the maintenance of communication facilities.

j) *Demobilisation plan*—Form 010 will be prepared by the PS in consultation with IC and other Section Chiefs. It will have to be approved by the RO and widely circulated in advance. It has often been experienced that because of lack of a proper demobilisation plan and a lack of its proper dissemination, resources (men and machines) mobilised for disaster response face difficulties in availing transportation while returning. Demobilisation plan therefore is very important.

Integrated Communications

Ability to communicate within the IRS structure is very important. Provision for a complete Communication Unit has been made in the LS. Several communication networks may be established depending upon the size, complexity of the incident, availability of various types of equipment and the simultaneous need to communicate by a number of responders and agencies. These may include Command Net, Operational Net, Logistics Net and Ground to Air Net. A suitable interoperable and compatible network between various agencies will have to be designed. This networking is also vital for the integration of agency capabilities like the NDRF, Armed Forces, etc. when they come in aid and support. The GoI is also concurrently working on a National Disaster Communication Network (NDCN) which will be useful in extreme disasters when all existing communication systems have failed.

Resource Management

Resources are managed and assigned under specific terminology to denote their employability. The terms used are as follows;

a) Resource Status: Tactical resources assigned to an incident will always be in any one of the following five status conditions.
   — *Required:* Resources that would be needed to respond to disasters effectively and which need to be obtained;
   — *Available:* Resources ready for deployment in the staging area;
   — *Assigned:* Resources on active assignment; and
   — *Out-of-Service:* Resources not assigned or not available because of repair or maintenance.

b) *Single Resource:* Single Resource includes both personnel and their equipment.

c) *Strike Team:* A Strike Team is a specified combination of a designated number of the same 'kind' and 'type' of resources with common communications and a leader. Strike Teams can be pre-designated or assembled at an incident site from the available Single Resources as per demand of the situation.

d) *Task Force:* A Task Force is any combination of Single Resource of different 'kinds' and 'types' within the ambit of a specific span of control to perform different types of functions simultaneously. They are assembled for a mult-tactical task in a particular location with common communications and a leader. Task Forces can be pre-determined or assembled for response in an incident site from available Single Resources according to the requirement.

Incident Action Plan (IAP), Briefing and Debriefing Meetings

Management of every incident needs an action plan and proper briefing of all personnel. The purpose of the action plan and briefing is to provide all concerned personnel with appropriate directions for the various tasks in hand.

Before taking up response activities, the RO/IC will need to take stock of the situation, availability and mobilisation of resources for listing out the various tasks and to provide proper briefing to the responders. For this, he will need to hold a proper briefing meeting at the beginning of each operational period. At the end of the operational period, a debriefing meeting is equally important where he will be able to again review whether the objectives were achieved or not and then decide what further steps need to be taken in the next operational period. Both the briefing and debriefing meetings are the basis on which the IAP will be prepared and tasks assigned. The briefing form—001 can also be used for briefing of senior officers who arrive on the scene. In certain circumstances when important developments take place and further immediate intervention is needed in-between the briefing and debriefing meetings, the IC may issue directions even before completion of one operational period.

IAP can be written or oral depending on the duration and magnitude of the incident. The incident may be of low, medium or large levels. Low level incident would be of less than 24 hours, medium would be of more than 24 hours and less than 36 hours and a large incident would be of more than 36 hours of emergency operations. In low or medium level incidents, oral action plan may surface. The directions given orally may be jotted down by the Command Staff and handed over to the PS to be integrated in the IAP.

At times there may be sudden disasters without warning and the IC may have to respond immediately. In such cases also the Command Staff will jot down the decisions taken for response and hand it over to the PS when it is activated and it should be incorporated in the IAP. In larger incidents when there is adequate early warning, a written IAP will be required. IAP may consist of incident objectives, organisation assignment and division assignment list, incident communication plan, traffic plan, safety plan and incident map etc.

Incident Response Teams (IRTs) at State and District Levels

The IRT is a team comprising of all positions of IRS organisation. The OS helps to prepare different tactical operations as required. The PS helps in obtaining different informations and preparing plans as required. The LS assesses the availability and requirement of resources and takes action for obtaining them.

IRTs will function at State, District, Sub-Division and the Tehsil/Block levels. These teams will respond to all natural and man-made disasters. The lowest administrative unit will be the first responder as the case may be. If the incident becomes complex and is beyond the control of local IRT, the higher level IRT will be informed and they will take over the response management. In such cases the lower level IRT will merge with higher level IRT.

When a lower level of IRT (e.g. Block/Tehsil) merges with a higher level (e.g. Sub-Division, District or State) the role of IC of lower level of IRT will change. When the Block level IRT merges with Sub-Division level IRT, IC of the Block level may play the role of Deputy IC or OSC or any other duty that the IC of higher authority assigns. This process will be applicable at all levels.

Disaster Response Management

India has a well defined, robust and time tested administrative structure. Section 22(2), 24, 30 and 34 of DM Act 2005 has clearly laid down various duties relating to DM to be performed by various agencies. No single agency or department can handle a disaster situation of any scale alone. Different departments have to work together to manage the disaster. For proper coordination and effective use of all available resources, the different departments and agencies need a formalised response management structure that lends consistency, fosters efficiency and provides appropriate direction during response. Response Management constitutes the functions of planning, execution and coordination. While planning in the pre-disaster phase is the responsibility of various authorities created under the DM Act, the execution of the plans has to be carried out by the various line departments of the Government and the existing administrative structure in the District and State. For coordination and ensuring smooth execution of the plans, bodies like NDMA, NEC, SDMA and SEC have been created at the National and State Level. At the District level, planning, execution and coordination of all the activities have been vested in the DDMA itself.

The IRS envisages and lays down various tasks that may need to be performed by the existing administrative machinery at various levels. It also recommends prior identification of officers for the performance of different tasks and getting them trained in their respective roles, and provides a structure under which all the line departments will function in tandem with the District and State administration.

The IRTs will be pre-designated at all levels. On receipt of early warning the RO may activate them. In case of occurrence of disaster without any warning, the local IRTs will respond and report to RO and request further support, if required.

In view of the provisions of the DM Act 2005 and the administrative structure existing in the country at the District and State levels, the roles of the Chief Secretary (CS) and the District Magistrates/DC is all encompassing as regards response. In the IRS, a need was felt to clearly identify a designated authority responsible and accountable by law to respond to disasters and therefore a position of Responsible Officer (RO) has been introduced. Incident response management may however not always require the direct intervention of the RO. On the ground, the management will be done by the IC to whom powers will have to be delegated by the RO. The CSs and the District Magistrates/DCs will perform the role of ROs in their respective administrative jurisdictions and will be overall responsible for all response activities during any incident or crisis.

As per the DM Act, it will be seen that the CS is the Chief Executive Officer (CEO) of the SDMA as well as Chairperson of the SEC. He is also the head of the administrative structure in the State. The District Magistrate/DC is the Chairperson of the DDMA and has been assigned all encompassing role of planning, coordination and execution of DM in his jurisdiction assisted by all line departments and local bodies. Though at the District level the Chairperson of the Zila Parishad has also been placed as the Co-Chairperson of the DDMA to elicit the community participation in DM, yet the responsibility for disaster response clearly lies with the District Magistrate/DC being the head of the District administration. It will only be the administrative machinery—CS, District Magistrate/DC and their team of officers who will be responsible and accountable for effective response in their jurisdictions. To elicit or mobilise the NGOs, PRIs and communities and other stakeholders for support at the District level, the Co-Chairperson of the DDMA may prove helpful.

Coordinating Arrangements

Though response to any disaster has to be mainly done by the State, even before the enactment of the DM Act, 2005, the GoI had already created an apex body for coordination of Crisis Response at the National level, headed by the Cabinet Secretary called the NCMC. The DM Act 2005, has also created a body called the NEC under the Home Secretary for coordination of response.

By convention, the NCMC gets involved in very serious crisis and disasters. The NEC has to statutorily get involved in all disasters. The chairperson of the NCMC/NEC will function as Chief Coordinator for the management of disasters at the National level. The chairperson may designate a Nodal Officer (NO) for this purpose. Various Ministries/ Departments of Government may also nominate NOs to perform the task of ESFs which may be required in a particular incident. The constitution of the NCMC/NEC has been designed with the purpose to cover all lead and support functions.

Lead Agency/Nodal Department

The National Policy on DM 2009, has stated that emergencies requiring the close involvement of the security forces and/or intelligence agencies such as terrorism (counter-insurgency), law and order situations, serial bomb blasts, hijacking, air accidents, CBRN, mine disasters, port and harbour emergencies, forest fires, oilfeld fires and oil spills will continue to be handled by the extant mechanism i.e. NCMC and the resources available with the DM Authorities at all levels with regard to cross cuting themes like medical, rescue & relief etc. will be made available to the Nodal ministries/agencies at times of such disasters/impending disasters.

Apart from the above, the management of other major natural and manmade disasters will also require Lead and Supporting agencies. Different disasters require different types of expertise for response. Thus, in case of rescue and relief in natural disaster, it will generally be the local Police and the NDRF/SDRF, in case of Fire it will be the Fire department, in case of drought it will be the Agriculture department, in case of Epidemics and other Biological disasters it will be the Health department that will have to play the lead role and the remaining departments will have to play the supporting role as per requirement and their core competencies. The Chief Coordinator at the national level and the ROs at the State and District level will ensure sensitsation of the concerned departments in advance regarding their roles as lead and supporting agencies.

Coordination of Response at the State Level

In any disaster response, the initial efforts would always be taken by the

District Administration. However, when Districts are overwhelmed in any situation, the support necessarily has to come from the State and National level. While the IRS is mainly relevant at the basic functional level, it is absolutely necessary that the support functionaries from the State and the National level also conform to the principles of IRS in the emergency support duties. This will be greatly beneficial for the proper coordination of the various response efforts at the National and State level with that of the District. It is therefore necessary to clearly understand the structure of the IRS in the context of State response.

For monitoring and support of the incident response, the RO will involve all required Emergency Support Functionaries (ESF) and headquarters IRT to support the on scene IC. The IC will work in close coordination with EOC and report to RO.

In case when central teams (NDRF, Armed Forces) are deployed, the RO should ensure resolution of all conflicts. For this purpose he may attach a representative of such agencies in the EOC. Though the teams so deployed will work in OS in the form of Strike Teams, Task Forces or Single Resource under the supervision of OSC all conflicts can easily be resolved at the highest level by the RO. IC will also exercise close supervision and resolve all conflicts at his level if required.

Roles and Responsibilities of CS as RO of the State

i) The CS who is the head of the State administration and also chairperson of SEC and CEO of SDMA, will perform responsibilities laid down under clause 22 (2) and 24 of the DM Act, 2005;

ii) The Section 22 (h) of the Act provides that the Chairperson of SEC will give directions to any department of the Government of the State or any other authority or body in the State regarding actions to be taken in response to any threatening disaster situation or disaster. Thus He will ensure active participation of all departments at State level;

Apart from the above, the CS will

iii) Ensure that IRTs at State, District, Sub-Division, Tehsil/Block are formed and IRS is integrated in the State and District DM Plan. This may be achieved by issuing a Standing Order to all District Magistrates/ DCs,

iv) Issue a Standing Order in advance to different departments and agencies, so that in any emergency, mobilisation of both equipment and personnel happens smoothly;

v) Ensure that a reasonable amount of imprest fund is sanctioned clearly delineating the procedure for emergency procurement;

vi) Ensure funds of 13th Finance Commission (FC) for capacity building of administrative machinery in DM is spent appropriately.

vii) Ensure that IRS is incorporated in the training syllabus of ATIs and other training institutions of the State. There should be proper faculty in the ATI for such purpose.

viii) Ensure effective communication and Web based/online Decision Support System (DSS) is in place in the EOC and connected with District, Sub-Division, Tehsil/Block level IRTs for support;

ix) Ensure that toll free emergency numbers existing in the State for Police, Fire and Medical support etc. will be linked to the EOC for response, command and control. For e.g., if there is any fire incident, the information should not only reach the fire station but also to the EOC and the nearest hospital to gear up to attend to any casualties and to the emergency medical service for the mobilisation of ambulance service to reach the spot;

x) Activate IRTs at State headquarters when the need arises and issue order for their demobilisation on completion of response;

xi) Set overall objectives and incident related priorities;

xii) Identify, mobilise and allocate critical resources according to established priorities;

xiii) Ensure that local Armed Forces Commanders are involved in the Planning Process and their resources are appropriately dovetailed, if required;

xiv) Ensure that when NDRF, Armed Forces arrive in support for disaster response, their logistic requirements like, camping ground, potable water, electricity and requirement of vehicles etc. are taken care of;

xv. Coordinate with the Central Government for mobilisation of Armed Forces, Air support etc. as and when required;

xvi) identify suitable NO to coordinate Air Operations and ensure that all District ROs are aware of it;

xvii) Ensure that incident management objectives do not conflict with each other;

xviii) consider the need for the establishment of AC, if required;

xix) Establish Unified Command (UC) if required and get the approval of Chief Minister (CM);

xx) Ensure that telephone directory of all ESF is prepared and available with EOC and IRTs;

xxi) Ensure use of Global Positioning System (GPS) technology in the vehicles (Police, Fire, Ambulance etc.) to get connectivity for their effective utilisation;

xxii) Keep the chairperson of SDMA informed of the progress of incident response;

xxiii. Ensure overall coordination of response, relief and other activities;

xxiv) Ensure that the Non-Governmental Organisations (NGOs) carry out their activities in an equitable and non-discriminatory manner;

xxv) Conduct post response review on performance of IRTs and take appropriate steps to improve performance; and

xxvi) take such other necessary action as the situation demands.

Coordination of Response at the District Level

The District Magistrate/DC is the head of the District administrative set up and chairperson of the DDMA as per the DM Act, 2005. He has been designated as the RO in the District.

The heads of different departments in the District will have separate roles to play depending on the nature and kind of disaster. The roles and responsibilities of the members of the DDMA will be decided in advance in consultation with the concerned members. The roles of other line departments also have to be clearly delineated in various disaster situations in the District DM Plan which will be duly approved by the State Government, so that there will be no ambiguity about their functions during response.

The District Magistrate/DC/RO will issue a Standing Order for formation of IRT at District headquarters/Sub-Division and Tehsil/Block levels. He will ensure that appropriate and experienced officers are selected for IRTs.

The selection of the OSC will however depend on the nature of the disaster. In case of food and earthquakes reaching the affected area, rescuing the affected people and providing relief to them is the main task of the responders. People have to leave their home in a hurry and they are not able to take away their valuables. These abandoned houses become vulnerable. The relief materials while being transported also become prone to loot. In such cases, Police and the Armed Forces are the best suited to handle and lead the operations. In case of fire at District level, it will be the District Fire Officer who will be appropriate officer to handle the situation. In case of health related disaster, it would be the District Chief Medical Officer and so on. There could even be such situations when the District officials may have no expertise in operationalising the response like CBRN disasters. For such disaster situations the OSC should be identified in advance, so that he could be easily mobilised to lead the OS as Section Chief. NDMA has already issued detailed guidelines on management of such response vide National Disaster Management Guidelines on the management of Nuclear and Radiological emergencies which should be followed. Other Section Chiefs will be selected according to the suitability and capability of the officer. In case of Sub-Division, Tehsil or Block, the respective heads, i.e. SDO, Tehsildar, BDO will function as the IC in their respective IRTs and the OSC will be selected as per nature of the disaster.

The structure depicted above may be activated as and when required. For monitoring and support of the incident response, the RO will involve all required ESF and headquarter IRT to support the on-scene IC. In case when central teams (NDRF, Armed Forces) are deployed, the RO will ensure resolution of all conflicts. For this purpose he may attach a representative of such agencies in the EOC where all conflicts can easily be resolved at the highest level. The teams so deployed will have to work in OS in the form of Single Resource, Strike Teams or Task Forces under the supervision of OSC. The IC will also exercise close supervision for resolution of all conflicts, if required.The IC will work in close coordination with EOC and report to RO. The RO will ensure that the strategic goals are achieved through the implementation of the IAP by the IRTs working in the field.

Roles and Responsibilities of District Magistrate as RO

The District Magistrate/RO will:

i) ensure that IRTs are formed at District, Sub-Division, Tehsil/Block levels and IRS is integrated in the District DM Plan as per Section 31 of the DM Act, 2005. This may be achieved by issuing a Standing Order by the RO to all SDOs, SDMs and Tehsildars/ BDOs;

ii) ensure web based/on line Decision Support System (DSS) is in place in EOC and connected with Sub-Division and Tehsil/Block level IRTs for support;

iii) ensure that toll free emergency numbers existing for Police, Fire and Medical support etc. are linked to the EOC for response, command and control. For e.g., if there is any fire incident, the information should not only reach the fire station but also the EOC and the nearest hospital to gear up the emergency medical service;

iv) obtain funds from State Government as recommended by the 13th FC and ensure that a training calendar for IRTs of District is prepared and members of IRTs are trained through ATIs and other training institutions of the District;

v) delegate authorities to the IC;

vi) activate IRTs at District headquarter, Sub-Division, Tehsil/Block levels, as and when required;

vii) appoint/deploy, terminate and demobilise IC and IRT(s) as and when required;

viii) decide overall incident objectives, priorities and ensure that various objectives do not conflict with each other;

ix) ensure that IAP is prepared by the IC and implemented;

x) remain fully briefed on the IAP and its implementation;

xi) coordinate all response activities;

xii) give directions for the release and use of resources available with any department of the Government, Local Authority, private sector etc. in the District;

xiii) ensure that local Armed Forces Commanders are involved in the planning process and their resources are appropriately dovetailed, if required;

xiv) ensure that when Armed Forces arrive in support for disaster response, their logistic requirements like camping grounds, potable water, electricity and requirement of vehicles etc. are sorted out;

xv) appoint a NO at the District level to organise Air Operations in coordination with the State and Central Government NO. Also ensure that all ICs of IRTs of the District are aware of it;

xvi) ensure that the NGOs carry out their activities in an equitable and non-discriminatory manner;

xvii) deploy the District Headquarter IRTs at the incident site, in case of need;

xviii) ensure that effective communications are in place;

xix) ensure that telephone directory of all ESF is prepared and available with EOC and members of IRTs;

xx) ensure provision for accountability of personnel and a safe operating environment;

xxi) in case the situation deterioraties, the RO may assume the role of the IC and may seek support from the State level RO;

xxii) mobilise experts and consultants in the relevant fields to advise and assist as he may deem necessary;

xxiii) procure exclusive or preferental use of amenities from any authority or person;

xxiv) conduct post response review on performance of IRTs and take appropriate steps to improve performance; and

xxv) take other necessary action as the situation demands.

Area Command

Area Command is activated when span of control becomes very large either because of geographical reasons or because of large number of incidents occurring at different places at the same time. Area Command may also be activated when a number of administrative jurisdictions are affected. It provides closer supervision, support to the IRTs and resolution of conflicts locally. When a number of Districts get affected, involving more than one Revenue Division, the concept of Area Command may be introduced Revenue Division wise by the State RO. In such cases the District Magistrate (RO) of the District will function as the IC. Similarly the District RO may introduce it Sub-Division wise when a large number of Tehsils/Blocks in different Sub-Divisions get affected. The RO will ensure adequate supporting Staff for the AC. The roles and responsibilities of AC are as follows.

The AC will

i) ensure that incident management objectives are met and do not conflict with each other;

ii) allocate critical resources according to identified priorities;

iii) ensure proper coordination in the management of incidents;

iv) ensure resolution of all conflicts in his jurisdiction;

v) ensure effective communications;

vi) identify critical resource needs and liaise with the EOC for their supply;

vii) provide for accountability of personnel and ensure a safe operating environment; and

viii) perform any other tasks as assigned by the RO.

Unified Command (UC)

In an incident involving multiple agencies, there is a critical need for integrating resources (men, materials and machines) into a single operational organisation that is managed and supported by one command structure. This is best established through an integrated, mult-disciplinary organisation. In the IRS this critical need is addressed by the UC.

UC is a framework headed by the Governor/LG/Administrator/CM and assisted by the CS that allows all agencies with jurisdictional responsibilities for an incident, either geographical or functional, to participate in the management of the incident. This participation is demonstrated by developing and implementing a common set of incident objectives and strategies that all can subscribe to, without losing or abdicating specific agency authority, responsibilities and accountability. The organisations that constitute the UC have the mandate for specific task and functional responsibilities to address the incident requirements.

UC incorporates the following components

a) A set of objectives for the entre incident;

b) A collective approach for developing strategies to achieve incident goals;

c) Improved information flow and inter-agency coordination;

d) Familiarity with responsibilities and constraints of other agencies;

e) Respect for the authority or legal responsibilities of all agencies;

f) Optimal synergy of all agencies for the smooth implementation of the IAP; and

g) Elimination of duplication of efforts.

Coordination of Response in Metropolitan Cities

The Metropolitan Cities are large and densely populated with a complex administrative setup. The different departments and agencies functioning within the cities are large with resources and independent hierarchical setups having autonomy and complete chain of command of their own. To visualize an IRT on the pattern of the other Districts of the country in such Metropolitan Cities would not be appropriate. A concept of UC will have to be introduced in such cases for effective disaster response.

For all Metropolitan Cities, the CM/Lt. Governor (LG)/CS will set up a UC involving all the existing departments and agencies like the existing District Administrations, Armed Forces, Municipal Corporations and Local Bodies etc. The CS will function as the RO and constitute IRTs in advance on the principle of IRS to respond to and manage disasters.

The IRT members will be identified in advance, roles assigned and trained accordingly. The existing District authorities of the Metropolitan Cities will function as per the directions of the UC.

Coordination of Response in Union Territories (UTs)

The Union Territories (UTs) are under the administrative control of GoI headed by LG. In some UTs, apart from the LG, there is a CM also. In some UTs the head of the administrative setup is the Administrator of the UT. The different departments and agencies functioning within the UTs have their own resources with independent hierarchical setups having a complete chain of command of their own. Therefore it would be appropriate that a concept of UC is introduced for effective disaster response in all the UTs of the country. The LG/CM/Administrator/GoI necessarily need to set up a UC in advance. It will include all the heads of the existing departments and agencies including the Armed Forces in the UTs. The Head/Administrator of the UTs will function as the RO and constitute IRTs at various levels. The IRT members should be assigned their roles in accordance to the principles of IRS. The existing District administration of the UTs will function as per the directions of the UC.

Coordination of response in remote areas of Andaman and Nicobar Islands, North East and other Hill Areas with a Slightly Different Administrative Structure and Set up

In some remote areas of Andaman and Nicobar Islands, North-East and in Hill areas of States like Utarakhand, the administrative structure is slightly different from that of the rest of the country. Some departments and agencies may have a dominating presence while others may not have any presence at all. In such areas, village chiefs and community level leaders are also important functionaries. It is therefore necessary that the RO of such UTs, States and Districts should design their IRTs according to their administrative structure and functionaries. They should select their village and ward level IRTs and get them sensitised and trained as per IRS principles for response. A proper communication set up should also be established.

Roles of Local Authorities

The DM Act, 2005 has defined the roles of NACs, Municipalities, Municipal Corporations, Municipal Councils and PRIs under section 41 (1)(2). These bodies will ensure that their officials and employees are trained in DM and resources relating to DM are also maintained in order to be readily available for use in any threatening disaster situation or disaster. These bodies are also required to carry out relief activities in the affected areas in accordance with State and District DM Plans. The SDMAs/DDMAs will lay down the specific roles and responsibilities of these local bodies in the DM Plan and suitably integrate them with relevant IRTs.

Community Participation in Disaster Response

A number of community based organisations like NGOs, Self Help Groups (SHGs), Youth Organisations, Volunteers of NYK, Civil Defence (CD) & Home Guard, etc., and workers of different projects funded by Government of India like National Rural Health Mission (NRHM), Integrated Child Development Services (ICDS), etc., normally volunteer their services in the aftermath of any disaster.

In the IRS structure, these organisations are placed in the OS where the skills and services of the community may be utilised systematically in the form of Single Resource, Strike Team and Task Force. The ROs of the State and District will ensure that such resources at village, ward or Gram Panchayat levels are organised with the help of leadership of PRIs and other community leaders. Their resources should be identified as per hazard and they should be encouraged and trained to be a part of the IRT.

The Community Based Disaster Management Teams should be appropriately integrated in the State and District level IRTs.

Emergency Operations Centre (EOC)

EOC is an offsite facility which will be functioning from the State/District headquarters and which is actually an augmented control room having communication facilities and space to accommodate the various ESFs. It is a combination of various line departments of Government and other agencies whose services are generally required during incident response. These officials will be able to take decisions on the spot under the guidance of RO and will be able to assist the RO in achieving the incident objectives. RO will also ensure that the line departments do not issue parallel and contradictory instructions to their field level officers.

The EOC will take stock of the emerging situation and assist the RO in mobilising the respective line department's resources, manpower and expertise along with appropriate delegated authorities for the on-scene IRT(s). EOC will keep the RO informed of the changing situation and support extended.

This responsibility can be discharged most effectively only if it has the required information through a fail safe communication facility and an ideal information technology solution with DSS. In addition to the above a web based connectivity will further help in accessing situational awareness, decision support and mult-agency coordination. It will allow all collaborating agencies and departments inside and outside EOC environment to share information, make decisions, activate plans, deploy IRTs, perform and log all necessary response and relief activities and make the EOC effective. It is very important to put the above capabilities in place.

EOC Norms

It will have

a) One Sr. Administrative Officer as EOC in-charge having experience in DM with required assistants;

b) Representation of all concerned line departments with authority to quickly mobilise their resources;

c) Adequate space with proper infrastructure to accommodate the participating agencies and departments;

d) Communication facilities with last mile connectivity;

e) A vehicle mounted with HF, VHF and satellite telephone for deployment in the affected site to provide immediate connectivity with the headquarters and ICP;

f) A representative of central teams whenever they are deployed to integrate their resources, expertise and to resolve conflicts that may arise during response effort;

g) Provision and plan for dovetailing the NDRF, Armed Forces communication capabilities with the local communication set up. There will be proper plan so that all are able to connect with each other in case of large scale disasters or failure of the local communication systems;

h) Map depicting affected site, resources deployed, facilities established like Incident Command Post, Staging Area, Incident Base, Camp, Relief Camp, Helibase, Helipad, etc.

i) DM plans of all line departments;

j) DM plans of the State and the District;

   — Directories with contact details of all emergency services and nodal officers;

   — Connectivity with all District headquarters and police stations;

   — Database of NGOs working in different geographical areas;

   — Demographic details of the State and Districts;

k) Online/Web based DSS with the availability of at least the following components:

   — Standardisation of Command Structure with the details of the earmarked and trained personnel in IRS;

   — Proactive planning facilities;

   — Comprehensive resource management system;

   — Geographic Information System (GIS) for decision support; and

   — Modelling capability for predicting casualties and resources for large scale incidents including CBRN emergencies.

l) Socio-economic, demographic and land use planning;

m) Resource inventories of all line departments and connectivity with database of India Disaster Resource Network (IDRN) India Disaster Knowledge Network (IDKN) and Corporate Disaster Resource Network (CDRN); and

Incident Command Post (ICP)

The ICP is the location at which the primary command functions are performed. The IC will be located at the ICP. There will only be one ICP for each incident. This also applies to situations with multi-agencies or multi jurisdictional incidents operating under a single or Unified command.

The ICP can be located with other incident facilities like Incident Base. For the initial location of the ICP, the nature of the incident, whether it is growing or moving and whether the ICP location will be suitable in size and safe for the expected duration of the incident should be taken into consideration. Larger and more complex incidents will require larger ICP.

The ICP may be located at Headquarters of various levels of administration of State (State, District, Sub-Division, Tehsil/Block). In case of total destruction or reasons of non availability of any other space, the ICP may be located in a vehicle, trailer or tent. It should however have adequate lighting, effective communication system and other such facilities so that one can function effectively. In such a situation the other components of IRT may function from a convenient location and the ICP should be in constant and regular touch with them.

General guidelines for Establishing the ICP

a) Position away from the general noise and confusion associated with the incident;

b) Position outside the present and potential hazard zone;

c) Position within view of the incident, when appropriate;

d) Have the ability to expand as the incident grows;

e) Have the ability to provide security and to control access to the ICP as necessary;

f) Should have distinctive banner or sign to identify location; and

g) Activation of ICP and its location should be announced via radio or other communications so that all concerned personnel are notified.

Incident Base

All primary services and support activities for the incident are usually located and performed at the Incident base. The LS will also be preferably located here. Normally base is the location where all uncommitted/out-of-service equipment and personnel to support operations are located.

There will be only one Base established for each incident and normally it will not be relocated. It will be designated by incident name. In locations where major incidents are known to occur frequently, it is advisable to pre-designate possible base locations and plan their layouts in advance.

The management of the Incident Base comes under the LS. If an Incident base is established, a Base Manager will be designated. The Base Manager in a fully activated IRS organization will be in the Facility Unit of the LS.

Camps

Camps are temporary locations within the general incident area which are equipped and Staffed to provide rest, food, drinking water and sanitary services to the responders. These are separate facilities which may not be located at the Incident Base. Camps may be in place for several days and they may be moved depending upon incident needs while the Incident Base remains at the same location.

Very large incidents may have one or more Camps located in strategic areas. All IRS functional unit activities performed at the incident Base may also be performed at camps. Each camp will have a Camp Manager assigned. The Camp Managers are responsible for managing the camp and for providing coordination to all organisational Units operating within the camp.

The Camp manager will report to the Facility Unit in the LS. If the FUL has not been activated he will report to the LSC. After the camp is established, additional personnel and support needs will normally be determined and ordered by the Camp manager. If Logistics Units are established at Camps they will be managed by assistants. Camps will be designated by a geographic name or by a number.

Relief Camp (RC)

All support services to the affected communities are usually provided in the Relief Camps (RCs). They will be established as per demands of the situation. The resources required for the establishment of RC will be provided by the LS and it will be maintained and managed by the Branch or Division of the OS deployed for the purpose. It may be established at the existing buildings like Schools, Community halls, Cyclone Shelters, etc. or tents may also be used for such purposes.

While establishing the RC, priority will be given for cleanliness of the RC. Each RC will have a Camp Manager assigned. After RC is established, additional personnel and support needs will normally be determined and requested for by the RC Manager. The RCs will be designated by a geographic name or by a number.

Triggering Mechanism for Deployment of IRT

Some of the natural hazards have a well established early warning system. States and Districts also have a functional 24 x 7 EOC/Control Room. On receipt of information regarding the impending disaster, the EOC will inform the RO, who in turn will activate the required IRT and mobilise resources. The scale of their deployment will depend on the magnitude of the incident. At times the information about an incident may be received only on its occurrence without any warning. In such cases the local IRT as the case may be, will respond and inform the higher authority and if required seek reinforcement and guidance.

The measures decided to be taken for response will be jotted down by the Command Staff and later handed over to PS. It will thus form the initial IAP.

IRS for Chemical, Biological, Radiological and Nuclear (CBRN) Emergency Response

All nuclear facilities have specialised Crisis Management Groups (CMGs) for on site response under the aegis of Department of Atomic Energy (DAE). For the offsite incident response at those locations, the RO/District Magistrate/DC will act as the IC and ensure that the stakeholders and communities are properly sensitsed in advance through regular mock exercises. Support from local experts for such purpose may be obtained wherever available. The State Government should train and equip its own SDRF for this purpose. The help of NDRF may be taken for immediate response and for training the SDRF.

For locations in other high risk towns where nuclear facilities do not exist, the IRTs need to be formed in advance and suitably trained to identify and manage such emergencies. CBRN emergencies require a specialised response. A brief description of the requirement is being given in the subsequent paragraph for general awareness.

For Radiological Emergencies in Metropolitan and larger cities having population of 20 lakhs and above with high vulnerability, the State RO will identify a Nodal Officer for Radiological Emergency to act as an IC. He should have designated experts to assist him in the discharge of his duties. Specially trained and equipped task forces will be earmarked which would be readily available with decontamination facilities. A concept of UC for this purpose is best suited to meet such contngencies.

Incident Commander (IC) and Command Staff

The IC is the overall in-charge for the management of onsite response to any incident. He is appointed by the RO. He may have a deputy with him depending upon the magnitude and nature of the incident. For his assistance and management of the incident there are two sets of Staff: a) Command Staff and b) General Staff. The command Staff comprises IC, Information & Media Officer (IMO), Safety Officer (SO), and the Liaison Officer (LO).

Roles and Responsibilities of IC

The IC will

i) Obtain information on:
   a) situation status like number of people and the area affected etc.;
   b) availability and procurement of resources;
   c) requirement of facilities like ICP, Staging Area, Incident Base, Camp, Relief Camp, etc.;
   d) availability and requirements of Communication system;
   e) future weather behaviour from IMD; and
   f) any other information required for response from all available sources and analyse the situation.

ii) determine incident objectives and strategies based on the available information and resources;

iii) establish immediate priorities, including search & rescue and relief distribution strategies;

iv) assess requirements for maintenance of law and order, traffic etc. if any at the incident site, and make arrangements with help of the local police;

v) brief higher authorities about the situation as per incident briefing form—001 enclosed;

vi) extend support for implementation of AC and UC if considered necessary by the RO;

vii) establish appropriate IRS organisation with Sections, Branches, Divisions and/or Units based on the span of control and scale of the incident;

viii) establish ICP at a suitable place. There will be one ICP even if the incident is mult-jurisdictional. Even a mobile van with complete communication equipment and appropriate personnel may be used as ICP. In case of total destruction of buildings, tents, or temporary shelters may be used. If appropriate or enough space is not available, other Sections can function from a different convenient location. But there should be proper and fail safe contact with the ICP in order to provide quick assistance;

ix) ensure that the IAP is prepared;

x) ensure that team members are briefed on performance of various activities as per IAP;

xi) approve and authorise the implementation of an IAP and ensure that IAP is regularly developed and updated as per debriefing of IRT members. It will be reviewed every 24 hours and circulated to all concerned;

xii) ensure that planning meetings are held at regular intervals. The meetings will draw out an implementation strategy and IAP for effective incident response. The decision to hold this meeting is solely the responsibility of the IC. Apart from other members, ensure that PSC attend all briefing and debriefing meetings;

xiii) ensure that all Sections or Units are working as per IAP;

xiv) ensure that adequate safety measures for responders and affected communities are in place;

xv) ensure proper coordination between all Sections of the IRT, agencies working in the response activities and make sure that all conflicts are resolved;

xvi) ensure that computerised and web based IT solutions are used for planning, resource mobilisation and deployment of trained IRT members;

xvii) consider requirement of resources, equipment which are not available in the functional jurisdiction, discuss with PSC and LSC and inform RO regarding their procurement;

xviii) approve and ensure that the required additional resources are procured and issued to the concerned Sections, Branches and Units etc. and are properly utilised. On completion of assigned work, the resources will be returned immediately for utilisation elsewhere or to the department concerned;

xix) if required, establish contact with PRIs, ULBs, CBOs, NGOs etc. and seek their cooperation in achieving the objectives of IAP and enlist their support to act as local guides in assisting the external rescue and relief teams; xx. approve the deployment of volunteers and such other personnel and ensure that they follow the chain of command;

xxi) authorise release of information to the media;

xxii) ensure that the record of resources mobilised from outside is maintained so that prompt payment can be made for hired resources;

xxiii) ensure that Incident Status Summary (ISS) is completed and forwarded to the RO;

xxiv) recommend demobilisation of the IRT, when appropriate;

xxv) review public complaints and recommend suitable grievance redressal measures to the RO;

xxvi) ensure that the NGOs and other social organisations deployed in the affected sites are working properly and in an equitable manner;

xxvii)ensure preparation of After Action Report (AAR) prior to the demobilisation of the IRT on completion of the incident response.

xxviii)perform any other duties that may be required for the management of the incident;

xxix) ensure that the record of various activities performed by members of Branches,

xxx) perform such other duties as assigned by RO.

Roles and Responsibilities of Information and Media Officer (IMO)

The IMO will

i) prepare and release information about the incident to the media agencies and others with the approval of IC;

ii) jot down decisions taken and directions issued in case of sudden disasters when the IRT has not been fully activated and hand it over to the PS on its activation for incorporation in the IAP;

iii) ask for additional personnel support depending on the scale of incident and workload;

iv) monitor and review various media reports regarding the incident that may be useful for incident planning;

v) organise IAP meetings as directed by the IC or when required;

vi) coordinate with IMD to collect weather information and disseminate it to all concerned;

vii) maintain record of various activities performed as per IRS Form-004; and

viii) perform such other duties as assigned by IC.

Roles and Responsibilities of Liaison Officer (LO)

The LO is the focal point of contact for various line departments, representatives of NGOs, PRIs and ULBs etc. participating in the response. The LO is the point of contact to assist the first responders, cooperating agencies and line departments. LO may be designated depending on the number of agencies involved and the spread of affected area.

The LO will

i) maintain a list of concerned line departments, agencies (CBOs, NGOs, etc.) and their representatives at various locations;

ii) carry out liaison with all concerned agencies including NDRF and Armed Forces and line departments of Government;

iii) monitor Operations to identify current or potential inter-agency problems;

iv) participate in planning meetings and provide information on response by participating agencies;

v) ask for personnel support if required;
vi) keep the IC informed about arrivals of all the Government and Non Government agencies and their resources;
vii) help in organising briefing sessions of all Governmental and Non Governmental agencies with the IC;
viii) maintain record of various activities performed as per IRS Form-004; and
ix) perform such other duties as assigned by IC.

Roles and Responsibilities of Safety Officer (SO)

The SO's function is to develop and recommend measures for ensuring safety of personnel, and to assess and/or anticipate hazardous and unsafe situations. The SO is authorised to stop or prevent unsafe acts. SO may also give general advice on safety of affected communities.

The SO will

i) recommend measures for assuring safety of responders and to assess or anticipate hazardous and unsafe situations and review it regularly;
ii) ask for assistants and assign responsibilities as required;
iii) participate in planning meetings for preparation of IAP;
iv) review the IAP for safety implications;
v) obtain details of accidents that have occurred within the incident area if required or as directed by IC and inform the appropriate authorities;
vi) review and approve the Site Safety Plan, as and when required;
vii) maintain record of various activities performed as per IRS Form-004; and
viii) perform such other duties as assigned by IC.

General Staff

The General Staff consists of the OS, PS and LS, each having a specific function in the overall response.

Operations Section (OS)

The OS deals with all types of field level tactical operations directly applicable to the management of an incident. OS is further sub-divided into Branches, Divisions and Groups which assist the OSC/IC in the execution of the field operations.

Planning Section (PS)

The PS deals with all matters relating to the planning of the incident response. It is headed by the Planning Section Chief (PSC). It maintains up-to-date information about the ongoing response and prepares IAP.

Logistics Section (LS)

The LS deals with matters relating to procurement of resources and establishment of facilities for the incident response. It also deals with all financial matters, concerning an incident.

Operations Section (OS)

The OS comprises Response Branch (RB), Transportation Branch (TB) and Staging Area (SA) and is headed by the OSC. The activation of the RB and TB is situational.

The RB consists of various Divisions and Groups depending upon the functional and geographical requirements of the incident response. The Groups are classified by their functional characteristics, such as Single Resource, Strike Teams and/or Task Force.

The TB may consist of Road Operations Group, Rail Operations Group, Water Operations Group and Air Operations Group. These Groups are also activated according to the transportation modes that may be required in the incident response.

SA is the area where resources mobilised are collected and accounted for. It is from this location that the resources are deployed for specific assignments or tasks.

RB is activated according to the nature of response required. For example in case of earthquake and food where a lot of houses get damaged or destroyed and people need to be rescued and provided relief and temporary shelter. The rescue and relief group of the Response Branch will be activated to provide these services.

The TB will manage the transportation of the affected people and the movement of relief materials. Groups within the TB like Road group or Water group will be activated as required for managing and providing the Road or Water transport. Since Air Operations in disaster response involves coordination between the Central Government, Ministry of Civil Aviation, Air Force, State and the Districts concerned and also require technical inputs.

Selection of the OSC depends on the nature of operations required. Rescuing people and taking them to shelter in case of earthquake or foods can best be handled by the police/Armed Forces and thus in such cases it should ideally be headed by them. However in cases of such disaster like bird fuel epidemic, the main requirement will be providing medical treatment to the victims, vaccinating and culling of birds. In such cases the OS shall have to be headed by Doctors for treatment of victims and supported by Animal husbandry department and Municipal institutions for vaccinating and culling of birds.

In disaster response a large number of duties and activities need to be performed. To meet the various duty requirements, the IRS provides for Single Resource, Task Force and Strike Teams.

As the operational activity increase because of the largeness and magnitude of the disaster, the OSC who is responsible for directing all tactical actions to meet the incident objectives will have to deploy more and more functional teams. It has been generally accepted that an ideal span of control is 1:5 that is one leader or supervisor can effectively manage five groups. In order to maintain close supervision, the IRS provides for the formation of Branches, Divisions and Groups.

Operations Section Chief (OSC)

On activation of the OS, the OSC will assume command of all the field operations and will be fully responsible for directing all tactical actions to meet the incident objectives.

As the operational activities increase and because of geographical reasons, the OSC will introduce or activate and expand the Branch into Divisions for proper span of control and effective supervision.

Roles and Responsibilities of OSC

The OSC will:

i) coordinate with the activated Section Chiefs;

ii) manage all field operations for the accomplishment of the incident objectives;

iii) ensure the overall safety of personnel involved in the OS and the affected communities;

iv) deploy, activate, expand and supervise organisational elements (Branch, Division, Group, etc,);

v) assign appropriate personnel, keeping their capabilities for the task in mind and maintain On Duty Officers list;

vi) request IC for providing a Deputy OSC for assistance, if required;

vii) brief the personnel in OS at the beginning of each operational period;

viii) ensure resolution of all conflicts, information sharing, coordination and cooperation between the various Branches;

ix) prepare Section Operational Plan in accordance with the IAP; if required;

x) suggest expedient changes in the IAP to the IC;

xi) consult the IC from time-to-time and keep him fully briefed;

xii) determine the need for additional resources and place demands accordingly and ensure their arrival;

xiii) ensure record of various activities performed by members of Branches, Divisions, Units/Groups are collected and maintained in the Unit Log IRS Form-003; and

xiv) perform such other duties as assigned by RO/IC.

Staging Area Manager (SAM)

The SA is an area where resources are collected and kept ready for deployment for field operations. These may include things like food, vehicles and other materials and equipment. The SA will be established at a suitable area near the affected site for immediate, effective and quick deployment of resources.

More than one SA may be established if required. If resources are mobilised at other locations to be ultimately despatched to the affected areas, these locations are also known as SAs. The overall in-charge of the SA is known as Staging Area Manager (SAM) and he needs to work in close liaison with both the LS and PS through the OSC.

School and college playgrounds, community halls, cyclone shelters and Panchayat Offices, stadia etc. may be used as SA. In case of total destruction of buildings in an incident, tents or temporary shelters may be used for such purposes.

For Air Operations, open space of Airport Authority of India (AAI) may be used for loading and unloading of relief materials. If area of AAI is not available, other suitable places near Helipads, Helibases etc. will have to be selected for such purpose.For parking of vehicles, playgrounds of the schools or any large plain areas may be used. Such parking area will preferably have separate entry and exit points. The SAM will arrange for separate entry and exit points to avoid and reduce traffic jam in an emergency.

The SAM will:

i) establish the SA with proper layout, maintain it in an orderly condition and ensure that there is no obstruction to the incoming and outgoing vehicles, resources etc;
ii) organise storage and despatch of resources received and despatch it as per IAP;
iii) report all receipts and despatches to OSC and maintain their records;
iv) manage all activities of the SA;
v) utilise all perishable supplies expeditiously;
vi) establish check-in function as appropriate;
vii) request maintenance and repair of equipment at SA, as needed;
viii) ensure that communications are established with the ICP and other required locations e.g. different SAs, Incident Base, Camp, Relief Camp etc;
ix) maintain and provide resource status to PS and LS.

REFERNCES

Alexander, D., (2002). *Principles of Emergency planning and Management*, Harpended: Terra publishing.

Anderson, Mary B. and Peter J. Woodrow. (1989). *Rising from the Ashes: Development Strategies at Times of Disasters.* Boulder: Westview Press and Paris: UNESCO Press.

Barton A.H., (1969). *Communities in Disaster. A Sociological Analysis of Collective Stress Situations.* SI: Ward Lock.

Carter, Nick. (1991). *Disaster Management: A Disaster Manager's Handbook.* Manila: Asian Development Bank.

Hagman, Gunnar. (1984). *Prevention Better Than Cure.* Stockholm and Geneva: The Swedish Red Cross.

8

Public Awareness for Disaster Risk Reduction

The importance of public awareness and education in promoting and enabling Disaster Risk Reduction (DRR) has already been identified by researchers and policy makers. In doing so, there is a renewed focus on disaster risk awareness and education in primary and secondary schools. Mainstreaming DRR into school curricula aims to raise awareness and provide a better understanding of disaster management for children, teachers and communities. Accompanying structural changes to improve safety in building schools will not only protect children and their access to education, but will also minimise long term costs.

There is increasing evidence that students of all ages can actively study and participate in school safety measures, and also work with teachers and other adults in the community towards minimising risk before, during and after disaster events. Methods of participatory vulnerability assessment, capacity assessment and hazard mapping have been be used with broader communities surrounding schools and other institutions of education and research. Government can effectively reach out to communities and protect them by focusing on schools in DRR initiatives to achieve greater resilience to disasters.

Recent disasters in Haiti and Pakistan in 2010 showed the need to "use knowledge, innovation and education to build a culture of safety and resilience at all levels" as articulated in the Hyogo Framework for Action 2005-2015. The role of education for disaster risk reduction strategies can thus be presented according to three types of activities: 1) Save lives and prevent injuries should a hazardous event occur, 2) Prevent interruptions to the provision of education, or ensure its swift resumption in the event of an interruption, and 3) Develop a resilient population that is able to reduce the economic, social and cultural impacts should a hazardous event occur.

Education for Disaster Risk Reduction (DRR) takes into account the relationships between society, environment, economy, and culture and their impacts. It also promotes critical thinking and problem-solving as well as social and emotional life skills that are essential to the empowerment of groups threatened or affected by disasters.

UNESCO has been playing a valuable role within the UN International Strategy for Disaster Reduction (ISDR) Thematic Platform on Knowledge and Education. With its ISDR partner agencies, UNESCO promotes the integration of Disaster Risk Reduction in national educational plans, school curricula and national strategies, as well as supporting natural disaster preparedness. UNESCO has promoted Education for Disaster Risk Reduction at a number of international events, including the workshop on "ESD and disaster risk reduction: building disaster-resilient societies", organized during the 2009 Bonn World Conference on ESD.

Community Disaster Awareness

Community disaster awareness (DA) initiatives which inform and train local populations about how to prepare for natural disasters and emergencies can reduce a population's vulnerability to specific hazards. These initiatives need not require large financial outlays nor do they require the work of a great number of people. What is required for planning purposes is a DA strategy that is opportunistic in its timing and which is integrated with other local and community development strategies

DA initiatives may consist of individual activities—such as touring villages to conduct earthquake awareness meetings, or posting earthquake preparedness posters at a local library. A second more comprehensive DA approach entails planning a series of coordinated activities—for example, a comprehensive DA campaign may be implemented during a disaster awareness week, when the media publicises disaster messages on the radio, T.V. and in newspapers; schools conduct poster contests and perform disaster drills; and community centres display disaster posters. Yet a third approach, and perhaps the most effective at the community level, is a strategy that integrates DA into broader community health and development goals— in

East Africa, for example, attempts have been made to link DP to branch level programmes through Community—Based First Aid (CBFA) programmes. In another case, disaster preparedness activities were conceptualised within Primary Health Care and Nutrition Initiatives.

Planning disaster awareness and disaster preparedness activities in isolation from people's daily lives and everyday concerns will rarely succeed. This is because people's interest in disaster preparedness fades if it has been a long time between disaster events. Therefore, disaster awareness activities will have the greatest impact when they are integrated into broader programme strategies that seek to alleviate everyday community problems and hazards —such as basic health care, water scarcity and potability, sanitation concerns such as garbage collection, employment and community based first aid.

While it is a fact that a community may be exposed to various natural and technological hazards, oftentimes, the reality of the situation is that people may not see the practicality of disaster preparedness suggestions and messages when they are trying to provide for themselves and their families in difficult and harsh economic environments. While this module focuses specifically on disaster preparedness awareness messages, it is important that National Societies explore ways to integrate these messages into a more holistic community education approach. In the Caribbean for example, some National Societies have assisted in the creation of community management committees which ultimately will take responsibility for carrying out DP activities and also for addressing other identified community needs—such as conflict resolution and garbage collection. National Society staff and volunteers with formal responsibilities for community disaster awareness gain greater credibility with residents and find it easier to discuss DP topics when they become more involved in the life of the community.

Designing a Disaster Awareness Effort

Proper planning is the key to launching successful DA initiatives. This section covers the following steps for planning a DA effort.

1. Define the purpose and objectives of the DA initiative
2. Select and analyse primary audience(s)
3. Form a DA planning team
4. Form collaborative community partnerships

5. Schedule the time and location of DA events for maximum impact
6. Brainstorm potential activities and resources
7. Determine the proper medium or format
8. Develop, implement and monitor the action plan

Define Purpose and Objectives of the DA Initiative

Planning should begin by outlining the general purpose and objectives of the DA initiative. It should be determined whether the initiative consists of an isolated activity, a series of activities, or a coordinated DA campaign. The purpose statement outlines what you hope to achieve, while statements of objectives offer specific, measurable details. For example, if the purpose is to increase children's knowledge of fire-safety practices in the home, then one specific objective might be to arrange for a local fire fighter to speak at three local schools within the next six months. Another specific objective might be to get the local Red Cross/Red Crescent Society and civil defence authorities to co-sponsor a contest for children to create fire-safety posters during an official Fire Awareness Week. While the overall purpose of an initiative may be to raise public awareness, specific objectives will depend on the nature of the target audience. In the previous example, schoolchildren might be taught about the dangers of playing near lit kerosene lamps. Homeowners, on the other hand, might be encouraged to purchase smoke detectors and fire extinguishers. For each audience, the following two questions must be asked:

1. What does this specific audience need to understand?
2. What action can they take?

Select Target Communities and Primary Audience

Each National Society should understand which communities and regions in their country are most vulnerable to disasters. Community disaster awareness activities can then be targeted to these communities and regions. Selection may be based on the location of a community in a highly vulnerable and hazard prone zone, its accessibility in the event of a disaster, its disaster history and its local resources. Once the priority communities have been identified, specific strategies can be developed for addressing them. There are many ways to categorise different segments of a population. Each situation requires a different type of segmentation. Categories of primary audiences include:

— Labourers in specific occupations
— Businessmen
— Children
— Teenagers
— Teachers
— Heads of families
— Women heads-of-household
— Senior citizens
— Village leaders
— Professional groups

Because resources are limited and not all audiences can be reached, DA planners need to prioritise which audience will receive the message. For example, planners may decide to target those most at risk such as schoolchildren, older adults, physically or mentally impaired individuals, or people with limited literacy skills.

Analyse Primary Audience Needs and Preferences

Once the primary audience has been identified, planners should try to learn as much as they can about its particular needs, preferences and characteristics. The more that is known about the primary audience the better the message can be designed, delivered and timed. To ensure maximum impact, it helps to know the following:

— What people make up this group? Are they children, adults, senior citizens, students, homemakers, business executives, blue-collar workers, single, married?
— What are the special characteristics and needs of this group? Consider such factors as age, education and literacy levels, gender, occupation, motivations, cultural and social interests, activities, and preferred entertainment options.
— What does this group already know about disasters?
— From what sources does this group typically get its information: newspapers, television, radio, mail, town meetings, word of mouth?
— Who are the most influential voices for this group: their teachers, parents, kinsmen,leaders?

— Are there other people in this community that this group listens to and respects (e.g. elders or clergy)?

Information on the primary audience can be obtained from a variety of sources. Ideally, face-to-face interviews or meetings should be arranged with representatives of the audience. When this is not possible, secondary sources of information can be useful. For example, if the DA initiative is singling out young school children, DA planners can speak with the children's teachers. Other sources of information include local social service agencies, schools, neighbourhood and community groups, religious establishments, the local fire department, local newspaper and radio stations, the civil defence official in the community, and others who have conducted DA activities. The primary audience will be more receptive to the message if the message is tailored to their situation.

Form a Planning Team

If one is tasked with planning a DA initiative, s/he might start by making a list of anyone and everyone who might be interested in joining the planning team. Next, one might consider what each person has to offer including expertise, volunteer time, organisational skills, contacts and professional networks, sponsorship, and financial support. Finally, those who would be of most use, who would be dedicated and who would work well together, should be invited to join the team. The individuals on a DA planning team need not be emergency management professionals. While the team might include firefighters or civil defence officials, it can also include teachers, respected community officials, businesspeople or leaders, and concerned parents and volunteers. Involving people with different backgrounds and experiences has many advantages including:

— Access to a wider range of ideas and perspectives

— Sharing work responsibilities among several people

— Expanding the network of potential contacts, supporters and sponsors

The team must consist of enthusiastic supporters who can help plan and promote the DA effort. Ideally, someone from the primary DA audience should be on the team or be available to advise the team. In small countries it may initially be necessary to form a planning team at the national level to ensure cooperation in the field. Quite often community organisations vie for limited resources and are more likely to compete than cooperate unless the planning process is sanctioned at the national level.

While it is important to have at least two or three people on a core planning team who can provide leadership and continuity throughout the planning and implementation effort, other members can rotate in and out as appropriate. Some may only be available for the initial planning meetings or for helping out at the actual event. Some, who are well-connected in the community, might be engaged early on to assist with contacting and gaining the support of influential and well-resourced friends and acquaintances in government or business.

Form Collaborative Community Partnerships

Opportunities for collaboration

One of the first tasks of the planning team is to identify potential collaborative community partnerships with other organisations, groups and agencies. Women's groups, teacher's associations, official emergency managers, fire fighters, community and voluntary organisations, businesses, corporations, foundations and the media all can help disseminate information, sponsor an event, provide space for an upcoming activity, underwrite the production of materials, or provide other much-needed resources. The planning team might begin by making a list of potential partners, what they might contribute, and how they will be contacted.

Potential partners need to know specifically what it is they are being asked to provide. They also might be more inclined to participate if they know what benefits they might derive from the partnership. Such benefits include:

- A forum for discussing and resolving community problems
- The opportunity to foster good community relations
- Increased awarenesss of the hazard by community residents
- The opportunity to improve the working relationships between government and civil society
- Local and collective ownership for resolving community problems
- Increased visibility in the community
- The opportunity to build organisational capacities and other skills
- Networking opportunity
- Increased positive media coverage, credibility and visibility
- An opportunity to contribute to the well-being of the community

List of Potential Partners

The following are all potential partners for supporting a DA initiative:

- Television stations
- Schools, colleges and universities
- Local community centres and groups
- Religious organisations
- Youth clubs, students' (hostels) dormitories
- Village elders
- Women's clubs, organisations
- Trade enterprises, associations
- Banks and credit unions
- Health centres, hospitals, clinics
- Sport clubs
- Libraries, cinemas, theatres, circuses
- Utility companies
- Newspapers, magazines
- Red Cross/Red Crescent Societies
- Civil Defence
- NGOs
- Fire brigade

Partnering with Local Businesses or Corporations

All organisations have a vested interest in protecting their employees and facilities in case of a disaster. Businesses depend on their employees and on their customers for their survival and profit. Local businesses and industries may be interested and willing to distribute information to protect their employees and customers and, as a result, reduce potential liabilities. Companies recognise that employees who are prepared for disasters at home will be less likely to be absent from work following a disaster—when businesses may need them most.

Large corporations and businesses might be willing to make "in-kind" contributions of expertise, time, facilities or equipment. A corporate partner can also help with the cost of printing materials or underwriting a special event. It is also possible for National Societies to work out some kind of mutually beneficial exchange with service industries.

The following are additional ideas for partnering with local businesses or corporations:

— Encourage local utilities (telephone, water, electric, gas) to include periodic emergency preparedness and mitigation information in customer bills or newsletters
— Encourage large businesses to distribute disaster preparedness information to and hold disaster preparedness workshops for all employees
— Ask them to print hazard and basic preparedness measures fact-sheets and brochures
— Ask local vendors to hang a poster or distribute brochures to customers

Finally, companies involved in the manufacture, storage and disposal of chemicals have a moral and often a legal responsibility to inform the surrounding community of the danger posed by their daily activities. Quite often, however, companies are reluctant to do this as they fear a public outcry. By working with these companies and bringing them into the mainstream preparedness and risk reduction planning process as it may be possible to work out solutions and compromises. The insert below provides an example of a chemical and industrial risk reduction programme which creates community partnership between government, industry and community-based organisations.

Partnering with Community Organisations

Community organisations can be valuable partners in a public outreach initiative. Community organisations include youth clubs, Red Cross/Red Crescent Societies, NGOs, law enforcement organisations, women's groups, veterans groups, religious organisations, etc.

Although community organisations cannot always provide financial resources, they often can provide people—an equally important resource. Often, members of these groups want to become involved in helping their community in a variety of ways. Each group has its own network that can help extend the reach of the disaster awareness activity. Some ideas for community partnerships include:

- Work with local school parents to incorporate a disaster preparedness workshop into one of their meetings
- Work with local school teachers to incorporate disaster preparedness messages into their lesson plans
- Sponsor a children's poster contest highlighting the steps to take in the event of a specific emergency or disaster
- Work with local organisations to present a disaster preparedness and mitigation workshop at one of their meetings
- Organise a display booth on disaster preparedness at an annual event, festival or fair
- Set up a display poster with brochures at the local library or community market
- Ask war veteran groups or youth clubs to assist with planning and setting up a disaster awareness booth or stage at a fair, festival or market

Partnering with the Local Media

Media partners can disseminate preparedness and mitigation messages through an article, editorial coverage or donated advertising space. Media contacts need to be cultivated early on and occasionally nourished and renewed.

Schedule the Time and Location of DA Assets

Timing and Location

When scheduling a DA event, it is important to select a time and place that encourages attendance and will best capture the attention of the intended audience. Generally, DA events should not be planned near or during holiday periods as they will compete for attention. The location for a DA event should coincide with a place where your primary audience commonly visits, works or plays.

"Piggy-back" on other events

Rather than organise an entirely new event, one can profit by "piggy-backing" on someone else's event. For example, DA planning teams might decide to coordinate their event with local festivals, fairs, town meetings, market days and community gatherings. The planning team may also approach a local health clinic and ask them to distribute flyers or brochures to their visitors. The idea is that efficiency and cost-savings can result from grafting your DA message or event onto an already ongoing effort or event.

Plan annual events

The chance that a DA activity will have an impact can be increased by making it an annual tradition. Many countries and communities, for example, have a disaster awareness week when many groups and organisations disseminate disaster awareness and community preparedness messages.

Disaster seasons

Some disasters are cyclical and are associated with specific seasons. For example, wildfires are likely to occur in the summer - autumn period. Severe flooding usually occurs in the spring. When potential disasters are seasonal, the pre-season period is a time when people are receptive to hearing messages related to preparedness: clean-up, warnings, possibility of evacuation, etc.

Post disaster activities

Public awareness of a disaster is highest following a disaster. For example, the entire world was attentive to the risks associated with nuclear power after the Chernobyl nuclear reactor accident in May 1986. Many local communities used this event as a way to publicise the dangers, risks and preparedness measures associated with nuclear reactor plants in their own vicinity.

Brainstorm Potential DA Activities

Generally, prior to developing a DA initiative, the planning team should spend some time brainstorming ideas about the kinds of activities and mediums they might use to deliver the message and information. For example, if the purpose is to increase the level of awareness among children ages 7 to 10 about home fire safety, a list of brainstormed ideas might include:

— Presentations in the school by local fire fighters
— Inclusion of disaster preparedness topics in teachers' lesson plans
— School game-quiz
— A "disaster preparedness" clown at the local circus
— A disaster preparedness colouring book

— Song to be played on the radio
— Cartoon on television
— Posters to hang in markets, libraries, and other public places
— TV program on disaster preparedness

After brainstorming a list of ideas, the planning team can more carefully consider a range of options. This broad approach is a more effective way to begin as opposed to choosing the first idea that is suggested. Once a generous list is developed, ideas can be evaluated according to a set of criteria. These criteria might include:

— Can the activity be completed in the given time-frame?
— Is it affordable (or, can the resources be found)?
— Are the necessary people and volunteers available?
— Will the activity reach the greatest number of people in our primary audience?

Select the Communication Medium and Activities

Communication mediums

Each primary audience will respond differently to various presentations and methods of information dissemination. If resources allow, it is best to vary the format of the message and communicate it in more than one way, and more than once. If the planning team knows its audience, it will be easier to select the most effective means of reaching them. If the planning team does not know the habits and preferences of their intended primary audience, this information must be researched. Once the message has been created and a medium selected, it is best to test it on people who are representative of the target audience and get their critical feedback.

The following is a non-exhaustive list of potential mediums:

— Fact sheets
— Brochures
— Newspaper articles or advertisements
— Booklets, leaflets
— Posters
— Bookmarks
— Gameboards

- Radio and television
- Cartoons
- Photographs
- Talks or presentations
- Theatre and plays
- Emergency drills and exercises
- Shopping bags
- Telephone directories
- Matchbox covers
- Special information displays, for example, at libraries or major stores
- Community gatherings/meetings of various kinds
- Existing government programs, which include short informational pieces on preparedness and other disaster-related matters

Activities and Events for Raising Disaster Awareness

Each disaster awareness initiative and activity is distinct and should be tailored to the particular population and primary audience. DA planning teams can benefit from studying the DA experiences and ideas of others. The following lists can be used to stimulate creative thinking among the planning team about how they might deliver DA messages and information.

- Create displays in public buildings or gathering places to portray past disasters and responses
- Set up markers to remind residents of past incidents
- Arrange tours to show local officials key locations, such as high water marks
- Ask the local telephone company to include emergency information in its annual directory, e.g., maps showing floodplains or the location of emergency shelters
- At times of seasonal risk, ask utility companies to include "stuffers" with their bills, identifying hazards and instructing citizens what to do when disasters strike
- Ask employers to distribute risk information brochures to their employees
- Post seasonal information in a variety of places—on milk cartons, bread wrappers, shopping bags, etc.

— Create a speaker's bureau to guarantee that any service organisation, parent-teacher group, or church group can learn about emergency planning
— Get your local mayor or governor to declare a Disaster Preparedness Day or Week. Each year, plan local events around this day (or week)
— Hold a poster contest for local students to design posters with preparedness messages. Invite an elected official and a member of the media to serve as judges. Sponsor a ceremony announcing the winner to provide an opportunity to promote your messages to a wider audience

Planning Community Disaster Awareness Strategies

Planning and implementing the actual DA strategy requires the use of basic project management skills. Once the broad objectives are set and the primary audience identified, planners should consider the detailed tasks and steps to implement the activity. The planning team also needs to identify required resources, develop a budget and locate the funds to implement the initiative. Useful planning tools include Gantt (or Bar) charts, action plans and project budgets.

Step in Developing Public Awareness

The frst step in developing public awareness or public education for disaster risk reduction is to bring together a small, dedicated and creative group to develop a plan of action. Whether you begin at national, district or local level, this guidance will help you involve others and develop a strong and effective plan that will gain the confdence and commitment of the organization. This process follows the familiar cycle promoted in programme development throughout the Movement. In the case of a public awareness or education initiative for disaster risk reduction, a good place to start is to ask the following set of familiar questions and review the answers.

Response alone is not sufficient to meet the increasing demand caused by hazard impacts on larger populations. It bears the obligation to share knowledge that can help with identifying hazards and risks, taking action to build safety and resilience, and reducing future hazard impacts. Communities and individuals usually can—and want to—become partners in this. Public awareness and public education for disaster risk reduction can empower normal people everywhere to participate in reducing future suffering.

The IFRC's *Disaster Response and Contingency Planning* provides detailed guidance on how to analyse risks, including hazards, vulnerabilities and capacities. Although it is challenging to be selective, we need to focus on those risks that are most likely to occur as well as having the most severe impact on the highest number of people. In some cases recurrent smaller risks add up to severe impacts. And in some cases chronic issues such as unclean water and poor sanitation are the key issues to be tackled. Today, urban areas account for more than half of the world's population, and are at the heart of economic and political life, so we must also be prepared to systematically tackle these risks in their urban contexts. And complex emergencies may layer these risks on top of one another, also demanding systematic approaches.

Who is the Initiative Aimed At?

The target audiences for public awareness and public education extend like ripples in a pond. At the core are those people that are already acting consistently to make themselves and those around them safer and more resilient. But this core (especially enthusiastic staff and volunteers) can always beneft from expanding itself.

Immediately outside that core are people who are receptive, and are thinking about acting, but need supportive information and more confdence in order to act. Next are those people who have heard about your efforts, and are beginning to think and talk about the issues. Then comes a larger group that seems resistant to acting, or that lacks wherewithal. People in this category are vaguely aware of the issues but have no intention to act yet. They are often mislabelled "fatalistic".

Finally, there are many more who have never heard about their risks, or thought much about what they might do about them. Public education and awareness efforts need to reach each of these layers and draw them towards the centre.

There really is no one, single 'general public'. Instead, there are many different publics, each affected on by a wide variety of social and cultural dynamics and vulnerabilities. Very early in the planning process, it is important to decide which of the various public market segments the initiative will target. Even those approaches that are intended to have broad appeal should be considered in relation to each of the targeted market segments.

Getting to know your market segments

Step 1: List all the different target groups that you can think of, and note down subsets of these. For example, consider:

— geographic location (including urban neighbourhoods, villages, remote areas, slums and suburbs)
— gender
— age
— education level
— language and ethnic groups
— type of workplace.

Include people with disabilities, recent immigrants, displaced or homeless people, non-literate people, street children and working youth, and identify the particular ways to reach these marginalized parts of your audience.

Step 2: List the kinds of organizations, associations and groups that people belong to. Include neighbourhood associations, workplaces, schools, places of worship, professional and alumni associations, clubs and teams, place-of-origin associations and gangs.

Step 3: Consider how people communicate within their social networks. Discuss and list the opportunities and barriers that each of these present.

This awareness will help you later to select approaches and tools appropriate to the different segments of your target audience.

What Could the Initiative Consist of?

Public awareness and public education for disaster reduction seek to turn available human knowledge into specifc local action to reduce disaster risks. It mobilizes people through clear messages, supported with detailed information.

Hazard awareness alone does not lead directly to people adopting risk-reduction measures. Researchers have found that people take action only when:

— they know what specifc actions can be taken to reduce their risks
— they are convinced that these actions will be effective
— they believe in their own ability to carry out the tasks.

Key research fndings can inform the design of successful public education. For example, the following facts are well established:

— People need to be stimulated to seek information.

— People seek consensus, and want validation from many sources before they act.

— People go along with what they think others are doing. (This means that it is important to focus on all of the positive and local examples: negative threats do not work.)

— Three types of people start 'pro-social epidemics': connectors who bring people together, information specialists (in other words, experts), and salespeople who have the ability to persuade.

— The most memorable lessons are learned from stories that are simple, unexpected, concrete, credible and emotional.

— The gradual process of behaviour change moves from contemplation to planning, then to action, and fnally to maintenance.

It is good practice start with the easy, little things that will make a difference, and to help people to experience, document and share their successes. It important to face and address the actual physical and environmental measures that reduce risk—for example, fastening furniture against earthquake shaking, or clearing drainage channels to prevent fooding. Similarly, frst aid cannot fll the gap if primary healthcare facilities are not open because they failed to take physical risk-reduction measures against wind and ground shaking. And people at risk of food, wind and earthquake need to learn the basics of disaster-resilient construction. If mitigation requires expertise that is not readily available, now is the time to access it.

Jumping directly from hazard awareness to response-preparedness skills can reinforce the view that disasters are inevitable, and that the only thing people can do is to react to them afterwards. This can inadvertently support a fatalistic attitude.

Who Should We Work With?

Partnerships are important to the success of public education and awareness efforts. Good strategies grow from collaboration, and cooperation is essential for developing consistent, harmonized and standardized messages that will be scaled up and repeated frequently enough to become common knowledge. Meaningful partnerships generally require a decision to invest in relationship building over a long period of time. Many stakeholders are ready to partner with National Societies, yet the mutual process of getting to know one another, developing trust and committing resources requires long-term dedication. If you start small, you can grow together from one success to the next. One post-disaster programme with staff responsible for outreach in separate sectors discovered that the team itself was most effective when members partnered each other, in order to saturate one geographic area at a time.Remember it is not necessary that National Societies lead every effort. Simply being a participant, and lending your weight and credibility, can play a valuable role in winning public support for shared goals. Your leadership, or your presence at the table, is powerful advocacy for the cause.

And fnally—your key partners for 'ground-truthing' (gathering on-site data to verify information gleaned from remote sources) are representatives of all of your intended benefciaries. Involve these individuals in the process of developing methods and approaches, as well as in reviewing programmes and materials. An advisory council of this kind will take its job seriously and help promote your objectives.

When and Where is the Initiative Appropriate?

National Societies are involved in a wide range of activities, most of which offer a ready opportunity to integrate public awareness and public education for disaster reduction. Strategic planning can help take full advantage of these, as well as identifying specifc opportunities to elevate public education and awareness as a main focus, and to reach out to high-risk areas and communities.

When woven together, the different strands of traditional Red Cross Red Crescent core activities combine to make communities safer and more resilient, contributing to the process of sustainable development. Public awareness and public education for disaster reduction are expected to fnd a heightened role in this process in the future. Many of the same measures that promote safe shelter, clean water, sanitation and hygiene, health, environmental restoration, food security and livelihood protection are the very same key behaviours needed for reducing disaster risks. All the accumulated technical expertise from these sectors is needed, along with additional inputs from multi-hazard risk assessment and specifc hazard mitigation measures, and cross-disciplinary problem solving.

Approaches to Create Public Awareness

This section sets out four key approaches to public awareness or public education for disaster risk reduction:

— campaigns
— participatory learning
— informal education
— formal school-based interventions.

For each of these approaches, the guide sets out background information, useful tools (such as checklists and templates), advantages and disadvantages of the approach, and tools that can be used within this approach.

Campaigns

The focus of campaigns is to provide uniform, large-scale impact with standard messages. There are many examples of large-scale national and international public awareness campaigns that have led to massive social change. Examples include childhood immunization, the wearing of seat belts in cars, and smoking restrictions.

Campaigns comprise a set of activities that may include:

— publications, including billboards, posters, newspaper or magazine coverage, information cards, fyers, bookmarks and brochures
— curricula, modules and presentations, including slide presentations and oral presentations
— e-learning
— performing and cultural arts
— games and competitions
— audio and video materials
— web pages and activities
— social media and telecommunications.

Most successful campaigns require a sustained, repeated and consistent thematic set of messages repeated over a long period of time, through activities in the public, education, private and civic sectors. These are often built by a unifying coalition under a single umbrella. Some recur seasonally. Others are ongoing, and select an annually changing sub-theme, or a monthly calendar with 10-12 messages per year.

The strongest, and most memorable, campaigns have been built around a single unifying and enduring slogan, expressed and delivered in a multitude of creative ways through both predictable and recurring outlets as well as new surprises. A good example is 'Clunk Click Every Trip'. This slogan was at the heart of road safety in the UK from 1971, and laid the groundwork for compulsory seat belt legislation introduced in 1983. Some campaigns have an enduring mascot. In the United States, Smokey Bear has delivered the slogan 'Only YOU can prevent forest fres' since 1944. About 95 per cent of adults and 77 per cent of children recognize him and his message..Where campaigns are short term and time limited because they successfully meet their goals, the tools developed can then be adapted and used at another time or place, when a similar intervention is needed.

Because campaigns need newsworthy moments and high visibility, participation is often focused around designated days such as a commemorative event, a community-wide drill, a festival, fair or exhibition, or through demonstrations and simulations. In between these focal events, volunteers continue to deliver the key messages through live interactions. These may take place in a range of ways. For example:

— at school assemblies and after-school activities
— at an outreach table at a local farmers' market
— at cultural or performing arts events
— during outreach and advocacy visits.

Actors such as community coalitions, scouts, civil defence organizations, university students and members of professional associations are often enthusiastic participants. Campaigns can also make excellent use of participatory learning approaches.

Participatory Learning

People are especially motivated by approaches in which they themselves participate in a solution, and especially when they believe it is their own idea. The focus of participatory learning is to engage people in discovery and problem solving for disaster risk reduction. At the heart of all of these activities is the community's own experience of empowerment.

This involves using language, stories, songs and traditions to strengthen the emerging culture of prevention. This is typically accomplished through tools such as:

— action-oriented research such as vulnerability and capacity assessment
— disaster management planning

— implementing risk reduction measures
— monitoring and improving on plans through drills and simulations.

These four elements of participatory learning can be applied at three levels:

— *The organizational level*—headquarters, branches, schools, businesses, workplaces, homes
— *The community level*—being scaled up to reach villages, towns, cities, school systems, and regions
— *The population level*—being expanded to incorporate entire urban populations, by taking advantage of internet-based tools and social media.

Parallel tools specifcally for use with children, and for marginalized populations can be valuable as well. Specifc tools within this approach include:

— publications such as booklets
— curricula, modules and presentations
— participatory activities such as transect walk, risk and asset mapping, seasonal calendar, group discussion, drills, simulations and tabletop exercises
— audio and video materials, including videos, audio clips and songs or other music
— web pages and activities such as workspaces
— social media and telephone-based initiatives, such as text messaging and polling.

Vulnerability and capacity assessment

More than 60 National Societies have some experience with vulnerability and capacity assessment (VCA) approaches, using traditional tools incorporated into facilitator training modules and supplementary toolkits for application in rural communities. These include:

— transect walk
— community risk and capacity mapping
— seasonal calendar
— focus-group discussions.

In recent innovations, National Societies such as Paraguay, Indonesia, Sri Lanka and China have used VCA effectively for integrated community-based disaster reduction. Meanwhile staff and volunteers are discovering a wide range of tools through the ProVention Consortium's CRA Toolkit, and are actively exploring ways of adapting and developing tools for urban settings and tools that integrate climate change concerns. In VCA, the focus of the learning is identifying and prioritizing threats and hazards, recognizing and mobilizing resources and capacities, and beginning disaster reduction action planning. This process may result in the community doing one of the following:

— fulfllling the task themselves and making their community safer (change)
— enlisting support from the municipality or other organizations (advocate for or infuence change)
— acknowledge that the solution is very complex and will require a longer-term process (transform). This may also lead to legislative advocacy.

Participatory disaster management planning

Participatory disaster management planning takes the VCA approach forward one more step by establishing a model for the long-term ongoing process of planning for risk reduction and response.

Step 1: Develop guidance and training materials

Guidance and training materials are needed for the following reasons:

— to evaluate and apply appropriate physical and/or environmental protection measures
— for risk reduction
— to develop disaster response skills.

Step 2: Learn and practise skills

Participatory learning takes place as skills are learned and practised, for example, in the following areas:

— evacuation route planning
— cyclone and food shelter construction and maintenance
— creating rainwater drainage channels and harvesting rainwater
— fastening furnishing and equipment against earthquake shaking
— response simulation drills.

Step 3: Provide training

The need for disaster response skills may be met through training in:

— community frst aid
— mass casualty triage
— response organization
— light search and rescue
— fre suppression
— emergency communications
— psychosocial support
— family reunifcation.

Step 4: Carry out drills and simulations

At their best, drills and simulations provide much more than simply an occasion for professional responders to practise their skills and monitor their plans. They also offer an opportunity for the public to do some reality testing, allowing lessons to be learned in advance of hazard impacts.

The most important part of the drill is the full participation of the communities, and the refection and renewed round of action planning that occurs after the drill, which leads to the plan being modifed. Large-scale annual community-wide drills can sustain public awareness and ongoing learning by doing.

Informal Education

The focus of informal education is taking advantage of brief moments and encounters to stimulate thinking and engage people in discovery of actions and behaviours to increase safety and resilience. Informal education in communities and schools is the most fexible of all approaches with respect to setting, audience and timeframe. Table 1 shows the various types of informal education available.

Table 1: Types of informal education

Public	**Group**	**Solitary**
Home	School	Work
Television	**Radio**	**Internet**
A few minutes	A couple of hours	A day or two
Specially planned	Infused into ongoing projects	Spontaneous or viral elements

Specifc tools that can be used for informal education include:

— *Publications*—posters, guidelines, fyers, brochures, booklets, activity books, paper models, comic books, story books, colouring books, assembly kits and teacher resources
— *Curricula, modules and presentations*—teacher briefngs and community training
— *E-learning*—self-study curricula
— *Performing and cultural arts*—plays, dances, poems, songs, street theatre, puppet theatre
— *Games and competitions*—card games, board games, cooperative, activities role play, drawing competitions, writing competitions, tournaments, radio quizzes
— *Audio and video materials*—short videos, radio programmes, television programmes
— *Web pages and activities*—web sites, online games, online quizzes
— *Social media and telecommunications*—SMS, early warning.

Informal education involves disseminating standard messaging but with the fexibility to accommodate the needs and concerns of specifc local audiences. This is particularly effective because peer information, social proof and social support are vital to shifting human behaviour. Volunteers are leaders and role models that offer powerful examples as they engage the wider public. Tools focused on stimulating discovery and problem solving allow scope for endless creative activities and materials to appeal to various target-audience segments. Many facilitation tools from the IFRC's Community-Based Health and First Aid in Action initiative are familiar models, including the facilitator's guide. Other examples include the Caribbean Red Cross Societies' *Better Be Ready campaign kit* and *Expect the Unexpected: Facilitator's guide* by the Canadian Red Cross. These include:

— presentations
— guided discussion
— demonstration, visual aids
— role play
— storytelling
— case studies.
— brainstorming
— small group discussion
— question box
— dramatization
— simulation

Similarly, a number of tools for social mobilization, such as the *Volunteer Manual for Community-Based Health and First Aid* are familiar to facilitators and volunteers trained in the Community-Based Health and First Aid (CBHFA) programme. They involve communicating and building relationships, and organizing, sensitizing and mobilizing communities.

Peer-to-peer activities work equally well with adults, youth and children. Much of the best informal education has cross-generational appeal. Often the energy, enthusiasm and curiosity of children and youth are the hooks for adult involvement. Tools can, and should, be attention grabbing, engaging, participatory and practical, so that learning and acting become one and the same thing.

Informal school-based disaster risk reduction has formed part of Red Cross Red Crescent activities since the 1970s. It is widely practised partly because it is much easier to access than formal education, and because it does not compete with the regular curriculum. Schools welcome the help, and students welcome some fun. Schools also offer the opportunity to develop junior or youth Red Cross Red Crescent groups—a continuous source of new members and volunteers. This is especially true if teachers can be identifed within the school to lead these ongoing groups. Informal education in schools can take many forms, including:

— disseminating publications
— giving presentations
— role play
— community-service projects
— after-school clubs.

One of the strengths of school-based informal education is that the school can act as a hub to attract the wider community, through special programmes, by showcasing student work and by sending messages home with students.Just like other strategies, the potential benefits of informal education will be reached through scaling up, consistent messaging and a focus on behaviour change.

Formal School-based Interventions

The focus of formal school-based interventions covers two areas: school disaster management and disaster risk reduction in school curricula. These are considered to be formal because accountability and responsibility for school safety and curricula belong exclusively to education authorities, so they require support for long-term planning and capacity building. Whether there is one such authority, many, or seemingly none, the same issues of caution remain.

Unless efforts are being offcially and systematically piloted or tested, inconsistency may undermine rather than support the goal.

No matter how schools are organized, where possible a proper approach should begin with a group of interested NGOs and intergovernmental organizations that approach school authorities in a spirit of collaboration, in order to offer support and identify a single focal point within the system. Expecting schools to contend separately, with multiple uncoordinated projects and programmes, places a burden on school authorities and is ultimately unproductive. The goal is not to run a parallel system, but to support and help develop capacity within existing public education systems. The team should also approach and involve national disaster management authorities.

School disaster management

The primary goals of school disaster management are to ensure the safety of students and staff, and for education to continue. Sustained school disaster management requires the familiar participatory and ongoing process of identi-fcation of hazards and risks, mitigation and reduction of risks, and developing response capacity. In order to be effective, these need to be led by school staff and supported by consistent policies throughout the jurisdiction.

A school disaster management plan, developed at the school level, should be the living document that expresses this. Standard operating procedures in response to various hazards should be consistent. Training in response skills is vital. The following elements are essential:

— an incident command type of system to organize the local responder

— fre suppression

— psychosocial support

— sanitation

— evacuation

— community-based frst aid

— mass casualty triage

— light search and rescue
— communications
— shelter
— nutrition
— student–family reunifcation procedures.

A recent global mapping of the Red Cross Red Crescent initiatives shows several elements of school disaster management have been successfully piloted, including:

— the Safer Schools campaign
— school disaster management training materials for teachers and students
— schools as emergency evacuation centres
— school frst aid
— community maintenance of schools.

Guidance materials for school is beginning to emerge and will play an important role.

School drills

School drills form a vital part of the school disaster management process, and provide an intensive learning experience. They should be followed by refection and assessment by all members of the school community. Lessons learned are incorporated into the school disaster management plan, and goals set for improvement next time. Depending on hazards faced, there several major types of drills that can be practised:

— building evacuation (if the building is unsafe)
— site evacuation (if the site is unsafe)
— shelter in place (a procedure for taking shelter if the outdoors is unsafe)
— lockdown (keeping students inside in case of violent attack).

Many individual skills and protocols can also be practised separately, and as part of more complete simulation drills:

— student release procedures (safe family reunifcation)
— drop, cover and hold (for earthquake)
— putting on life jackets and practising water safety (for food or tsunami)
— extinguishing small fres
— stop, drop, and roll (when on fre)

— light search and rescue
— ightning strike safety
— mass casualty non-medical triage
— frst aid
— emergency communications
— incident command systems
— fexible organization and
— availability of response provisions assignment of response roles
— transportation and procedures
— public relations, communications for locations away from school and documentation
— reverse building evacuation.

Schools need to master building evacuation rules to ensure that staff and children can respond safely if an emergency arises.

School building evacuation drill rules

— Don't push. Don't run. Don't talk. Don't go back.
— Teachers should buddy up, with one leading of and one behind two classes.
— On exit, move away from building for safety.
— Assemble quietly and account for all students.

Curriculum work

School-based curriculum work in disaster reduction takes three main forms, each appropriate to different contexts:

— standalone courses
— integrating short modules (specifc subjects and grade levels)
— infusion throughout the curriculum (multi-subject, using readings, examples, problems and activities).

Tools in this area fall into the category of curricula, modules and presentations, including:

— textbooks
— modules
— case studies

- exercises
- hands-on learning materials
- informal education tools.

Standalone courses are much easier for 'outsiders' to contribute to, but much harder to incorporate into the available time in the curriculum. All forms require roughly the same sequence of steps and leadership from skilled curriculum experts, as described below.

Step-by-step guide: Developing a standalone course:

- *Step 1*: Identify public education curriculum development focal points and content experts with whom you can work in partnership.
- *Step 2*: Familiarize yourself with, or audit, the existing school curriculum to fnd out where disaster reduction and climate adaptation and mitigation issues are already being addressed, and where they can be enhanced or introduced.
- *Step 3*: Articulate and agree on the scope and sequence of competency outcomes.
- *Step 4*: Develop content for students.
- *Step 5*: Develop support materials and/or training for teachers (self-study, in-service, and/or training through teacher-training colleges or universities).

Well-developed education systems go through curriculum adoption cycles that typically last fve-to-ten years. Professional educators look at the scope and sequence of knowledge, competencies and skills for each subject area, aligning reading, problem solving, and discovery activities. Printed and digital curriculum materials must be identifed or developed to support this. This means that integrating new modules in a specifc subject and grade level, or ensuring infusion throughout the curriculum in many grade levels and subjects, is typically a long-term undertaking. Many educators believe that the curriculum should be designed to come alive, and should be fexible enough to incorporate local content about local realities. For example, while science and geography courses often include information about natural hazards, this can be structured so that teachers can link it to local concerns, such as:

- identifying the precursors of landslides

— incorporating local rainfall monitoring into the design and delivery of people-centred early warning systems
— methods of stabilizing slopes and preventing landslides
— land-use planning
— safe evacuation routes and procedures.

In other words, simple hazard awareness and abstract science or geography education is not enough.

Initially, capable staff or volunteers can build teacher capacity through a cascading model. However, sustainability requires capacity building through formal ongoing teacher-training institutions. E-learning, in the form of digital self-study courses for teachers and students, may also be developed for delivery via DVD or the internet, where resources permit.

References

Campbell, J. R. (1993). *Disaster Preparedness and Mitigation in the Republic of Maldives.* Manila, Asian Development Bank and Male, Ministry of Planning and Environment.

CBSE. (2004). *Towards a Safer India: Education in Disaster Management.* Delhi, Central Board of Secondary Education.

Kuberan, R. (2007). *Disaster Risk Reduction Education Efforts in India.* New Delhi: Risk RED and Sustainable Environment and Ecological Development Society.

Petal, M. (2008). 'Disaster risk reduction education' in Shaw, R. and Krishnamurty, R. (eds.) *Disaster Management: Global challenges and local solutions.* Hyderabad: Universities Press.

UN/ISDR. (2004). *Living with Risk: A Global Review of Disaster Reduction Initiatives.* Version, Inter-Agency Secretariat of the ISDR, Volume 1. Geneva, United Nations International Strategy for Disaster Reduction.

Bibliography

Alexander, D., (2002). *Principles of Emergency planning and Management*, Harpended: Terra publishing.

Allen, E., (1994), 'Political responses to flood disaster: the example of Rio de Janeiro', in: A. Varley (ed.) *Disasters, development and the environment*, Chichester: John Wiley.

Anderson, M. B. & P. J. Woodrow, (1989), *Rising from the ashes: development strategies in times of disaster*, Boulder: Westview Press/London: Intermediate Technology Publications.

Barton A.H., (1969). *Communities in Disaster. A Sociological Analysis of Collective Stress Situations*. SI: Ward Lock.

Bates, F. L. & W. G. Peacock, (1993), *Living conditions, disasters and development: an approach to cross-cultural comparisons*, Athens, USA: University of Georgia Press.

Blaikie, P., T. Cannon, I. Davis & B. Wisner, (1994), *At Risk: Natural Hazards, Peoples' Vulnerability and Disasters*, London: Routledge.

Bohem, Hilda. (1978).*Disaster Prevention and Disaster Preparedness* . Berkeley: University of California.

Business Executives for National Security (BENS). "A Company Primer on Preparedness and Response Planning for Terrorist and Bioterrorist Attacks." BENS.

Campbell, J. R. (1993). *Disaster Preparedness and Mitigation in the Republic of Maldives.* Manila, Asian Development Bank and Male, Ministry of Planning and Environment.

Cannon, T. (1994). 'Vulnerability analysis and the explanation of "natural" disasters', in A. Varley (ed.) *Disasters, development and the environment*, Chichester: John Wiley.

Carter, N. (1991).*Disaster Management, A disaster Manager's Handbook,* Asian Development Bank, Manilla.

CBSE. (2004). *Towards a Safer India: Education in Disaster Management.* Delhi, Central Board of Secondary Education.

Comfort, Louise K., ed. (1988). *Managing Disaster: Strategies and Policy Perspectives*, Durham: Duke University Press.

Donald Hyndman, David Hyndman (2009). *Natural Hazards and Disasters*. Brooks/ Cole: Cengage Learning.

Environment Waikato, (1999). Volcanic Risk Mitigation Plan, *Environment Waikato Policy Series* 1999/10.

Genovese, Robert, Trish Taylor and Edward White. (1989). *Disaster Preparedness Manual*, Buffalo, N.Y.: W.S. Hein.

Haddow, George D. and Jane A. Bullock, (2003). *Introduction to Emergency Management*, Amsterdam: Butterworth-Heinemann.

Hagman, Gunnar. (1984). *Prevention Better Than Cure.* Stockholm and Geneva: The Swedish Red Cross.

Hewitt, K.,(1997), *Regions of Risk: a geographical introduction to disasters*, Harlow: Addison Wesley Longman.

International Federation of Red Cross and Red Crescent Societies. (1984). *Prevention Better than Cure*. Geneva: IFRC.

Keeney, J. (2007). *In Case of Emergency*. Sydney: Design Masters Press.

Kuberan, R. (2007). *Disaster Risk Reduction Education Efforts in India.* New Delhi: Risk RED and Sustainable Environment and Ecological Development Society.

Lopes, R. (1992). *Public Perception of Disaster Preparedness Presentations Using Disaster Damage Images.* Boulder, CO: Natural Hazard Research.

Maskrey, A., (1989), *Disaster mitigation: a community based approach*, Oxford: Oxfam.

Mileti, Dennis S. and Paul W. O'Brien. (1992). "Warnings During Disaster: Normalizing Communicated Risk", *Social Problems*.

Petal, M. (2008). 'Disaster risk reduction education' in Shaw, R. and Krishnamurty, R. (eds.) *Disaster Management: Global challenges and local solutions.* Hyderabad: Universities Press.

Sharma, Vinod K. (ed.), (2001). *Disaster management*, New Delhi: National Centre for Disaster Management, Indian Institute of Public Administration.

Twigg J., (2003). *Early Warning Systems for Natural Disasters Reduction*, Zschau J. and Kuppers A. Editors, Springer.

UN/ISDR. (2004). *Living with Risk: A Global Review of Disaster Reduction Initiatives.* Version, Inter-Agency Secretariat of the ISDR, Volume 1. Geneva, United Nations International Strategy for Disaster Reduction.

UNDRO. (1984). Disaster Prevention and Mitigation. Vol. 11, Preparedness Aspects. New York: United Nations.

United Nations, (2006). *Global Survey of Early Warning Systems*, United Nations report.

Varley (ed.), (1994), *Disasters, development and the environment*, Chichester: John Wiley.

Waugh, William L. (2000). *Living with Hazards Dealing with Disasters: An Introduction to Emergency Management.* M.E. Sharpe: Armonk, New York.

World Meteorological Organization, (2006). *Drought Monitoring and Early Warning: Concepts, Progress and Future Challenges,* WMO Report No. 1006.